Lecture Notes in Computer Science   12494

More information about this series at http://www.springer.com/series/7407

Carlos Martín-Vide · Miguel A. Vega-Rodríguez ·
Miin-Shen Yang (Eds.)

Theory and Practice of Natural Computing

9th International Conference, TPNC 2020
Taoyuan, Taiwan, December 7–9, 2020
Proceedings

 Springer

Editors
Carlos Martín-Vide 🆔
Rovira i Virgili University
Tarragona, Spain

Miguel A. Vega-Rodríguez 🆔
University of Extremadura
Cáceres, Spain

Miin-Shen Yang 🆔
Chung Yuan Christian University
Taoyuan, Taiwan

ISSN 0302-9743 ISSN 1611-3349 (electronic)
Lecture Notes in Computer Science
ISBN 978-3-030-62999-1 ISBN 978-3-030-63000-3 (eBook)
https://doi.org/10.1007/978-3-030-63000-3

LNCS Sublibrary: SL1 – Theoretical Computer Science and General Issues

This Springer imprint is published by the registered company Springer Nature Switzerland AG
The registered company address is: Gewerbestrasse 11, 6330 Cham, Switzerland

Preface

These proceedings contain the papers that were presented at the 9th International Conference on the Theory and Practice of Natural Computing (TPNC 2020), held in Taoyuan, Taiwan, during December 7–9, 2020.

The scope of TPNC is rather broad, including:

- Theoretical contributions to: affective computing, ambient intelligence, ant colony optimization, approximate reasoning, artificial immune systems, artificial life, cellular automata, cognitive computing, cognitive robotics, collective intelligence, combinatorial optimization, computational intelligence, computing with words, developmental systems, DNA computing, evolutionary algorithms, evolutionary computing, evolutionary game theory, fuzzy logic, fuzzy sets, fuzzy systems, genetic algorithms, genetic programming, global optimization, granular computing, heuristics, intelligent agents, intelligent control, intelligent manufacturing, intelligent systems, intelligent user interfaces, machine intelligence, membrane computing, metaheuristics, molecular programming, multi-objective optimization, neural networks, quantum communication, quantum computing, quantum information, quantum metrology, rough sets, soft computing, swarm intelligence, swarm robotics, and unconventional computing.
- Applications of natural computing to: algorithmics, bioinformatics, cryptography, design, economics, graphics, hardware, human-computer interaction, knowledge discovery, learning, logistics, medicine, natural language processing, pattern recognition, planning and scheduling, programming, telecommunications, and web intelligence.

TPNC 2020 received 24 submissions and the papers were reviewed by three Program Committee members. There were also a few external reviewers consulted. After a thorough and vivid discussion phase, the committee decided to accept 12 papers (which represents an acceptance rate of 50%). The conference program also included three invited talks as well as some presentations of work in progress.

The excellent facilities provided by the EasyChair conference management system allowed us to deal with the submissions successfully and handle the preparation of these proceedings in time.

We would like to thank all invited speakers and authors for their contributions, the Program Committee and the external reviewers for their cooperation, and Springer for its very professional publishing work.

September 2020

Carlos Martín-Vide
Miguel A. Vega-Rodríguez
Miin-Shen Yang

Organization

TPNC 2020 was organized by the Chung Yuan Christian University, from Taoyuan, Taiwan, and the Institute for Research Development, Training and Advice (IRDTA), from Brussels, Belgium, and London, UK.

Program Committee

Andrew Adamatzky	University of the West of England, UK
Shawkat Ali	Central Queensland University, Australia
Elisabeth André	University of Augsburg, Germany
Peter J. Bentley	University College London, UK
Erik Cambria	Nanyang Technological University, Singapore
Christer Carlsson	Åbo Akademi University, Finland
Shyi-Ming Chen	National Taiwan University of Science and Technology, Taiwan
Claude Crépeau	McGill University, Canada
Leroy Cronin	University of Glasgow, UK
Ernesto Damiani	University of Milan, Italy
Yong Deng	University of Electronic Science and Technology of China, China
Matthias Ehrgott	Lancaster University, UK
Deborah M. Gordon	Stanford University, USA
Étienne Kerre	Ghent University, Belgium
Sam Kwong	City University of Hong Kong, Hong Kong
Chung-Sheng Li	PricewaterhouseCoopers, USA
Jing Liang	Zhengzhou University, China
Gui Lu Long	Tsinghua University, China
Jie Lu	University of Technology Sydney, Australia
Robert Mann	University of Waterloo, Canada
Carlos Martín-Vide (Chair)	Rovira i Virgili University, Spain
Luis Martínez López	University of Jaén, Spain
Serge Massar	Université Libre de Bruxelles, Belgium
Marjan Mernik	University of Maribor, Slovenia
Seyedali Mirjalili	Torrens University, Australia
Saeid Nahavandi	Deakin University, Australia
Ngoc Thanh Nguyen	Wrocław University of Science and Technology, Poland
Leandro Nunes de Castro	Mackenzie Presbyterian University, Brazil
Arun Kumar Pati	Harish-Chandra Research Institute, India
Matjaž Perc	University of Maribor, Slovenia
Brian M. Sadler	Army Research Laboratory, USA

Patrick Siarry	Paris-Est Créteil University, France
Dan Simon	Cleveland State University, USA
Andrzej Skowron	University of Warsaw, Poland
Stephen Smith	University of York, UK
Ponnuthurai N. Suganthan	Nanyang Technological University, Singapore
Vicenç Torra	Umeå University, Sweden
Rufin VanRullen	CNRS Toulouse, France
Miin-Shen Yang	Chung Yuan Christian University, Taiwan
Simon X. Yang	University of Guelph, Canada
Yi Zhang	Sichuan University, China

Additional Reviewers

Kaushik Das Sharma
Tao He
Han Wang
Zhou Yao

Organizing Committee

Meng-Hui Li (Co-chair)	Chung Yuan Christian University, Taiwan
Sara Morales	IRDTA, Belgium
Manuel Parra-Royón	University of Granada, Spain
David Silva (Co-chair)	IRDTA, UK
Miguel A. Vega-Rodríguez	University of Extremadura, Spain
Miin-Shen Yang (Co-chair)	Chung Yuan Christian University, Taiwan

Contents

Swarm Intelligence, Evolutionary Algorithms, and DNA Computing

Invited Talk

Adaptive Coordination of Multiple Learning Strategies in Brains and Robots

Mehdi Khamassi$^{(\boxtimes)}$

Sorbonne Université, CNRS, Institut des Systèmes Intelligents et de Robotique (ISIR), 75005 Paris, France
`mehdi.khamassi@sorbonne-universite.fr`

Abstract. Engineering approaches to machine learning (including robot learning) typically seek for the best learning algorithm for a particular problem, or a set problems. In contrast, the mammalian brain appears as a toolbox of different learning strategies, so that any newly encountered situation can be autonomously learned by an animal with a combination of existing learning strategies. For example, when facing a new navigation problem, a rat can either learn a map of the environment and then plan to find a path to its goal within this map. Alternatively, it can learn sequences of egocentric movements in response to identifiable features of the environment. For about 15 years, computational neuroscientists have searched for the mammalian brain's coordination mechanisms which enable it to find efficient, if not necessarily optimal, combinations of existing learning strategies to solve new problems. Understanding such coordination principles of multiple learning strategies could have great implications in robotics, to enable robots to autonomously determine which learning strategies are appropriate in different contexts. Here, we review some of the main neuroscience models for the coordination of learning strategies and present some of the early results obtained when applying these models to robot learning. We moreover highlight important energy costs which can be reduced with such bio-inspired solutions compared to current deep reinforcement learning approaches. We conclude by sketching a roadmap for further developing such bio-inspired hybrid learning approaches to robotics.

Keywords: Adaptive coordination · Multiple learning strategies · Brains and robots

1 Introduction

The mammalian brain combines multiple learning systems whose interactions, sometimes in a competitive way, sometimes in a cooperative way, are thought to be largely responsible for the high degree of behavioral flexibility observed in mammals [13,18,34,35,37,46,51,53,57]. For instance, the hippocampus is a brain region playing an important role in the rapid acquisition of episodic memories – the memory of individual episodes previously experienced, such as

© Springer Nature Switzerland AG 2020
C. Martín-Vide et al. (Eds.): TPNC 2020, LNCS 12494, pp. 3–22, 2020.
https://doi.org/10.1007/978-3-030-63000-3_1

sequences of visited places while visiting a new city [4,25,42]. Together with the prefrontal cortex, the hippocampus can link these episodes so as to store in long-term memory a mental representation (or 'model') of statistical regularities of the environment [18,26,66]. In the spatial domain, such a mental model can take the form of a 'cognitive map' [53]. Even if it constitutes an imperfect and incomplete representation of the environment, it can be used to mentally explore the map [8,27], or to plan potential trajectories to a desired goal before acting [32,45]. Such a *model-based strategy* enables to rapidly and flexibly adapt to changes in goal location, since the map can be updated instantaneously with the new goal location so that the animal can plan the new correct trajectory in a one-trial learning manner [18]. Nevertheless, such a flexibility comes at the expense of time- and energy-consuming planning phases (the larger the map, the longer it takes to find the shortest path between two locations). This is typically observed when a human or an animal takes longer decision time after task changes, putatively implying a re-planning phase [32,70].

In contrast, the basal ganglia, and especially its main input region called the striatum, is involved in the slow acquisition of procedural memories [37,55,73]. This type of memories is typically acquired through the repetition of sequences of egocentric movements (*e.g.,* turn left, go straight, turn right) or sequences of stimulus-triggered responses (*e.g.,* start moving in response to a flash light, then stop in response to a sound) which become behavioral 'habits' [16,31]. These habits are known to be inflexible, resulting in slow adaptation to both changes in the environment (*e.g.,* change in goal location) and changes in motivation (*e.g.,* an overtrained rat habitually presses a food-delivering lever, even when it is satiated) [17]. Nevertheless, when these habits have been well acquired in a familiar environment, they enable the animal to make fast decisions and to perform efficient action sequences without relying on the time-consuming planning system [13,37]. Such a learning strategy is thus called *model-free* because making a decision does not require the manipulation of an internal model to mentally represent the potential long-term consequences of the actions before acting. In contrast, it is the perception of a stimulus or the recognition of a familiar location which triggers the execution of a habitual behavioral sequence.

It is fascinating how lesion studies have highlighted some degree of modularity of the organization of learning systems within the brain. Lesioning the hippocampus impairs behavioral flexibility as well as behavioral strategies relying on a cognitive map (see [37] for a review). As a consequence, hippocampus-lesioned animals only display stimulus-response behaviors in a maze and do not seem to remember the location of previously encountered food. In contrast, animals with a lesion to what is called the dorsolateral striatum have an intact map-based behavioral strategy and perform less egocentric movements during navigation (see [37] for a review). Nevertheless, the modularity is not perfect and an important degree of distributed information processing also exists. For instance, lesions to what is called the ventral striatum seem to impair representations of reward value which are required for both model-based and model-free learning strategies (again see [37] for a review). Moreover, some brain regions do not seem to play a specific role in learning one particular strategy, but rather a role in the coordination of these strategies. For instance, lesions to the medial prefrontal cortex only impair the initial acquisition of model-based strategies, but not their later expression [54]. Indeed, it seems that the medial prefrontal cortex plays a central role in the arbitration between model-based and model-free strategies [39]. As a consequence, lesioning a subpart of the medial prefrontal cortex can even restore flexible model-based strategies in overtrained rats [11].

This paper is particularly aimed at illustrating how neuroscience studies of decision-making have progressively helped understanding (and are still currently investigating) the neural mechanisms underlying animals' ability to adaptively coordinate model-based and model-free learning, and to illustrate how this biological knowledge can help towards developing behaviorally flexible autonomous robots. Since the computational models of these processes largely rely on the reinforcement learning theoretical framework, the next section will first describe the employed formalism. Then the third section will briefly review some of the neuroscience results which contribute to deciphering the principles of this coordination, and how this coordination was mathematically formalized by computational neuroscience models. The fourth section will then review some of the experimental tests of these principles in robotic scenarios. We will finally discuss the perspectives of this field of research, and how it could not only contribute to improving robots' behavioral flexibility, but also to reducing the computational cost of machine learning algorithms for robots (by enabling to skip model-based strategies when the robot autonomously recognizes that model-free strategies are sufficient).

2 Formalism Adopted to Describe Model-Based and Model-Free Reinforcement Learning

For simplicity, existing computational models are most often framed within standard Markov Decision Problem (MDP) settings, where an agent visits discrete states $s \in \mathcal{S}$, using a finite set of discrete actions $a \in \mathcal{A}$. They can encounter reward scalar values $r \in \mathbb{R}$ after performing some actions a in some states s, which they have to discover. And there is a transition probability function $\mathcal{T}(s, a, s') : (\mathcal{S}, \mathcal{A}, \mathcal{S}) \rightarrow [0; 1]$, which is a generative model underlying the statistics of the task that the agent will face, and which basically determines what is the probability of ending up in a state s' after performing an action a in state s.

In navigation scenarios, states represent unique locations in space. In neuroscience modeling studies, these states are usually equally spaced on a square grid, an information expected to be provided by place cell activity in the hippocampus, which are neurons that participate in the estimation of the animal's current location within the map. In the robot navigation experiments that will be presented later on, the state space discretization process is autonomously performed by the robot after an initial exploration of the environment. As a consequence, different states have different sizes and are unevenly distributed. It is important

to note that these models can easily be extended to more distributed or continuous state representations [1], for instance when facing Partially Observable
Markov Decision Process (POMDP) settings [7]. The models reviewed here can
also be generalized to more continuous representations of space and actions (*e.g.*,
[22,38]). Nevertheless, we stick here to the discrete state representation for the
sake of simplicity and because it has a high explanatory power.

As classically assumed within the Reinforcement Learning (RL) theoretical framework, the agent's goal is here considered to be the maximization
of the expected value of the long-term reward, that is the maximization
of the discounted sum of future rewards over a potentially infinite horizon:
$\mathbb{E}\left[\sum_{t=0}^{\infty}\gamma^t r(s_t, a_t)\right]$, where γ ($\gamma < 1$) is a discount factor which basically
assigns a weaker weights to long-term rewards than to short-term rewards. In
order to meet this objective, the agent will learn a state-action value function
$Q : (\mathcal{S}, \mathcal{A}) \rightarrow \mathbb{R}$ which evaluates the total discounted sum of future rewards that
the agent expects to receive when starting from a given state s, taking the action
a and then following a certain (eventually learned) behavioral policy π:

$$Q^\pi(s, a) = \mathbb{E}\left[\sum_t \gamma^t r(s_t, a_t) \mid s_0 = s, a_0 = a, a_t = \pi(s_t), s_{t+1} \sim \mathcal{T}(s_t, a_t, .)\right]$$
$$(1)$$

Saying that the agent adopts a *model-based* RL strategy means that the
agent will progressively try to estimate an internal model of its environment.
Conventionally, this model is the combination of the estimated transition func-
tion $\hat{\mathcal{T}}(s, a, s')$ and the estimated reward function $\hat{\mathcal{R}}(s, a)$ that aims at capturing
the rules that the human experimenter chooses to determine which (state, action)
couples yield reward in the considered task.

Various ways to learn these two functions exist. Here, we will simply consider that the agent estimates the frequencies of occurrence of states, actions
and rewards from its observations. Then, the learned internal model can be used
by the agent to infer the value of each action in each possible state. This inference can be a computationally costly process, especially when all (s, a) are to
be visited multiple times before reaching an accurate estimation of the state-
action value function Q. Some heuristics exist to simplify the computations, or
to make it less costly, like *trajectory sampling* [68] or *prioritized sweeping* [49,56],
which we review in [8]. Some alternatives to full model-based strategies exist,
like the *successor representation* [14], which provides the agent with more flexibility and generalization ability than a pure model-free strategy, at a smaller
computational cost than a pure model-based strategy, and at the same time can
contribute to describe some neural learning mechanisms in the hippocampus
[48,65]. Nevertheless, for the sake of simplicity, here we will consider that the
inference process in the model-based (MB) RL agent is performed through a
value iteration process [68]:

$$Q_{MB}^{(t+1)}(s, a) = \hat{\mathcal{R}}^{(t)}(s, a) + \gamma \sum_{s'} \hat{\mathcal{T}}^{(t)}(s, a, s') \max_{k \in \mathcal{A}} Q_{MB}^{(t)}(s', k) \qquad (2)$$

In contrast, an agent adopting a *model-free* RL strategy will not have access to nor try to estimate any internal model of the environment. Instead, the agent will iteratively update its estimation of the state-action value function through its interactions with the environment. Each of these interactions consist in performing an action a in a state s and observing the consequence in terms of the reward r that this yields and the new state s' of the environment. Again, if we address a navigation problem, the possible actions are typically movements towards cardinal directions (North, South, East, West) and the new state s' is the new location of the agent within the environment after acting. A classical and widely used model-free RL algorithm is Q-learning [71]:

$$Q_{MF}^{(t+1)}(s_t, a_t) = Q_{MF}^{(t)}(s_t, a_t) + \alpha(r_t + \gamma \max_{k \in \mathcal{A}} Q_{MF}^{(t)}(s_{t+1}, k) - Q_{MF}^{(t)}(s_t, a_t)) \quad (3)$$

where $\alpha \in [0; 1]$ is the learning rate, and the term between parentheses, often written δ_t is called the *temporal-difference error* [68] or the *reward prediction error* [64] because it constitutes a reinforcement signal which compares the new estimation of value $(r_t + \gamma \max_{k \in \mathcal{A}} Q_{MF}^{(t)}(s_{t+1}, k))$ after performing action a_t in state s_t, arriving in state s_{t+1} and receiving a reward r_t, with the expected value $Q_{MF}^{(t)}(s_t, a_t)$ before executing this action. Any deviation between the two is used as an error signal to correct the current estimation of the state-action value function Q.

Finally, for the decision-making phase, no matter if the agent is model-free or model-based, the agent selects the next action a to perform from a probability distribution over actions in the current state s computed from the estimated state-action value function $x^{(t)}(s, a)$ (with $x^{(t)}(s, a) = Q_{MB}^{(t)}(s, a)$ if the agent is model-based, or $x^{(t)}(s, a) = Q_{MF}^{(t)}(s, a)$ if the agent is model-free), using a Boltzmann softmax function:

$$P^{(t)}(a|s) = \frac{e^{\beta x^{(t)}(s,a)}}{\sum_{k \in \mathcal{A}} e^{\beta x^{(t)}(s,k)}} \quad (4)$$

where β is called the *inverse temperature* which regulates the exploration/exploitation trade-off by modulating the level of stochasticity of choice: the closer β is to zero, the more the contrast between Q-values will be attenuated, the extreme being for $\beta = 0$ which produces a flat action probability distribution (random exploration); in contrast, the larger the value of β, the more the contrast between Q-values will be enhanced, which makes the probability of the action with the highest Q-value close to 1 when β tends towards ∞ (exploitation).

3   Neuroscience Studies of the Coordination of Model-Based and Model-Free Reinforcement Learning

Reinforcement learning models (initially only from the model-free family) have started to become popular in neuroscience in the mid 90s, when researchers discovered that a part of the brain called the dopaminergic system (because it inner-vates the rest of the brain with a neuromodulator called *dopamine*) increases its activity in response to unpredicted reward, decreases its activity in response to the absence of a predicted reward, but does not respond to predicted ones, as can be modeled when δ_t, the right part between parentheses in Eq. 3, is positive, negative or null, respectively [64]. This discovery was followed by a large set of diverse neuroscience experiments to verify that other parts of the brain could show neural activity compatible with other variables of reinforcement learning models like state-action values (see examples of comparisons of neuroscience results with RL models' predictions in [2,3]; and see [35] for a review).

More important for the topic of this paper, since about 10 years, an increasing number of neuroscience studies have started to investigate whether human and animal behavior during reward-based learning tasks could involve some sort of combination of model-based (MB) and model-free (MF) learning processes, and what are the neural mechanisms underlying such a coordination.

The simplest possible way of combining MB and MF RL processes is to con-sider that they occur in parallel in the brain, and that any decision made by the subject results from the simple weighted sum of MB and MF state-action values (*i.e.*, replacing $x^{(t)}(s, a)$ in Eq. 4 by $(1 - \omega)Q_{MB}^{(t)}(s_t, a_t) + \omega Q_{MF}^{(t)}(s_t, a_t)$, with $\omega \in [0; 1]$ a weighting parameter). This works well to have a first approx-imation of the degree with which different individual subjects, whether human adults [12], human children [15], or animals [41], rely on a model-based sys-tem to make decisions while considering the ensemble of trials made by the subject during a whole experiment. This has for instance helped understand that children make more model-free decisions than adults because their brain area subserving model-based decisions (their prefrontal cortex) takes years to mature [15]. This has also helped better model why some subjects are more prone than others to be influenced by reward predicting stimuli (which has implica-tion to understand stimulus-triggered drug-taking behaviors in humans): roughly because their model-based process contributes less to their decisions [41].

Nevertheless, a systematic weighted sum of MB's and MF's decisions has the disadvantage of systematically requiring the (potentially heavy) computations from both learning systems. In contrast, it is thought that relying on habit-ual behaviors learned by the model-free system when the environment is stable and familiar is useful to avoid the costly inference-related computations of the model-based system [13,35]. There could thus be some evolutionary reasons why humans do not always perform rational choices as could be (more often) the case if they were relying more on their model-based system [33]: namely that they would not be able to make fast decisions in easy familiar situations. Instead, they would always need to make long inferences with their internal models before deciding. Thus, they would be exhausted at the end of the day if they had to think deeply for all the simple decisions they have to make everyday, like whether they should drink a coffee before taking a shower or the opposite, whether they should wear a blue or a red shirt, where to go for lunch, etc.

Alternatively, early neuroscience studies of the coordination of MB and MF process hypothesized a sequential activation of the two systems: humans and animals should initially rely on their MB system when facing a new task, so as to figure out what are the statistics of the task and what is the optimal thing to do; and as they repeat over and over the same task and get habituated to it (making it become familiar), they should switch to the less costly MF system which hopefully will have had time to learn during a long repetition phase. Moreover, if suddenly the task changes, they should restart using their MB system (and thus break their previously acquired habit) in order to figure out what has changed and what is the new optimal behavioral policy. And then again after many repetitions with the new task settings, they can acquire a new behavioral habit with the MF system.

An illustrative example is the case where someone has to visit a new city. In that case, people usually look at a map, which is an allocentric representation of the city, and try to remember the parts of the maps that are useful to reach a desired location. And then, once people walk through the city, if they suddenly find themselves in front of some landmark that they thought would not be encountered during their planned trip (*e.g.*, a monument), they can close their eyes and try and understand where they might actually be located within their mental map, and which change in their trajectory they should operate. This is typically a MB inference process. In contrast, when one always takes the same path from their home until their workplace, they rarely perform MB inference, and rather let their body automatically turn at the right corner and lead them to their usual arrival point. This works well even if one is discussing with a friend while walking, or is not fully awake. We thus think that in such a case the brain has shifted its decisions to the MF system. This permits to free other parts of the brain which can be used to think while we walk about the last book we read, or to try and solve the maths problem we are currently addressing.

One initial computational proposal for the coordination of MB and MF learning systems which can well capture this dynamics consists in comparing the uncertainty of the MB and MF systems and relying on the most certain one [13]. This can be achieved if a Bayesian formulation of RL is adopted where the agent does not simply learns point estimates of state-action value functions, but rather full distributions over each (state, action) pair value. In that case, the precision of the distribution can be used to represent the level of uncertainty. In practice, when facing a new task, the uncertainty in both systems is high. But the uncertainty in the MB system decreases faster with learning (*i.e.*, after less observations made following interactions of the agent with the world, even if these observations are processed during a long inference phase). As a consequence, the agent will rely more on the MB system during early learning. In parallel the uncertainty in the MF system slowly decreases, until the MF system is sufficiently certain to take control over the agent's actions. When the task changes (*e.g.*, the goal location changes, or a path is now obstructed by an obstacle), uncertainty re-increases in both systems, but again it decreases faster in the MB system, so that again a sequence of MB decisions followed by MF decisions after a long second learning phase can be produced.

However, systematically monitoring uncertainty in the MB system can be computational heavy, and does not really permit the avoidance of the costly computations of the MB system when the MF system is currently leading. Alternatively, a more recent computational neuroscience model proposes to only monitor uncertainty within the MF system, and considers that the MB system is by default providing *perfect information*, so that it should be chosen when the MF system is uncertain, and avoided only when the MF system is sufficiently certain [34]. This works well in a number of situations and enables to well capture the behavior of animals in a number of experiments. However, there are situations where this assumption cannot be true. In particular, as we will illustrate with some robotic tests of this kind of models in the next section, if the agent has an inaccurate internal model, it is better to rely on the more reactive MF system even when it is still uncertain [6,59]. Less costly alternative estimations of uncertainty can be used to permanently monitor both the MB and the MF system [40]. For instance, the degree of instability of Q-values (MB or MF) before convergence is reached can be a good proxy to uncertainty [8,36]. Choice confidence can also give a relatively good proxy to choice uncertainty in simple situations, by measuring the entropy of the probability distribution over all possible actions in a given state and comparing MB and MF estimations of this measure [70]. This moreover enables to well capture not only choices made by human subjects during simple decision-making tasks, but also their decision time (the more uncertain they are, the more time they need to make their decision). Finally, this type of mechanism also enables to explain why the ideal MB-to-MF sequence is not always true, since early choices of human subjects can sometimes significantly rely on the MF system because their MF system might initially be overconfident [70].

Another important current question is whether uncertainty alone is sufficient to arbitrate between MB and MF systems [52], or whether, when the two systems are equally uncertain, the agent should rely on the least computationally costly one [24]. If we want the agent to be initially agnostic about which system is more costly, and if we even want the agent to be able to potentially arbitrate between N different learning systems with different a priori unknown computational characteristics, then one proposal is simply to measure the average time taken by each system when it has to make decisions [24]. In some of the robotic experiments that we will describe in the next section, we found that this principle works robustly, enables to produce the ideal MB-to-MF sequence, not only during initial learning but also after a task change. We will come back to this later.

Finally, other current outstanding questions are whether the two systems shall always be in competition, or whether they shall sometimes also cooperate (as can be achieved with the weighted sum of their contribution described above); and whether an efficient coordination mechanism shall arbitrate between MB and MF at each timestep from the current available measures (*e.g.,* uncertainty,

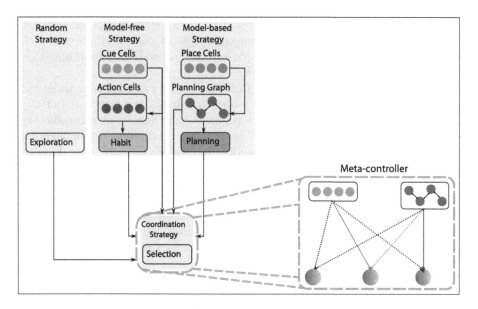

Fig. 1. The generic architecture for the coordination of multiple learning strategies applied to navigation proposed by Dollé and colleagues [18]. Three main learning strategies are considered here (but the paper tests other variants, such as the combination of multiple instances of the same strategy, which would correspond to a case of ensemble learning [72]): a model-based planning strategy; a model-free habitual strategy; and a distinct random exploration strategy in order to avoid cumulating the exploratory decisions of the two other strategies. A so-called 'meta-controller' performs the high-level strategy coordination process. This process can consists in different manners of coordinating strategy, such as giving the hand to the least uncertain one [13]. Nevertheless, in [18] the meta-controller learns which strategy yields the largest amount of reward in different locations of the environment or in the presence of different stimuli. Adapted from [18].

computational cost, etc.), or whether it is sometimes more efficient to learn and remember that the MF system is usually better in situation type A while the MB system is better in situation type B. The latter could enable the agent to instantaneously rely on the best memorized system without needing to fully experience a new situation identified as belonging from a recognized type. This issue relates to current investigations in subfields of machine learning known as transfer learning, life-long learning and open-ended learning [21,62,69]. One solution to this coordination memory problem consists in adopting a hierarchical organization where a second, higher-level, learning process (in what Dollé and colleagues call a 'meta-controller') learns which strategy (model-based, model-free or random exploration) is the best (in terms of the amount of reward it yields) in different parts of the environment [18] (Fig. 1). This model learns through RL which strategy is the most efficient in each part of the environment. It can moreover learn that a certain equilibrium between MB and MF processes is required for good performance, thus resulting in cooperation between systems. It can even learn to change through time the weight of the contribution of each system, as learning in the MF system progresses, thus producing something that looks like the ideal MB-to-MF sequence.

With these principles in hand, the Dollé model [18] can explain a variety of rat navigation behaviors experimentally observed, including data that initially appeared as either contradictory to the cognitive map theory, or contradictory to the associative learning theory which approximately considers that navigation behaviors shall all be learned through model-free reinforcement learning. Finally, it is worthy of note that performing offline replay of the MB system can result in learning by observation in the MF system, so that the two somehow cooperate [8], as inspired by the now classical DYNA architecture [67].

Overall, this short review highlights that the investigation of the principles underlying the adaptive coordination of model-based and model-free reinforcement learning mechanisms in humans and animals is currently an active area of research in neuroscience.

4   Robotic Tests of Bio-Inspired Principles for the Coordination of Model-Based and Model-Free Reinforcement Learning

The importation of these bio-inspired ideas to robotics is quite recent, and is still an emerging field of research. Nevertheless, a few studies and their outcomes deserve to be mentioned here.

To our knowledge, the first test with a real robot of a bio-inspired algorithm for the online coordination of model-based and model-free reinforcement learning has been presented in [6]. This work included an indoor robot navigation scenario with the Psikharpax rat robot [47] within a 2 m × 2.5 m arena (Fig. 2). The robot first explored the environment to autonomously learn a cognitive map of the environment (hence a mental model used by its model-based learning strategy). In addition, the robot could use a model-free reinforcement learning strategy to learn movements in 8 cardinal directions in response to perceived salient features within the environment (*i.e., stimuli* in the vocabulary of psychology). The latter MF RL component of the model was later improved in [5] to make it able to learn movements away from visual features when needed. The proposed algorithm for the online coordination of MB and MF RL was based on the computational neuroscience model of Dollé and colleagues [18–20], which has been presented in the previous section and sketched in Fig. 1.

The first important result of this robotic work is that the algorithm could autonomously learn the appropriate coordination of MB and MF systems for each specific configuration of the environment that was presented to the robot. For a first configuration associated to an initial goal location (where the robot can obtain a scalar reward), the algorithm learned that the MB strategy was appropriate to guide the robot from far away towards the goal, and that the MF strategy was appropriate to control the fine movements of the robot when

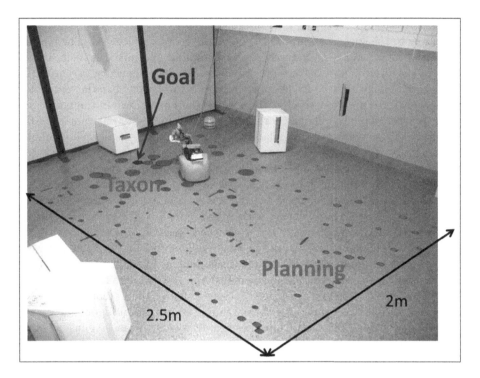

Fig. 2. Robotic experiments presented in [6] and aiming at testing the performance of a bio-inspired algorithm for the online coordination of model-based and model-free reinforcement learning. The algorithm itself is based on the computational neuroscience model of Dollé and colleagues [18], which is presented in Fig. 1. The photo shows the Psikharpax rat robot [47] within a 2 m × 2.5 m indoor arena. Salient features are displayed on the surrounding walls and objects because the purpose of this research work was not on vision, but how to make the robot use the noisy perception of these features with its cameras in order to learn a simple cognitive map that can be used for model-based navigation. The green and red dots superimposed on the photo show the location of the *place cells* of the cognitive map learned by the robot. The blue dot (invisible to the robot) shows the current location of the goal, where the robot receives a scalar reward during the first part of the experiment. Later on this goal location is moved without informing the robot, so that it needs to detect this change and learn a new appropriate coordination of model-based and model-free strategies to quickly reach a good performance. In the last part of the experiment, the goal is again moved back to its initial location, to show that the coordination algorithm can, after detecting this new change, instantaneously retrieve its memory of the first appropriate coordination and thus quickly re-display a good performance without re-learning. Finally, the green dots are labelled 'taxon' (a *taxon* strategy in neuroscience consists in learning actions in response to visual cues), which corresponds to areas where the algorithm considers the model-free strategy as the best strategy, while red dots are labelled 'planning' because the algorithm considers that the model-based strategy is the most appropriate there. Adapted from [6].

closer to the goal. This was an emergent property of the coordination that was not designed by human. Instead, it was autonomously learned by the algorithm in response to the specific environment where the robot was located. The reason is that the robot had less explored the area around the initial goal location. Thus, its cognitive map was less precise there. As a consequence, a pure MB version of the algorithm could learn to approach the robot near the goal, but could not learn to precisely reach it (because of the imprecision in the map). As a consequence, the autonomous coordination algorithm found out that the MF system could compensate for this lack of precision. From this simple example we can learn two things: first, that in contradiction to the assumption made by some previously discussed computational models that the MB system has access to *perfect information*, the map (*i.e.,* model) learned by the MB system can be imperfect, and the coordination algorithm has to cope with it. More generally, we think that when experimenting with robots, there will always be a situation where the map cannot be accurately learned, because of noisy perceptions, problems with the light, etc. So, rather than endlessly trying to refine the MB system to make it appropriate for each new situation at hand, it might be better to let the coordination algorithm autonomously find out what is the appropriate alternation between MB and MF for the present situation. The second thing that we can learn from this example is that a simple coordination algorithm which puts MB and MF systems in competition, and selects the most efficient one, can sometimes produce a sort of cooperation between them. In this particular example, a learned trajectory of the robot to the goal can be hybrid, involving a first use of the MB strategy when far away from the goal, and then a shift to the MF strategy when getting closer. This enables us to draw a model-driven prediction for neuroscience: that sometimes animals solving these types of task may display a trajectory within a maze or an arena that is not the result of a single learning system, but rather a hybrid byproduct of the coordination of multiple systems.

Another important result of this robotic work relates to its ability to learn context-specific coordination patterns, which can relate to what people call *episodic control*. This occurred when we changed the goal location after some time, and let the robot adapt to the new configuration. What happened is that the algorithm first detected the change because of the different profile of reward propagation through its mental map that this induced. Then the algorithm decided to store in memory the previously learned coordination pattern between MB and MF, and to learn a new one. After a new learning phase, the algorithm found a new coordination pattern adapted to the new condition, thus producing good performance again. Finally, we suddenly moved the goal location back to its initial location. The algorithm could detect the change and recognize the previous configuration (again thanks to the profile of reward propagation through its mental map). As a consequence, the algorithm retrieved the previously learned coordination pattern, which enabled the robot to instantaneously restore the appropriate behavior without re-learning.

Nevertheless, some limitations and perspectives of this seminal work ought to be mentioned here. First, the coordination component of the algorithm (which is called the *meta-controller* in [5,6,18]) slowly learns through MF RL (in addition to the MF RL mechanism used within the MF system dedicated to the MF strategy) which strategy is the most appropriate in each part of the environment (In other words, the model involves a hierarchical learning process in addition to the parallel learning process between MB and MF strategies). While this is good for the robot to be able to memorize specific coordination patterns for each context (*i.e.,* for each configuration of the goal location within the arena), this nevertheless requires a long time to achieve a good coordination within each context. Thus, it would be interesting to also test coordination mechanisms based on instantaneous measures such as uncertainty, as discussed in the previous section. A second limitation is that this experiment involved a specific adaptation of a coordination model to a simple indoor navigation task, with a small map, a small number of states to learn, and an action repertoire which is specific to navigation scenarios. A third limitation is at the technical level, involving an old custom robot. Thus, it it not clear if these results could be generalized to other robotic platforms facing a wider variety of tasks, and sometimes more complex tasks involving a larger number of states.

Fig. 3. (Left) Human-Robot Interaction task tested in [9]: the human and the robot collaborate to put all boxes in a trashbin. (Right) Navigation task autonomously mapped and discretized by the robot during exploration [9,24]. The red area indicates the goal location whereas the green areas indicate starting locations of the robot. Red numbers are starting location indexes; blue numbers are some states where some changes in the configuration of the environment can occur. Adapted from [9]. (Color figure online)

A more recent series of robotic experiments with the same research goal (*i.e.,* assessing the efficiency and robustness of bio-inspired coordination principles of MB and MF learning) has been presented in [58–60] and later in [9,23,24]. First, [58–60] compared different coordination principles, including methods coming from ensemble learning [72] in several different simulated robotic tasks. They found again that the MB system was not always the most reliable system, especially in tasks with hundreds of states, where the MB system requires long inference durations to come up with a good approximation of the state-action value function Q. These experiments highlighted the respective advantages and disadvantages of MB and MF reinforcement learning in a variety of simulated robotic situations, and concluded again for the added value of coordinating them. In [9,23,24], simulated and real robotic experiments were presented, some involving navigation with a Turtlebot, and others involving simulated tasks with the PR2 robot and the Baxter robot (Fig. 3).

The first important result of these new series of experiments to highlight is that the coordination of MB and MF RL was efficient in a variety of tasks, including navigation tasks with detours, non-stationarity of the configuration of the environment (*i.e.*, sudden introduction of obstacles obstructing some corridors), but also simple human-robot interaction tasks. In the latters, the human and the robot had to cooperate to clean a table by putting objects in a trashbin. Importantly, some objects were reachable by the human, some by the robots, thus forcing them to communicate and cooperate. In that case, the model-based system could compute joint action plans where actions by the robot and actions by the humans alternated. In all these situations, the robot could autonomously learn the task and reach good performance.

The second important result to highlight is that instantaneous measures of uncertainty in MB and MF systems allow a quicker reaction of the coordination mechanism to changes in the environment. Nevertheless, this does not permit memorization nor episodic control, which the work of [6] did. Thus, the results are in good complementarity and in the future it would interesting to test combinations of these two principles.

The last important result to highlight here is that an efficient coordination mechanism proposed by [23,24], and successfully applied to robot navigation and human-robot interaction scenarios, consists in taking into account not only the uncertainty but also the computational cost of each learning system. In practice, the proposed algorithm monitored the average time taken by each system to make its inference phase before deciding. It learned that the MB system takes on average 10 times longer than the MF system, in these specific tasks, before making a decision. As a consequence, the coordination algorithm gave the lead to the MF system in cases of equal uncertainty, and even in cases of slightly higher uncertainty in the MF system. As a result, the algorithm mostly relied on the MF system but transiently and efficiently gave the lead to the MB system, only when needed. This occurred during initial learning as well as after task changes. As a consequence, the algorithm could reproduce the nice MB-to-MF sequence that we discussed in previous sections, both during initial learning and after task changes. Moreover, with this new coordination principle, the robot could achieve the same optimal performance as a pure MB system (which was optimal in these cases) while requiring a cumulated computational cost which was closer to that of a pure MF system (which achieves a lower bound on computational cost in these experiments). Thus, the coordination algorithm not only allowed for an efficient and flexible behavior of the robot in these non-stationary tasks, but it also permitted to reduce the computational cost of the algorithm controlling the robot. Finally, the authors also compared their algorithm with a state-of-the-art deep reinforcement learning algorithm. They found that the latter requires a very large number of iterations to learn, much more than their proposed MB-MF coordination algorithm.

Finally, it is interesting to mention that in the meantime, several other research groups throughout the world have also started to test hybrid MB/MF algorithms for robot learning applications [29, 30, 43, 44, 61, 63]. In particular, the deep reinforcement learning community is showing a growing interest for such hybrid learning algorithms [10, 28, 50]. This illustrates the potentially broad interest that this type of hybrid solutions to reinforcement learning can have in different research communities.

5   Conclusion

This paper aimed at first illustrating current outstanding questions and investigations to better understand and model neural mechanisms for the online adaptive coordination of multiple learning strategies in humans and animals. Secondly, the paper reviewed a series of recent robot learning experiments aimed at testing such bio-inspired principles for the coordination of model-based and model-free reinforcement learning strategies.

We discussed the respective advantages and disadvantages of different coordination mechanisms: on the one hand, mechanisms relying on instantaneous measures of uncertainty, choice confidence, performance, as well as computational cost; on the other hand, mechanisms relying on hierarchical learning where a high-level *meta-controller* autonomously learns which strategy is the most efficient in each situation.

The robotic experiments discussed here showed that this type of coordination principle can work efficiently, robustly and at a reduced computational cost in a variety of robotic scenarios (navigation, human-robot interaction). This is of particular importance at a time where energy saving is a critical issue for the planet and to slow down global warming. In contrast, many current machine learning techniques, especially those relying on deep learning, require tremendous amounts of energy and long pre-training phases.

Finally, the paper aimed at also illustrating the interest of testing neuro-inspired models in real robots interacting with the real world so as to generate novel model-driven predictions for neuroscience and psychology. In the particular case of the adaptive coordination of model-based and model-free reinforcement learning strategies, we showed that some situations can induce cooperation between learning strategies. We moreover showed that not only taking into account the uncertainty of each learning system but also its computational cost could work efficiently in a variety of task. This raises the prediction that the mammalian brain may also monitor and memorize the average computational cost (for instance in terms of the duration required for inference) of different learning strategies in different memory systems, in order to favor those which cost less when they are equally efficient. This paves the way for novel neuroscience experiments aimed at testing these new model-driven predictions and understanding the underlying neural mechanisms.

Acknowledgments. The author would like to thank all his collaborators who have contributed through the years to this line of research. In particular, Andrea Brovelli, Romain Cazé, Ricardo Chavarriaga, Laurent Dollé, Benoît Girard, Agnes Guillot, Mark Humphries, Florian Lesaint, Olivier Sigaud, Guillaume Viejo for their contribution to the design, implementation, test, and analysis of computational models of the coordination of learning processes in humans and animals. And Rachid Alami, Lise Aubin, Ken Caluwaerts, Raja Chatila, Aurélie Clodic, Sandra Devin, Rémi Dromnelle, Antoine Favre-Félix, Benoît Girard, Christophe Grand, Agnes Guillot, Jean-Arcady Meyer, Steve N'Guyen, Guillaume Pourcel, Erwan Renaudo, Mariacarla Staffa for their contribution to the design, implementation, test and analysis of robotic experiments aimed at testing neuro-inspired principles for the coordination of learning processes.

Funding. This work has been funded by the Centre National de la Recherche Scientifique (CNRS)'s interdisciplinary programs (MITI) under the grant name 'Hippocampal replay through the prism of reinforcement learning'.

Disclosure/Conflict-of-Interest Statement. The author declares that the research was conducted in the absence of any commercial or financial relationships that could be construed as a potential conflict of interest.

References

1. Arleo, A., Smeraldi, F., Gerstner, W.: Cognitive navigation based on nonuniform Gabor space sampling, unsupervised growing networks, and reinforcement learning. IEEE Trans. Neural Netw. **15**(3), 639–652 (2004). https://doi.org/10.1109/TNN.2004.826221
2. Bellot, J., Sigaud, O., Khamassi, M.: Which temporal difference learning algorithm best reproduces dopamine activity in a multi-choice task? In: Ziemke, T., Balkenius, C., Hallam, J. (eds.) SAB 2012. LNCS (LNAI), vol. 7426, pp. 289–298. Springer, Heidelberg (2012). https://doi.org/10.1007/978-3-642-33093-3_29
3. Bellot, J., Sigaud, O., Roesch, M.R., Schoenbaum, G., Girard, B., Khamassi, M.: Dopamine neurons activity in a multi-choice task: reward prediction error or value function? In: Proceedings of the French Computational Neuroscience NeuroComp12 Workshop, pp. 1–7 (2012)
4. Burgess, N., Maguire, E.A., O'Keefe, J.: The human hippocampus and spatial and episodic memory. Neuron **35**(4), 625–641 (2002)
5. Caluwaerts, K., et al.: Neuro-inspired navigation strategies shifting for robots: integration of a multiple landmark taxon strategy. In: Prescott, T.J., Lepora, N.F., Mura, A., Verschure, P.F.M.J. (eds.) Living Machines 2012. LNCS (LNAI), vol. 7375, pp. 62–73. Springer, Heidelberg (2012). https://doi.org/10.1007/978-3-642-31525-1_6
6. Caluwaerts, K., et al.: A biologically inspired meta-control navigation system for the Psikharpax rat robot. Bioinspiration Biomim. **7**, 025009 (2012)
7. Cassandra, A.R., Kaelbling, L.P., Littman, M.L.: Acting optimally in partially observable stochastic domains. In: AAAI, vol. 94, pp. 1023–1028 (1994)
8. Cazé, R., Khamassi, M., Aubin, L., Girard, B.: Hippocampal replays under the scrutiny of reinforcement learning models. J. Neurophysiol. **120**(6), 2877–2896 (2018)

9. Chatila, R., et al.: Toward self-aware robots. Front. Robot. AI **5**(1), 88–108 (2018)
10. Chebotar, Y., Hausman, K., Zhang, M., Sukhatme, G., Schaal, S., Levine, S.: Combining model-based and model-free updates for trajectory-centric reinforcement learning. arXiv preprint arXiv:1703.03078 (2017)
11. Coutureau, E., Killcross, S.: Inactivation of the infralimbic prefrontal cortex reinstates goal-directed responding in overtrained rats. Behav. Brain Res. **146**(1–2), 167–174 (2003)
12. Daw, N.D., Gershman, S.J., Seymour, B., Dayan, P., Dolan, R.J.: Model-based influences on humans' choices and striatal prediction errors. Neuron **69**(6), 1204–1215 (2011)
13. Daw, N.D., Niv, Y., Dayan, P.: Uncertainty-based competition between prefrontal and dorsolateral striatal systems for behavioral control. Nat. Neurosci. **8**(12), 1704–1711 (2005)
14. Dayan, P.: Improving generalization for temporal difference learning: the successor representation. Neural Comput. **5**(4), 613–624 (1993)
15. Decker, J.H., Otto, A.R., Daw, N.D., Hartley, C.A.: From creatures of habit to goal-directed learners: tracking the developmental emergence of model-based reinforcement learning. Psychol. Sci. **27**(6), 848–858 (2016)
16. Dezfouli, A., Balleine, B.W.: Habits, action sequences and reinforcement learning. Eur. J. Neurosci. **35**(7), 1036–1051 (2012)
17. Dickinson, A., Balleine, B.: Motivational control of goal-directed action. Anim. Learn. Behav. **22**(1), 1–18 (1994)
18. Dollé, L., Chavarriaga, R., Guillot, A., Khamassi, M.: Interactions of spatial strategies producing generalization gradient and blocking: a computational approach. PLoS Comput. Biol. **14**(4), e1006092 (2018)
19. Dollé, L., Khamassi, M., Girard, B., Guillot, A., Chavarriaga, R.: Analyzing interactions between navigation strategies using a computational model of action selection. In: Freksa, C., Newcombe, N.S., Gärdenfors, P., Wölfl, S. (eds.) Spatial Cognition 2008. LNCS (LNAI), vol. 5248, pp. 71–86. Springer, Heidelberg (2008). https://doi.org/10.1007/978-3-540-87601-4_8
20. Dollé, L., Sheynikhovich, D., Girard, B., Chavarriaga, R., Guillot, A.: Path planning versus cue responding: a bio-inspired model of switching between navigation strategies. Biol. Cybern. **103**(4), 299–317 (2010)
21. Doncieux, S., et al.: Dream architecture: a developmental approach to open-ended learning in robotics. arXiv preprint arXiv:2005.06223 (2020)
22. Doya, K.: Reinforcement learning in continuous time and space. Neural Comput. **12**(1), 219–245 (2000)
23. Dromnelle, R., Girard, B., Renaudo, E., Chatila, R., Khamassi, M.: Coping with the variability in humans reward during simulated human-robot interactions through the coordination of multiple learning strategies. In: Proceedings of the 29th IEEE International Conference on Robot and Human Interactive Communication (RO-MAN 2020), Naples, Italy (2020)
24. Dromnelle, R., Renaudo, E., Pourcel, G., Chatila, R., Girard, B., Khamassi, M.: How to reduce computation time while sparing performance during robot navigation? A neuro-inspired architecture for autonomous shifting between model-based and model-free learning. In: 9th International Conference on Biomimetic & Biohybrid Systems (Living Machines 2020). pp. 1–12. LNAI, Online Conference (Initially Planned in Freiburg, Germany) (2020)
25. Eichenbaum, H.: Prefrontal-hippocampal interactions in episodic memory. Nat. Rev. Neurosci. **18**(9), 547–558 (2017)

26. Frankland, P.W., Bontempi, B.: The organization of recent and remote memories. Nat. Rev. Neurosci. **6**(2), 119–130 (2005)
27. Gupta, A.S., van der Meer, M.A., Touretzky, D.S., Redish, A.D.: Hippocampal replay is not a simple function of experience. Neuron **65**(5), 695–705 (2010)
28. Hafez, M.B., Weber, C., Kerzel, M., Wermter, S.: Curious meta-controller: adaptive alternation between model-based and model-free control in deep reinforcement learning. In: 2019 International Joint Conference on Neural Networks (IJCNN), pp. 1–8. IEEE (2019)
29. Hangl, S., Dunjko, V., Briegel, H.J., Piater, J.: Skill learning by autonomous robotic playing using active learning and creativity. arXiv preprint arXiv:1706.08560 (2017)
30. Jauffret, A., Cuperlier, N., Gaussier, P., Tarroux, P.: From self-assessment to frustration, a small step toward autonomy in robotic navigation. Front. Neurorobotics **7**, 16 (2013)
31. Jog, M.S., Kubota, Y., Connolly, C.I., Hillegaart, V., Graybiel, A.M.: Building neural representations of habits. Science **286**(5445), 1745–1749 (1999)
32. Johnson, A., Redish, A.D.: Neural ensembles in CA3 transiently encode paths forward of the animal at a decision point. J. Neurosci. **27**(45), 12176–12189 (2007)
33. Kahneman, D.: Thinking, Fast and Slow. Macmillan, New York (2011)
34. Keramati, M., Dezfouli, A., Piray, P.: Speed/accuracy trade-off between the habitual and the goal-directed processes. PLoS Comput. Biol. **7**(5), e1002055 (2011)
35. Khamassi, M.: Complementary roles of the rat prefrontal cortex and striatum in reward-based learning and shifting navigation strategies. Ph.D. thesis, Université Pierre et Marie Curie-Paris VI (2007)
36. Khamassi, M., Girard, B.: Modeling awake hippocampal reactivations with model-based bidirectional search. Biol. Cybern. (114), 231–248 (2020)
37. Khamassi, M., Humphries, M.D.: Integrating cortico-limbic-basal ganglia architectures for learning model-based and model-free navigation strategies. Front. Behav. Neurosci. **6**, 79 (2012)
38. Khamassi, M., Velentzas, G., Tsitsimis, T., Tzafestas, C.: Robot fast adaptation to changes in human engagement during simulated dynamic social interaction with active exploration in parameterized reinforcement learning. IEEE Trans. Cogn. Dev. Syst. **10**(4), 881–893 (2018)
39. Killcross, S., Coutureau, E.: Coordination of actions and habits in the medial prefrontal cortex of rats. Cereb. Cortex **13**(4), 400–408 (2003)
40. Lee, S.W., Shimojo, S., O'Doherty, J.P.: Neural computations underlying arbitration between model-based and model-free learning. Neuron **81**(3), 687–699 (2014)
41. Lesaint, F., Sigaud, O., Flagel, S.B., Robinson, T.E., Khamassi, M.: Modelling Individual differences in the form of Pavlovian conditioned approach responses: a dual learning systems approach with factored representations. PLoS Comp. Biol. **10**(2) (2014). https://doi.org/10.1371/journal.pcbi.1003466
42. Leutgeb, S., Leutgeb, J.K., Barnes, C.A., Moser, E.I., McNaughton, B.L., Moser, M.B.: Independent codes for spatial and episodic memory in hippocampal neuronal ensembles. Science **309**(5734), 619–623 (2005)
43. Llofriu, M., et al.: A computational model for a multi-goal spatial navigation task inspired by rodent studies. In: 2019 International Joint Conference on Neural Networks (IJCNN), pp. 1–8. IEEE (2019)
44. Maffei, G., Santos-Pata, D., Marcos, E., Sánchez-Fibla, M., Verschure, P.F.: An embodied biologically constrained model of foraging: from classical and operant conditioning to adaptive real-world behavior in DAC-X. Neural Netw. **72**, 88–108 (2015)

45. Mattar, M.G., Daw, N.D.: Prioritized memory access explains planning and hippocampal replay. Nat. Neurosci. **21**(11), 1609–1617 (2018)
46. McClelland, J.L., McNaughton, B.L., O'Reilly, R.C.: Why there are complementary learning systems in the hippocampus and neocortex: insights from the successes and failures of connectionist models of learning and memory. Psychol. Rev. **102**(3), 419 (1995)
47. Meyer, J.A., Guillot, A., Girard, B., Khamassi, M., Pirim, P., Berthoz, A.: The Psikharpax project: towards building an artificial rat. Robot. Auton. Syst. **50**(4), 211–223 (2005)
48. Momennejad, I.: Learning structures: predictive representations, replay, and generalization. Curr. Opin. Behav. Sci. **32**, 155–166 (2020)
49. Moore, A.W., Atkeson, C.G.: Prioritized sweeping: reinforcement learning with less data and less time. Mach. Learn. **13**(1), 103–130 (1993)
50. Nagabandi, A., Kahn, G., Fearing, R.S., Levine, S.: Neural network dynamics for model-based deep reinforcement learning with model-free fine-tuning. In: 2018 IEEE International Conference on Robotics and Automation (ICRA), pp. 7559–7566. IEEE (2018)
51. Nakahara, H., Doya, K., Hikosaka, O.: Parallel cortico-basal ganglia mechanisms for acquisition and execution of visuomotor sequences-a computational approach. J. Cogn. Neurosci. **13**(5), 626–647 (2001)
52. O'Doherty, J.P., Lee, S., Tadayonnejad, R., Cockburn, J., Iigaya, K., Charpentier, C.J.: Why and how the brain weights contributions from a mixture of experts (2020)
53. O'keefe, J., Nadel, L.: The Hippocampus as a Cognitive Map. Clarendon Press, Oxford (1978)
54. Ostlund, S.B., Balleine, B.W.: Lesions of medial prefrontal cortex disrupt the acquisition but not the expression of goal-directed learning. J. Neurosci. **25**(34), 7763–7770 (2005)
55. Packard, M.G., Knowlton, B.J.: Learning and memory functions of the basal ganglia. Annu. Rev. Neurosci. **25**(1), 563–593 (2002)
56. Peng, J., Williams, R.J.: Efficient learning and planning within the Dyna framework. Adapt. Behav. **1**(4), 437–454 (1993)
57. Pezzulo, G., Rigoli, F., Chersi, F.: The mixed instrumental controller: using value of information to combine habitual choice and mental simulation. Front. Psychol. **4**, 92 (2013)
58. Renaudo, E., Girard, B., Chatila, R., Khamassi, M.: Design of a control architecture for habit learning in robots. In: Duff, A., Lepora, N.F., Mura, A., Prescott, T.J., Verschure, P.F.M.J. (eds.) Living Machines 2014. LNCS (LNAI), vol. 8608, pp. 249–260. Springer, Cham (2014). https://doi.org/10.1007/978-3-319-09435-9_22
59. Renaudo, E., Girard, B., Chatila, R., Khamassi, M.: Respective advantages and disadvantages of model-based and model-free reinforcement learning in a robotics neuro-inspired cognitive architecture. In: Biologically Inspired Cognitive Architectures BICA 2015, Lyon, France, pp. 178–184 (2015)
60. Renaudo, E., Girard, B., Chatila, R., Khamassi, M.: Which criteria for autonomously shifting between goal-directed and habitual behaviors in robots? In: 5th International Conference on Development and Learning and on Epigenetic Robotics (ICDL-EPIROB), Providence, RI, USA, pp. 254–260. (2015)
61. Rojas-Castro, D.M., Revel, A., Menard, M.: Rhizome architecture: an adaptive neurobehavioral control architecture for cognitive mobile robots' application in a vision-based indoor robot navigation context. Int. J. Soc. Robot. (3), 1–30 (2020)

62. Ruvolo, P., Eaton, E.: ELLA: an efficient lifelong learning algorithm. In: International Conference on Machine Learning, pp. 507–515 (2013)
63. Santos-Pata, D., Zucca, R., Verschure, P.F.M.J.: Navigate the unknown: implications of grid-cells "Mental Travel" in vicarious trial and error. In: Lepora, N.F.F., Mura, A., Mangan, M., Verschure, P.F.M.J.F.M.J., Desmulliez, M., Prescott, T.J.J. (eds.) Living Machines 2016. LNCS (LNAI), vol. 9793, pp. 251–262. Springer, Cham (2016). https://doi.org/10.1007/978-3-319-42417-0_23
64. Schultz, W., Dayan, P., Montague, P.R.: A neural substrate of prediction and reward. Science **275**, 1593–1599 (1997)
65. Stachenfeld, K.L., Botvinick, M.M., Gershman, S.J.: The hippocampus as a predictive map. Nat. Neurosci. **20**(11), 1643 (2017)
66. Stoianov, I., Maisto, D., Pezzulo, G.: The hippocampal formation as a hierarchical generative model supporting generative replay and continual learning. bioRxiv (2020)
67. Sutton, R.S.: Integrated architectures for learning, planning, and reacting based on approximating dynamic programming. In: Proceedings of the Seventh International Conference on Machine Learning, pp. 216–224 (1990)
68. Sutton, R.S., Barto, A.G.: Introduction to Reinforcement Learning, 1st edn. MIT Press, Cambridge (1998)
69. Thrun, S.: Lifelong learning algorithms. In: Thrun, S., Pratt, L. (eds.) Learning to Learn, pp. 181–209. Springer, Boston (1998). https://doi.org/10.1007/978-1-4615-5529-2_8
70. Viejo, G., Khamassi, M., Brovelli, A., Girard, B.: Modeling choice and reaction time during arbitrary visuomotor learning through the coordination of adaptive working memory and reinforcement learning. Front. Behav. Neurosci. **9**, 225 (2015)
71. Watkins, C.J., Dayan, P.: Q-learning. Mach. Learn. **8**(3–4), 279–292 (1992)
72. Wiering, M.A., van Hasselt, H.: Ensemble algorithms in reinforcement learning. IEEE Trans. Syst. Man Cybern. Part B **38**(4), 930–936 (2008). https://doi.org/10.1109/TSMCB.2008.920231
73. Wise, S.P.: The role of the basal ganglia in procedural memory. In: Seminars in Neuroscience, vol. 8, pp. 39–46. Elsevier (1996)

Applications of Natural Computing

Interactive Sensor-Based Virtual Experiment Digital Textbook System on Smart Phone and Learning Cloud

Kwang Sik Chung[1]([⊠]) [iD], Yeon Sin Kim[2] [iD], Sang Im Jung[2] [iD], Chung Hun Lee[3] [iD], Sooyoul Kwon[4] [iD], and Namhyeong Lee[5] [iD]

[1] Department of Computer Science, Korea National Open University, Dongsung-dong, Jongno-gu, Seoul 110-791, Korea
kchung0825@knou.ac.kr

[2] Information & Computer Center, Korea National Open University, Dongsung-dong, Jongno-gu, Seoul 110-791, Korea
{yskim,jsn}@knou.ac.kr

[3] Digital Media Center, Korea National Open University, Dongsung-dong, Jongno-gu, Seoul 110-791, Korea
chlee@knou.ac.kr

[4] Department of Environmental Health, Korea National Open University, Dongsung-dong, Jongno-gu, Seoul 110-791, Korea
sykwon@knou.ac.kr

[5] Department of Economics, Korea National Open University, Dongsung-dong, Jongno-gu, Seoul 110-791, Korea
namhyunglee@knou.ac.kr

Abstract. This study looks at digital learning material as its qualified virtual practice/virtual experiment learning content and designs the best learning content to satisfy the existing definition of functions and services of digital learning material. The virtual practice/virtual experiment learning content service should meet the requirements. It is created considering a link to/synchronization with future learning content services built and operated by distance universities.

This research defined learning model scenarios based on failure-experience learning model in oxygen titration for chemical experiments. The research developed the failure-experience learning scenario for chemical experiments' oxygen titration and developed a prototype for digital learning material service which will be provided to learners. It also conducted a survey asking learners on the developed virtual experiment learning material service. The survey results found that the service could be effective to improve the learning efficiency.

Keywords: Digital textbook system · Interactive Sensor-based Virtual Experiment · Smart learning · Virtual experiment · Smart phone · Learning cloud

1 Introduction

Mobile learning based on smartphones is getting more effective as a variety of content for smartphones or tablet PCs are being introduced along with the advancement of IT

© Springer Nature Switzerland AG 2020
C. Martín-Vide et al. (Eds.): TPNC 2020, LNCS 12494, pp. 25–35, 2020.
https://doi.org/10.1007/978-3-030-63000-3_2

technology. The mobile learning content vary. Some use various sensors installed in smartphones (i.e. acceleration sensor, G sensor, access sensor, and brightness sensor) and others use communications functions (i.e. Bluetooth, 5G, and HSDPA). Accordingly, the needs for smartphone-based digital learning material are rising. Particularly, the demands among natural science students for digital content such as virtual experiment are getting higher. The existing virtual experiment content, which was developed when people commonly used desktop computers with flash memories, have limits requiring a mouse and keyboard in a certain environment. Under the circumstances, dynamic interactions in natural science experiments were not available and the learners were not able to fully enjoy a virtual experiment. The students had static learning devices and no or limited access to proper content.

It is time to create really effective digital learning content which can lead learners to concentrate on a virtual experiment class and fully use mobile functions through interactive activities. Unfortunately, a prototype development of digital learning content providing a virtual experiment started by Korea National Open University is at a standstill producing no study results.

In remains of this paper, Sect. 2 discusses previous research related to virtual experiment service on e-learning. Sect. 3 presents Interactive Sensor-based Virtual Experiment Digital Textbook service and platform system. Finally, Sect. 5 concludes after discussing some improvements and future research plans.

2   Related Research

ERICA-MOOC was developed to introduce an open SW learning system on a coding class platform and is now in service. Basically, it is a web browser-based coding platform providing a cloud-based virtual class. It has an interactive coding program which includes an automated learner tracking service (informing the progress, test, and results), graded content, and recyclable learning content. ERICA-MOOC was launched in 2018 and ran on a trial basis in 2019. 2020 will be the year of online opening. Through the ERICA-MOOC, web-based live interactive coding education platform, learners can practice Python, Java, Scratch, and C. They can get an automated feedback and results after submitting an online code thanks to the real-time publishing service. The ERICA-MOOC also provides distance tutoring services as it is an openlab system [1].

Four institutes of science and technology in Korea such as KAIST, GIST, DGIST, and UNIST and POSTECH (science technology university) launched Science & Technology Advanced Research (STAR)-MOOC aimed at developing and introducing an online open class named Massive Online Open Courses (MOOC) [2]. The STAR-MOOC is designed to integrate online open classes of the science technology university and institutes and offer classes to public free of charge related to science and technology like the 4th industrial revolution. Anyone can get the free education service after a member subscription on the website (starmooc.kr). Fifteen classes were open in earlier 2018 and the number increased to 25 at the end of 2018.

Korea Institute of Science and Technology Information (KISTI) independently developed an intelligent R&D platform called EDISON [3]. The EDISON, which combined 7 research achievements in calculation science and engineering with advanced IT technologies like AI, is an open platform enabling a web-based simulation and data-based research environment buildup in education or research online. The web-based open simulation platform is created to put the local simulation SW to practical use and develop competent science and engineering personnel in the area of simulation SW development, application, and distribution. Due to its promising goal, it was subsidized by Ministry of Science and Technology since 2011. Its services can be used for many purposes including supercomputers.

Analyses on the virtual experiment practice and services have been made and there are three issues coming from the analyses. First, the platform does not support a failure-based learning. The learning scenario is created under the assumption that all learners will be successful. There is no learning process for failed learners. Therefore, the failed learning cannot be led to learning experiences or achievements. What is particularly needed is an extra learning content responsive to any failure but there is nothing like that. Second, the virtual experiment practice content and its side content are linear and asynchronous. That is, no synchronization occurs between the two content not allowing learners to track their learning process and study consistently. Third, learners have little access to a learning device losing a chance to use sensor functions. They cannot respond actively to features of various devices due to the web-based platform. They depend only on two-dimensional virtual experiments whereas smartphones have a lot of sensors which are effective as a learning tool.

3 Interactive Sensor-Based Virtual Experiment Digital Textbook System

The present digital learning material service for distance university, which enables learners to get access to both on and offline data synchronizing and providing textbooks, video lecture, and question samples, is a comprehensive service where the learning process can be traced. With the help of this material people can start online learning at will at anywhere anytime and at any device. The service is composed of learning material, personalized learning for a self-study, and class participation as like in Fig. 1.

3.1 Learning Material Service

A distance learning material is defined as one (or more) of textbooks, video lectures (by a professor or lecture), virtual experiment practice content, question samples, assignments, discussion minutes, the Internet search-based content (i.e. Google scholar, Coursera, Google news, NAVER news, and YouTube), and material produced by learners (i.e. Answers to questions, video, and explanations on problems). Its manufactures are distance universities, learners, and professional learning content producers. The learning material given to learners varies depending on the learning purpose. Distance universities, teachers (class managers) and students all should be able to register a variety of learning material in the Learning Content Management System (LCMS) online. In addition, the LCMS should be able to keep watching and manage issues like intellectual property rights, learning content metadata, access routes, and access permissions which are necessary to provide learners with content manufactured by professional producers.

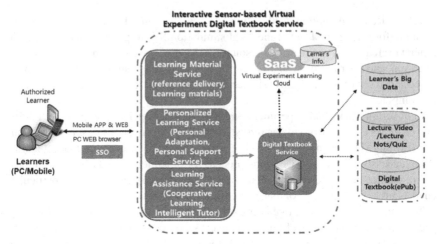

Fig. 1. Concept of Interactive Sensor-based Virtual Experiment Digital Textbook System

The learning material service can be enjoyed at anytime and anywhere regardless of the learning device, type of web browser, or type of communications service as like in Fig. 2. The service provides the following material to learners.

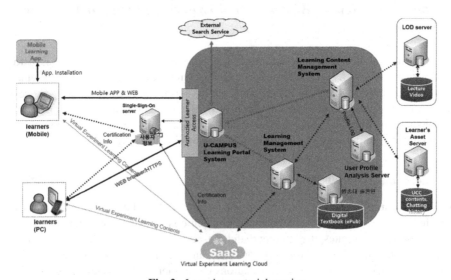

Fig. 2. Learning material service

– Learning content: Textbooks, video lectures (by a professor or lecture), virtual experiment practice content, question samples, lecture material, teaching plan on the web, class material, supplementary data, and sample questions manufactured to satisfy the educational purpose by Korea National Open University

– Learning activity outcomes: Virtual experiment/practice results, assignments, outputs after discussion (At the request of the teacher, the learners make a discussion or discuss with the teacher by team and submit the discussion minute), individual notes for learning, learners' glossary, and learning content manufactured by professional content producers (explanations on problems, learning video, and explanatory material)
– External learning material: The Internet-based learning content (Google scholar, Coursera, Google news, NAVER news, YouTube, etc.)

The detailed functions of the learning material service system are as follows:

The learning content includes internal material like textbooks, video lectures (by a professor or lecture), virtual experiment practice content, question samples, lecture material, teaching plan on the web, class material, supplementary data, and sample questions designed and manufactured by distance universities. In order to make learners use the content, the instructional design should be registered in the LCMS storage. Then, the LCMS should have the lecture list according to the teaching plan and be able to make the learners call the content from the storage or lead them to a URL link. For external learning material (i.e. supplementary textbooks, sample questions, and teaching plan), the learners may download them on the webpage they currently stay or make up settings from the user's menu to download. Such a function necessary to use the content will be synchronized with the current learning page and each relevant content will be connected to be operated and managed.

Learners save their learning activity outcomes such as virtual experiment/practice results, assignments, outputs after discussion (At the request of the teacher, the learners make a discussion or discuss with the teacher by team and submit the discussion minute), individual notes for learning, learners' glossary, and learning content manufactured by professional content producers (explanations on problems, learning video, and explanatory material). Teachers as well as the learners themselves are allowed to access to the learning activity outcomes. The data also can be shared among learners. The outcomes should be managed by the learners themselves in their own online space (cloud environment). The individual cloud storage for submitting experiments results, assignments, and discussion minutes is linked to the learning content. It should be searched and classified by the curriculum/subject/class priority/learner/learner group/online study/SNS/region. The learners should be able to write and save their own comments through an individual memo function including a memo button at each unit and find the writings in serial order or at random. Particularly, glossaries and memos need to be managed by the version in order to allow not only the student but also the other learners permitted to share the data to build up the learner's content. Learners may be able to see how much they improved by keeping glossaries and comments in record.

To make learners use the external learning material (i.e. the Internet-based learning content like Google scholar, Coursera, Google news, NAVER news, YouTube, etc.) and any data from SNS activity, some necessary functions should be completed. For an information collection from outside, learners should be able to get access to external search services and the relevant intellectual property rights and metadata should be watched and updated continuously. In this environment, the learners may be able to obtain learning material via the external route through a keyword-based search. It is also necessary to provide a function in which learners can track their learning history and see effectiveness of external material and use them in statistics to help distance universities better design and create a learning content.

3.2 Personalized Learning Service

This service not only provides pre-organized content according to an instructional design but also leads learners to study by themselves and achieve the learning goal allowing them to choose a class fit for their level as like in Fig. 3.

– Select a content at own level
– Personalized learning course
– Choose a test category fit for you (the learner) and check the feedback
– Manage the learning progress for a self-study

Learners will be able to control their learning capacity if they get access to a proper learning course personalized according to their preferences and learning goals.

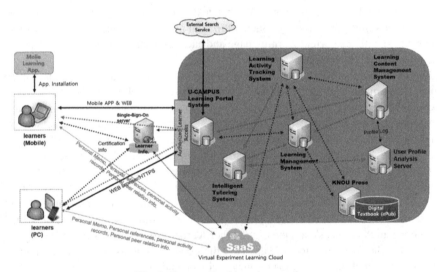

Fig. 3. Personalized learning service

The detailed functions of the learning material service system are as follows:

In order to enable learners to study by themselves there should be various learning levels to meet each learner's needs. The content should be able to reflect a user's personal learning data such as the learner's background knowledge, prerequisite unit and grade, relevant learning activities to recommend the best content allowing the learner to make decisions on which course they will take. First of all, when the content is in process of manufacture/design and operation the learning list needs to be fragmented more than the current level.

Until now, learners have passively studied as one unit is assigned to a single learning content. However, future distance universities will be required to establish a function allowing individual learners to control their learning schedule and experiences. The learners should be able to choose to take a pre-set program or make up the course by themselves. To this end, the content should be full of various learning material and identify which is the most searched and preferred from the class lists. A detailed analysis on the content and correlation with learners will be a must.

For a correct test, tests implemented at each level should well reflect the level of difficulty. More detailed and fragmented categories are needed than those generally used like an upper, intermediate, or lower level to effectively show the learners' capacity. Under the grading system, those who completed answers in the lower level must be able to solve problems in the intermediate level and those who cannot pass from a lower level to an upper level should be able to see the cause and repeat the learning again. If the levels are more fragmented the analysis will be more accurate leading to a better learning achievement.

Multiple features should be prepared to enable the learners to diagnose their capacity by themselves. The users should be able to check the learning progress, test feedback and results, the number of visits to each lecture, access hour, remaining time limits, and recommended schedule. Furthermore, students who failed to reach a proper level after completing the course should be able to partly or fully repeat taking the class.

3.3 Learning Assistance Service

Learners should access to other options to obtain knowledge, for example, by sharing the learning content or activities created among the learners as well as from the pre-organized content or textbooks provided by teachers as like in Fig. 4.

– Enable to help each other to achieve more
– Give a learning assistance service to prevent a dropout
– Analyze the learning progress to manage in an intelligent way
– Give access to the personal learning cloud

The knowledge that they collect and organize by themselves through online communications can give them more practical experiences.

The detailed functions of the learning material service system are as follows:

To realize this environment, there should exist a virtual space to interact and cooperate with other learners. An extra assistance service in addition to general SNS platforms is necessary to create a chat room or online study room keep studying together. The online chat room is required for group, team-based, or temporary discussions for a project success. The chat room should be effective for a real-time or non-real-time meeting and provide a place only for a team-based project in the short- and long-term. The learners should be able to save and submit the outputs from group discussions, or receive the feedbacks and share grades with the same team members. Teachers should be able to freely upload and download feedbacks, good outcomes, and relevant data. The assistant learning service should provide best examples of Q&A and self-manufactured video lectures as it is more effective for learners to achieve academic results if they see how

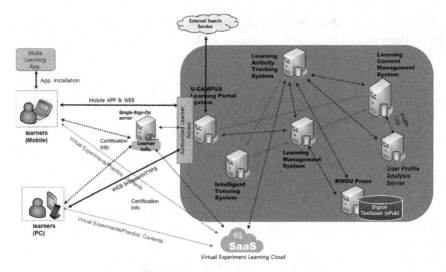

Fig. 4. Learning assistance service

other students solve problems and share each personal note including right and wrong answers.

In addition, there should be an intelligent learning management function to track the learners' study activities, provide learning content for each individual, manage test results, and give an opportunity to study in group. The function will help recommend a content fit for each learner and establish a study strategy. The intelligent management system which collects and analyzes students' learning data and their performance will influence on most functions of the digital learning material service operated by distance universities in the future.

In the middle of learning, both teachers and students have to be able to ask questions at any time and the Q&A platform should vary including a counselling with a teacher, e-mail, SMS, PC app or mobile app. Text messages or mobile instant messaging application like Kakao Talk can be used. But whether the messaging tool is allowed or not will be determined by the responsible institution. When users are permitted to use the tool, personal information must be tightly protected and any slander or defamation restricted.

4   Satisfaction of the Proposed Interactive Sensor-Based Virtual Experiment Digital Textbook

Figure 5 shows the satisfaction level of learners with the prior stage contents of proposed Interactive Sensor-based Virtual Experiment Digital Textbook. The questionnaire for the satisfaction level of learners with the prior stage contents of proposed Interactive Sensor-based Virtual Experiment Digital Textbook is 'the prior stage contents of proposed Interactive Sensor-based Virtual Experiment Digital Textbook were useful for understanding the experiment'. Before learning the prior stage contents of proposed Interactive Sensor-based Virtual Experiment Digital Textbook, learners go through the steps to understand the whole experiment contents through the proposed Interactive Sensor-based Virtual Experiment Digital Textbook. 82.1% of learners answered that the proposed Interactive Sensor-based Virtual Experiment Digital Textbook before the experiment helps them understand the real experiment. In particular, they responded that their understanding of how to use experiment tools and experiment scenarios will increase.

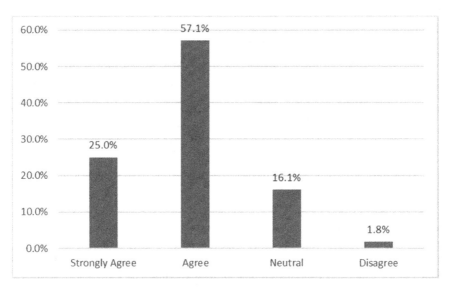

Fig. 5. The satisfaction level of the prior stage contents

Figure 6 shows the satisfaction level of learners with the function and operation of the actual experimental equipment and tools by using the proposed Interactive Sensor-based Virtual Experiment Digital Textbook. The questionnaire question is [It was easy to recognize the function or operation of the actual experimental equipment and tools through the proposed Interactive Sensor-based Virtual Experiment Digital Textbook]. Learners responded that they could improve their understanding of the experiment equipment and tools through the proposed Interactive Sensor-based Virtual Experiment Digital Textbook. 76.1% of learners answered that the pre-learning of the proposed Interactive Sensor-based Virtual Experiment Digital Textbook helps them understand the function and usage of the actual experimental equipment and tools. In particular, they responded that it was helpful in the selection of experimental equipment and tools in each experimental stage, the method of moving and operating the equipment and tools for actual experiments.

The response result for the applicability of the proposed Interactive Sensor-based Virtual Experiment Digital Textbook is shown in Fig. 7. If the proposed Interactive Sensor-based Virtual Experiment Digital Textbook is applied to the actual experiment subject or class, 85.7% of respondents said that it would be helpful for offline experiment learning, and 0% said that it would not be helpful. The questionnaire question is [the proposed Interactive Sensor-based Virtual Experiment Digital Textbook content will

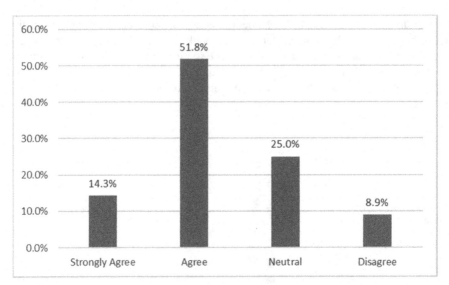

Fig. 6. Satisfaction level with the function and operation of the actual experimental equipment and tools

help you learn actual experiment in offline class. In particular, they responded that it would be helpful in preventing risks and accidents of offline experiment class, that may occur in each experiment stage, and that it would be helpful in understanding the overall contents of the experiment and the purpose of the experiment.

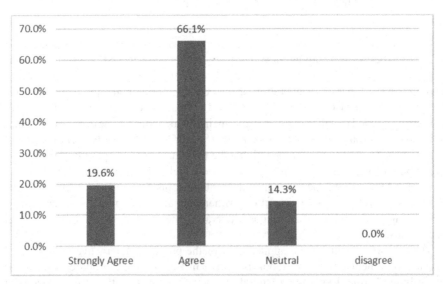

Fig. 7. The applicability of the proposed Interactive Sensor-based Virtual Experiment Digital Textbook

5   Conclusion

With the development of IT technology and sensor networks, collecting IT users' information has been possible, and accordingly, virtual learning content have been created. Particularly, virtual experiment and practice learning content serve as a motivation for students to learn something. It is often said that the content is what the Korea National Open University must introduce for future education.

This study applied the existing textbook-based learning activities to the future digital-based service. Under the digital system, learners can use video lectures and virtual experiment content. The virtual learning content may encourage the students to actively get involved in learning leading to more experiences. It may also help those who want to study in advance as virtual videos make them better understand. The digital material, learning video streams, test questions, and virtual experiment content will be assigned to the same unit. There are two versions of the learning device: HTML5 and smartphone app.

The learners can choose one of them. This study also proposed the development method of virtual experiment learning content. The method defined a necessary mutual cooperation between and among the parties concerned who are engaged in the content development and their work scope, enabling an assumption of the development budget and required staff size. It is practical standards for the development environment and management that can be applied to distance universities in Korea. It is an outcome created after eliminating or improving errors from the existing content.

References

1. http://computer.hanyang.ac.kr/value/mooc.php
2. https://www.starmooc.kr/
3. http://elearning.edison.re.kr/

Solving Hard Problems by Protein Folding?

Andrzej Lingas[✉]

Department of Computer Science, Lund University, Box 118, 221 00 Lund, Sweden
Andrzej.Lingas@cs.lth.se

Abstract. Inspired by the NP-hardness of string folding problems modeling the natural process of protein folding, we discuss the idea of solving instances of NP-hard problems (e.g., string folding problems) of moderate size by letting artificially assembled proteins to fold. The accuracy with which one can combinatorially model the protein folding process, e.g., by string folding, as well as the precision with which one could experimentally estimate the energy of folded artificial proteins are crucial issues.

Keywords: Hard problems · Protein folding

1 Introduction

The overwhelming majority of algorithmic and complexity communities believes that NP is not equal P. Since the $P = NP$? problem has been posed almost 50 years ago no strong arguments for the equality of these two classes have been provided. Hence, it seems that the only way to attack larger hard instances of NP-complete problems is to adhere to unconventional computation models, in particular natural ones.

Protein folding is a multi-phase process where a protein originally in linear form (primary structure) conforms to a complicated three dimensional form (tertiary or quaternary structure) that is believed to minimize free energy. Levinthal observed that usually a protein has a huge number of possible ways (pathways) to conform to the final native structure that uses to be unique [8]. The conformation process seems to be driven by the second law of thermodynamic tending to the minimization of the free energy of the folded protein (energy tunnel).

On the other hand, for the purpose of the prediction of the native structure of a protein on the basis of its primary structure, i.e., a sequence of amino acids, one has developed simplified combinatorial models of protein folding, e.g., string folding problems with finite alphabet over two or three dimensional grids. Interestingly enough, the latter problems tend to be NP-hard. This suggests that perhaps the natural process of protein folding modeled by the string folding problems could be used in order to solve instances of an NP-hard problem (e.g., a string folding problem) of moderate size. It could be done by assembling an

C. Martín-Vide et al. (Eds.): TPNC 2020, LNCS 12494, pp. 36–41, 2020.
https://doi.org/10.1007/978-3-030-63000-3_3

artificial sequence of amino acids corresponding to the input instance of the NP hard problem, letting the sequence to fold and then by experimentally measuring the energy of the folded artificial protein.

The aforementioned idea might seem naive, note however that the preliminary ideas of several recognized methods of unconventional computation were regarded as naive at their beginnings too.

In this paper, we discuss the idea and its potential implementation in more details. We develop a theorem identifying the lower limit for the number of H-H bindings subsequent to an artificial protein folding process corresponding to 'yes' instances. The accuracy with which one could combinatorially model the protein folding process, e.g., by string folding, as well as the precision with which one could experimentally estimate the energy of (more precisely, the number of H-H bindings in) the folded artificial protein appear to be crucial issues.

Our paper is structured as follows. In the next short section, we discuss shortly combinatorial models of protein folding. In Sect. 3, we outline the idea of a process solving a hard problem by protein folding. In Sect. 4, we present sufficient conditions for the implementation of the process. We conclude with final remarks.

2   Combinatorial Models of Protein Folding

In computational biology, the problem of protein folding is to predict the three-dimensional structure of a protein molecule specified by a sequence of amino acids solely on the basis of the sequence.

Dill proposed a simple model, the so called HP-model of a protein in [5]. In this model, the amino acids are classified as being either hydrophilic (H) or hydrophobic (P) and then a protein is modeled as a consecutive chain of hydrophilic and hydrophobic elements. The folding of a protein is modeled by defining a bond as a pair of adjacent hydrophobic elements that are not neighbors in the chain. It is generally assumed that the folding of a protein which maximizes the number of bonds in this model corresponds to the folding of the protein in the nature that is believed to minimize its free energy.

The problem of protein folding in the HP model can be further simplified into the following problem of *string folding*: given a string over a fixed alphabet, determine its embedding onto Z^2 or Z^3 such that any two consecutive elements in the string are mapped on neighboring grid points and the number of pairs of adjacent grid points which are images of alphabet symbols of the same type corresponding to hydrophilic amino acids is maximized [11]. (Note that the maximization of the latter number is equivalent to the maximization of the number of pairs of such adjacent grid points that are not images of consecutive alphabet symbols in the sequence).

Initially, different versions of the string folding problem with infinite alphabet have been shown to NP-hard (e.g., [11]). In a breakthrough paper, Nayak et al. presented a framework allowing for proving NP-hardness even in case of a finite alphabet [10] (see also [10]). Because of the NP-hardness of different variants of the string folding problem [2,3,10,11], approximation algorithms [9] as well as sub-exponential exact algorithms have been developed for some of these variants [4,6].

3 An Outline of the Solving Process

Our idea of *problem solving by protein folding* is inspired by the NP-completeness of combinatorial problems modeling protein folding [2,3,10,11], and the following known conjecture [10].

Conjecture 1. A protein folds in such a manner that the number of H-H bindings is maximized so the free energy is minimized.

This conjecture implicitly assumes suitable thermodynamic conditions. Frequently, one needs to cool the protein but not necessarily closely to the absolute zero [7].

The aforementioned combinatorial problems modeling protein folding are simply string folding problems over finite alphabets in two or three dimensional grids, where the objective is to maximize the number of neighboring symbols corresponding to hydrophilic amino acids.

The proposed process of solving by protein folding consists of the following steps:

1. Combinatorial reduction of the input problem instance to an instance of a combinatorial problem realistically modeling protein folding (CRPF for short).
2. Assembly of an artificial protein chain corresponding to the instance of CRPF.
3. Experiment consisting in letting the artificial protein chain to fold.
4. Measurement pertaining to an estimation of the number of H-H bindings (e.g., of the free energy) in the resulting folding of the artificial protein.

Of course, the assembly and folding steps can take long time which hopefully should be only a polynomial function of the size of an instance to the input problem.

Note that the potential computational power of protein folding would not be based on a variant of *massive* parallelism as in case of DNA-computing, but on the conjectured optimization properties of physical protein folding (Conjecture 1).

4 Sufficient Conditions

As a realistic model of protein folding, we can pick the string folding problem with the alphabet corresponding to amino acids on a relaxed, dense, three-dimensional grid with non-necessarily 90 degrees angles. We shall say that the latter string problem models protein folding with an accuracy δ if the following condition holds:

The instance of the string problem modeling an instance K of protein folding conforms to a folded string with the number of HH neighboring pairs falling in the interval $[(1 - \delta)k, (1 + \delta)k]$, where k is the number of H-H bindings in the folded protein to which conforms K.

Note that conversely if ℓ stands for the number of HH neighboring pairs in the folded instance of the string problem then k falls in the interval $[\frac{1}{1+\delta}\ell, \frac{1}{1-\delta}\ell]$,

Conjecture 2. There is a positive constant $\delta < 1$ such that the refined string folding problem models protein folding with accuracy δ.

Nayak et al. [10] established the NP-hardness of several string folding problems over finite alphabet. By using their framework, hopefully one should be able to prove the following conjecture.

Conjecture 3. The refined string folding problem (on a relaxed, dense, three-dimensional grid) is NP-hard.

Also, we need a many-one polynomial-time reduction ϕ of the original decision problem to the refined string problem to have the following gap property:

There is a natural function ψ and a positive constant $c < 1$ such that an instance I of the original decision problem is reduced to an instance $\phi(I)$ of the refined string folding problem, where if I is a YES instance then $\phi(I)$ has $\psi(I)$ HH neighboring pairs and otherwise it has less than $c\psi(I)$ HH neighboring pairs.

Conjecture 4. Any decision problem in NP admits such a gap polynomial-time reduction ϕ with some natural function ψ and some positive constant $c < 1$.

Finally, we assume that the estimation of the number H-H bindings in a folded artificial protein has a precision ϵ. This means that it yields an answer falling in the interval $[(1 - \epsilon)q, (1 + \epsilon)q]$, where q is the actual number of H-H bindings. Perhaps, such an estimation could be obtained by measuring the free energy in the folded protein that should be minimized. At present, one uses tens of different experimental techniques in order to investigate the structure of folded proteins. Hopefully, some of them, e.g., Circular dichroism [1], could be used to provide good estimations of the energy of folded artificial proteins. Likely, the aforementioned methods do not work on a single protein so one would need to assemble a number of artificial proteins in parallel.

Conjecture 5. There is a nonnegative constant $\epsilon < 1$ such that the number of H-H bindings in the folded artificial protein can be experimentally estimated with precision ϵ.

Under all these conjectures and assumptions, we can implement the solving by protein folding process so the following theorem holds.

Theorem 6. *If the inequality $\frac{1+\epsilon}{1-\delta}c < \frac{1-\epsilon}{1+\delta}$ holds then an instance I of the original combinatorial decision problem is a YES instance if and only if the number of H-H bindings estimated at the end of the solving by protein folding process is at least $\frac{1-\epsilon}{1+\delta}\psi(I)$.*

Proof. In Step 1 of the process, we use a many-one polynomial-time reduction ϕ of the original decision problem to the refined string folding problem. By Conjecture 4, there is a natural function ψ and a positive constant $c < 1$ such that an instance I of the original decision problem is reduced to an instance $\phi(I)$ of the refined string folding problem, where if I is a YES instance then $\phi(I)$ has $\psi(I)$ HH neighboring pairs and otherwise it has less than $c\psi(I)$ HH neighboring pairs. Recall that in Step 2 of the process an artificial protein corresponding to $\phi(I)$ is assembled. It follows by Conjecture 2 and the observation below it that the number k of H-H bindings in the folded protein in Step 3 of the process is not less than $\frac{1}{1+\delta}\psi(I)d$ if I is a YES instance and otherwise it is not greater than $\frac{1}{1-\delta}c\psi(I)$. In Step 4 of the process, the number k is estimated with precision ϵ by Conjecture 5. Hence, the value of the estimation is at least $\frac{1-\epsilon}{1+\delta}\psi(I)$ if I is a YES instance and otherwise it is not greater than $\frac{1+\epsilon}{1-\delta}c\psi(I)$. By the inequality assumed in the theorem, the latter (upper) bound is smaller than the former (lower) bound which completes the proof. $\square$

It follows that the constants δ, and ϵ or c have to be sufficiently small in order to be able to use the process to solve the original decision problem for some instances.

5   Final Remarks

Of course, the assumption on a constant accuracy of modeling protein folding by a refined version of the string folding problem as well as that on a constant precision of estimating the total number of H-H bindings in the folded artificial protein are very optimistic. They are bottlenecks in the implementation of the process of solving the original problem by protein folding. On the other hand, providing a reduction of the original problem to the string folding problem with enough large gap seems easier. Unfortunately, it can potentially blow up the size of the resulting instance of the string problem which in turn would force an assembly of huge artificial proteins. The maximum length of sequences of amino acids that could be assembled limits the size of instances of the original problem that could be decided by the proposed process.

Another difficulty is the likely necessity of substantially cooling the artificial proteins in order to make Conjecture 1 valid. To soften this technical problem, one could consider a weakened conjecture guaranteeing a folding of the input protein closely approximating the maximum number of H-H bindings already in feasible low temperatures. Consequently, one would need to strengthen Conjecture 3 to include MAXSNP-hardness of the refined string folding problem (cf. [10]).

The verification and possible development of the ideas outlined in this paper, in particular the verification of the large number of conjectures involved, would require long-term multi-disciplinary research efforts. A positive outcome of the verifications could open for possible implementations of these ideas for limited-size instances of hard problems in the reality.

Acknowledgments. The author is thankful to Eva-Marta Lundell and Mia Persson for some preliminary discussions and to Anders Irbäck for answering my question on the temperatures required by Conjecture 1. The research has been supported in part by Swedish Research Council grant 621-2017-03750.

References

1. Atkins, P., de Paula, J.: Elements of Physical Chemistry, 4th edn. Oxford University Press, Oxford (2005)
2. Berger, B., Leighton, T.: Protein folding in the hydrophobic-hydrophilic (HP) model is NP-complete. In: Proceedings of the RECOMB 1998, New York (1998)
3. Crescenzi, P., Goldman, D., Papadimitriou, C.H., Piccolboni, A., Yannakakis, M.: On the complexity of protein folding. J. Comput. Biol. **5**(3), 423–466 (1998)
4. Dessmark, A., Lingas, A., Lundell, E.-M.: Subexponential-time framework for optimal embeddings of graphs in integer lattices. In: Hagerup, T., Katajainen, J. (eds.) SWAT 2004. LNCS, vol. 3111, pp. 248–259. Springer, Heidelberg (2004). https://doi.org/10.1007/978-3-540-27810-8_22
5. Dill, K.A.: Theory for the folding and stability of globular proteins. Biochemistry **24**, 1501 (1985)
6. Fu, B., Wang, W.: A $2^{O(n^{1-\frac{1}{d}}\log n)}$ time algorithm for d-dimensional protein folding in the HP-model. In: Díaz, J., Karhumäki, J., Lepistö, A., Sannella, D. (eds.) ICALP 2004. LNCS, vol. 3142, pp. 630–644. Springer, Heidelberg (2004). https://doi.org/10.1007/978-3-540-27836-8_54
7. Irbäck, A.: Personal communication, 2019 December
8. Levinthal, C.: Are there pathways for protein folding? Journal de Chimie Physique et de Physico-Chimie Biologique **65**, 44–45 (1968)
9. Mauri, G., Pavesi, G., Piccolboni, A.: Approximation algorithms for protein folding prediction. In: Proceedings of the SODA 1999, pp. S945–S946 (1999)
10. Nayak, A., Sinclair, A., Zwick, U.: Spatial codes and the hardness of string folding problems (extended abstract). In: Proceedings of the SODA 1998, pp. 639–648 (1998)
11. Paterson, M., Przytycka, T.: On the complexity of string folding. In: Meyer, F., Monien, B. (eds.) ICALP 1996. LNCS, vol. 1099, pp. 658–669. Springer, Heidelberg (1996). https://doi.org/10.1007/3-540-61440-0_167

A Three-Player Envy-Free Discrete Division Protocol for Mixed Manna

Yuki Okano and Yoshifumi Manabe$^{(\boxtimes)}$ [ID]

Faculty of Informatics, Kogakuin University,
Shinjuku, Tokyo, Japan
manabe@cc.kogakuin.ac.jp

Abstract. This paper proposes a three-player envy-free discrete assignment protocol of a divisible good, in which the utility of some portion of the good can be positive for some players and negative for the others. Such a good is called mixed manna. For mixed manna, current discrete envy-free cake-cutting or chore-division protocols cannot be applied. A naive protocol to achieve an envy-free division of mixed manna for three players needs an initial division of given mixed manna into eight pieces. This paper shows a new three-player envy-free discrete division protocol that needs an initial division into two pieces. After the initial division, it is shown that each of the pieces can be divided by modifying current envy-free cake-cutting and chore-division protocols.

Keywords: Cake-cutting · Mixed manna · Chore-division · Divisible good · Envy-free

1 Introduction

This paper proposes a three-player envy-free assignment protocol of a divisible good in which the utility of some portion of the good can be positive for some players and negative for the others. Many works have been done for the cake-cutting problem, where a divisible good has some positive utility to every player. There are some surveys to these problems [7,8,14,17,18]. Some number of works have been done for a chore division problem, where a divisible good has some negative utility to every player [9,10,12,16]. The problem can be used to assign dirty work among people. There are some cases when a portion of a divisible good has some positive utility to some players but the same portion has some negative utility to the other players. For example, a child does not like chocolate but another child likes chocolate on a cake. A nation does not want a region where the religion believed by the residents is different from the national religion. A good which has such a property is called mixed manna. Very few works have been done for fair divisions of divisible mixed manna [19].

There are several assignment results for a given number of indivisible mixed manna [1–3,5,6,11]. Ref. [19] proved the existence of a connected envy-free division of divisible mixed manna by three players. However, finding such a division

© Springer Nature Switzerland AG 2020
C. Martín-Vide et al. (Eds.): TPNC 2020, LNCS 12494, pp. 42–53, 2020.
https://doi.org/10.1007/978-3-030-63000-3_4

cannot be done by a finite number of queries. Thus, a simple protocol to divide divisible mixed manna is necessary. The most widely discussed property that fair division protocols must satisfy is envy-freeness [7,18]. An envy-free cake division among any number of players can be done by a fixed number of discrete operations [4]. An envy-free chore division among any number of players can also be done by a fixed number of discrete operations [9]. This paper discusses an envy-free division of mixed manna. The above cake-cutting or chore-division protocols cannot be used to divide mixed manna. A naive envy-free division protocol is shown in [19], which works for any number of players, needs many initial divisions. When the number of players is three, the manna must be initially divided into eight pieces. Thus, the protocol is not efficient. The protocol in [15] for three players needs an initial division into two pieces. Though the protocol achieves envy-free, the protocol is not discrete sine it uses a moving-knife procedure. We show a new discrete protocol for three players in which the initial division is the same as the one in [15]. After the initial division, it is shown that each of the pieces can be divided by modifying current envy-free cake-cutting and chore-division protocols.

Section 2 defines the problem. Section 3 shows the naive protocol. Section 4 shows the new protocol. Section 5 concludes the paper.

2 Preliminaries

Throughout the paper, mixed manna is a heterogeneous good that is represented by the interval $[0, 1]$ on a real line. It can be cut anywhere between 0 and 1. Each player P_i has a utility function, μ_i, which has the following properties.

1. $\mu_i(X)$ can be positive or negative for any $X = [a, b](0 \leq a < b \leq 1)$.
2. For any X_1 and X_2 such that $X_1 \cap X_2 = \emptyset$, $\mu_i(X_1 \cup X_2) = \mu_i(X_1) + \mu_i(X_2)$.

Note that $\mu_i(X)$ and $\mu_j(X)(i \neq j)$ are independent, thus $\mu_i(X) > 0$ and $\mu_j(X) < 0$ for some X might occur.

Note that if the first condition is changed as $\mu_i([a, b]) \geq 0$ for any a, b, and i, the problem becomes cake-cutting. If the condition is changed as $\mu_i([a, b]) \leq 0$ for any a, b, and i, the problem becomes chore-division.

The tuple of the utility function of $P_i(i = 1, 2, \ldots, n)$ is denoted as $(\mu_1, \mu_2, \ldots, \mu_n)$. No player knows the utility functions of the other players.

An n-player division protocol, f, assigns some portions of $[0, 1]$ to each player such that every portion of $[0, 1]$ is assigned to some player. This means that no portion of the manna is discarded. We denote $f_i(\mu_1, \mu_2, \ldots, \mu_n)$ as the set of portions assigned to the player P_i by f when the tuple of the utility functions is $(\mu_1, \mu_2, \ldots, \mu_n)$.

All players are risk-averse, namely, they avoid gambling. They try to maximize the worst utility they might obtain.

Several desirable properties of fair division protocols have been defined [7,18]. One of the most widely considered property is envy-freeness. The definition of envy-free is as follows: for any $i, j(i \neq j), \mu_i(f_i(\mu_1, \mu_2, \ldots, \mu_n)) \geq$

$\mu_i(f_j(\mu_1, \mu_2, \ldots, \mu_n))$. Envy-free means that every player thinks he has obtained more than or equal value to any other player.

3   A Naive Protocol for Mixed Manna

First, let us review an easy example of the two-player case shown in [19]. The Divide-and-chose protocol for the cake-cutting problem by two players works for any mixed manna. The Divide-and-choose is as follows: the first player, called Divider, cuts the cake into two pieces. The other player, called Chooser, selects the piece he wants among the two pieces. Divider obtains the remaining piece. The reason that Divide-and-choose works for mixed manna is as follows. Since Divider is a risk-averse player, Divider cuts the manna into two pieces $[0, x]$ and $[x, 1]$, such that $\mu_D([0, x]) = \mu_D([x, 1]) = 1/2\mu_D([0, 1])$ for Divider, whenever $\mu_D([0, 1]) \geq 0$ or $\mu_D([0, 1]) < 0$ holds. Otherwise, Chooser might select the better piece and Divider might obtain the worse piece. Since Divider cuts the manna into two equal utility pieces, Divider does not envy Chooser. Chooser selects the better piece among the two pieces. Thus, Chooser does not envy Divider. Therefore, Divide-and-choose can be used for an envy-free division of any mixed manna.

Next, let us consider a three-player case. Selfridge-Conway protocol [18], shown in Fig. 1, is a discrete cake-cutting protocol to achieve envy-freeness. The outline of the protocol is as follows. First, P_1 cuts the cake into three pieces whose utilities are the same for P_1. If P_2 thinks the utility of the largest piece, $\mu_2(X_1)$, is larger than the one of the second-best piece, $\mu_2(X_2)$, P_2 cuts L from X_1 so that $\mu_2(X_1 - L) = \mu_2(X_2)$. If P_2 thinks $\mu_2(X_1) = \mu_2(X_2)$, P_2 does nothing. Then, P_3 selects the best piece among $X_1 - L$, X_2, and X_3. Next, P_2 selects one piece between the remaining two pieces. In this case, if $X_1 - L$ remains, P_2 must select the piece. P_1 obtains the remaining piece. Note that this assignment is envy-free. Since P_3 first selects, P_3 obtains the best piece for P_3. Since P_2 makes two equal-value pieces, P_2 can obtain one of the best pieces whatever P_3 selects. Though P_1 obtains the remaining piece, the piece is not cut by P_2, thus it is one of the best pieces for P_1.

Next, L needs to be assigned if L is cut from X_1 at Step 5. Let P_b be the player who obtained $X_1 - L$ between P_2 and P_3. Let P_a be the other player. P_a cuts L into three pieces whose utilities are the same for P_a. Then P_b, P_1, and P_a select one piece in this order. P_b does not envy the other players since P_b selects first. P_a does not envy the other players because the utilities of the three pieces are the same. P_1 does not envy P_a because P_1 selects earlier than P_a. The reason why P_1 does not envy P_b is as follows. Since P_b obtains $X_1 - L$, the total utility of P_b is less than the utility of X_1 for P_1. P_1 obtains at least $\mu_1(X_1)$, thus P_1 does not envy P_b.

This protocol cannot be used for mixed manna for several reasons. Though P_1 can cut the manna into three pieces X_1, X_2, and X_3 whose utilities are the same for P_1, there can be a case when $\mu_2(X_1) > 0$ and $\mu_2(X_2) < 0$. In this case, P_2 might not be able to cut L from X_1 so that $\mu_2(X_1 - L) = \mu_2(X_2)$. Even if

```
1  Begin
2    P₁ cuts into three pieces so that the utilities of the pieces is the
         same for P₁.
3    Let X₁, X₂, X₃ be the pieces where μ₂(X₁) ≥ μ₂(X₂) ≥ μ₂(X₃).
4    If μ₂(X₁) > μ₂(X₂) Then
5      P₂ cuts L from X₁ so that μ₂(X₁') = μ₂(X₂), where X₁' = X₁ - L.
6      P₃ selects the largest (for P₃) among X₁', X₂, and X₃.
7      If X₁' remains Then
8        P₂ must select X₁'.
9        Let (Pₐ, P_b) be (P₃, P₂).
10   Else
11     P₂ selects X₂. /* the largest for P₂ */
12     Let (Pₐ, P_b) be (P₂, P₃).
13     P₁ obtains the remaining piece.
14   If L is not empty Then
15     Pₐ cuts L into three pieces so that Pₐ considers their utilities
         are the same.
16     P_b, P₁, and Pₐ selects one piece in this order.
17 End.
```

Fig. 1. Selfridge-Conway three-player envy-free cake-cutting protocol [18].

$\mu_2(X_1) > 0$, $\mu_2(X_2) > 0$, and P_2 can cut L from X_1, there can be a case when $\mu_1(L) < 0$ and $X_1' = X_1 - L$ becomes the best piece for P_1. If P_2 or P_3 selects X_1', P_1 envies the player. A similar situation occurs at the assignment of L. P_a cuts L into three pieces L_1, L_2, and L_3 such that $\mu_a(L_1) = \mu_a(L_2) = \mu_a(L_3)$. P_b selects the best piece, say L_1. P_1 then selects one of the remaining pieces, say L_2. In this situation, $\mu_1(L_1) > \mu_1(L) + \mu_1(L_2)$ might occur if $\mu_1(L_3)$ is a very large negative value. In this case, $\mu_1(X_1 - L) + \mu_1(L_1) > \mu_1(X_3) + \mu_1(L_2)$ holds, where X_3 is the piece selected by P_1 at Step 13. Thus, P_1 envies P_b and envy-freeness is not satisfied. Therefore, the Selfridge-Conway protocol cannot be used for mixed manna.

Oskui's three-player envy-free chore division protocol [18], shown in Fig. 2, cannot be used for mixed manna for similar reasons. After P_1 cuts the manna into X_1, X_2, and X_3 and X_1 is the best piece for P_2 and P_3, P_2 cannot cut the manna so that $\mu_2(X_1) = \mu_2(X_2 - E) = \mu_2(X_3 - F)$ is satisfied, if $\mu_2(X_1) > 0$, $\mu_2(X_2) < 0$, and $\mu_2(X_3) < 0$. Even if $\mu_2(X_1) < 0$, $\mu_2(X_2) < 0$, $\mu_2(X_3) < 0$ and P_2 cuts E from X_2 and F from X_3 so that $\mu_2(X_1) = \mu_2(X_2 - E) = \mu_2(X_3 - F)$ is satisfied, there can be a case when $\mu_1(E) > 0$, $\mu_1(F) > 0$, and P_1 envies P_3 by the assignment at Step 11. Therefore, protocols for mixed manna must be newly considered.

A naive envy-free assignment protocol for mixed manna is shown in [19]. First, divide the manna as follows:

- X_{123} such that any portion $x \subseteq X_{123}$ satisfies $\mu_i(x) \geq 0$ for every player $P_i(i = 1, 2, 3)$.
- $X_{ij}(i, j = 1, 2, 3, i < j)$ such that any portion $x \subseteq X_{ij}$ satisfies $\mu_i(x) \geq 0$, $\mu_j(x) \geq 0$, and $\mu_k(x) < 0$ for the other player P_k.

```
1  Begin
2  P₁ cuts into three pieces X₁, X₂, X₃ so that μ₁(X₁) = μ₁(X₂) = μ₁(X₃)
      is satisfied.
3  If the best piece for P₂ and P₃ differs Then
4    P₂ and P₃ select the best piece. P₁ obtains the remaining piece.
5  Else /* Let X₁ be the best piece for P₂ and P₃. */
6    P₂ cuts E from X₂ and F from X₃ so that
         μ₂(X₁) = μ₂(X₂ − E) = μ₂(X₃ − F) is satisfied.
7    If μ₃(X₂ − E) ≤ μ₃(X₁) and μ₃(X₃ − F) ≤ μ₃(X₁) Then
8      P₁, P₃, and P₂ select one piece in this order among X₁, X₂ − E, and
          X₃ − F.
9      Wlog P₁ selects X₂ − E. P₃ selects X₁. P₂ obtains X₃ − F.
10     P₂ cuts E and F into three pieces E₁, E₂, E₃ and F₁, F₂, F₃ so that
          μ₂(E₁) = μ₂(E₂) = μ₂(E₃) and μ₂(F₁) = μ₂(F₂) = μ₂(F₃) are
          satisfied.
11     P₃, P₁, and P₂ select one piece among Es and Fs in this order.
12   Else if μ₃(X₁) ≤ μ₃(X₂ − E) and μ₃(X₁) ≤ μ₃(X₃ − F) Then
13     P₃ cuts E′ ⊆ E and F′ ⊆ F so that
          μ₃(X₂ − E′) = μ₃(X₃ − F′) = μ₃(X₁) are satisfied.
14     Execute Step 8-11 by changing the roles of P₂ and P₃ and renaming
          (E′, F′) to (E, F).
15   Else /* μ₃(X₁) is between μ₃(X₂ − E) and μ₃(X₃ − F). */
16     Wlog μ₃(X₂ − E) ≤ μ₃(X₁) ≤ μ₃(X₃ − F) holds.
17     P₃ cuts F′ ⊆ F so that μ₃(X₃ − F′) = μ₃(X₁) is satisfied.
18     P₁ selects the best piece between X₂ − E and X₃ − F′.
19     If P₁ selects X₂ − E Then
20       P₂ obtains X₁. P₃ obtains X₃ − F′.
21       P₃ cuts E and F′ into three pieces E₁, E₂, E₃ and F₁′, F₂′, F₃′ so
            that μ₃(E₁) = μ₃(E₂) = μ₃(E₃) and μ₃(F₁′) = μ₃(F₂′) = μ₃(F₃′) are
            satisfied.
22       P₂, P₁, and P₃ select one piece among Es and F′s in this order.
23     Else /* P₁ selects X₃ − F′. */
24       P₂ obtains X₂ − E. P₃ obtains X₁.
25       P₂ cuts E and F′ into three pieces E₁, E₂, E₃ and F₁′, F₂′, F₃′ so
            that μ₂(E₁) = μ₂(E₂) = μ₂(E₃) and μ₂(F₁′) = μ₂(F₂′) = μ₂(F₃′) are
            satisfied.
26       P₃, P₁, and P₂ select one piece among Es and F′s in this order.
27 End
```

Fig. 2. Oskui's three-player envy-free chore division protocol [18].

- $X_i (i = 1, 2, 3)$ such that any portion $x \subseteq X_i$ satisfies $\mu_i(x) \geq 0$ and $\mu_j(x) < 0$ for $j \neq i$.
- The remaining portion X_0 such that any portion $x \subseteq X_0$ satisfies $\mu_i(x) < 0$ for $i = 1, 2, 3$.

Then, the Selfridge-Conway protocol is executed among all players for X_{123}. Divide-and-choose is executed to X_{ij} between P_i and P_j. X_i is given to P_i. Last, three-player envy-free chore division protocol [18] is executed for X_0. Similar procedures can be considered for any number of players. Though this procedure achieves an envy-free assignment, the procedure to initially divide the manna is complicated. The mixed manna must be divided into the above eight pieces. Note that each of the eight pieces might not be connected. For example, disconnected multiple portions might satisfy $\mu_i(x) \geq 0$ for all players, thus X_{123} might consist of multiple portions. Thus, the number of cuts to obtain the above eight pieces might be more than eight. When $P_i(i = 1, 2, 3)$ needs to cut the manna c_i times to divide into non-negative regions and negative regions for P_i, the manna needs to be cut $c_1 + c_2 + c_3$ times in the worst case. This paper considers reducing the procedure of the initial division. The protocol in [15] is not discrete since the protocol uses a moving-knife procedure. Thus this paper proposes a new discrete protocol that does not use a moving-knife procedure.

4 A New Protocol for Mixed Manna

This section shows a new three-player envy-free division protocol for mixed manna in which the number of the initial division is reduced. Initially, cut the manna as follows: X^+ such that any portion $x \subseteq X^+$ satisfies $\mu_1(x) \geq 0$. X^- such that any portion $x \subseteq X^-$ satisfies $\mu_1(x) < 0$. $X^+(X^-)$ is the portion with non-negative (negative) utility for P_1. The manna must be cut c_1 times. Note that by a renaming of the players, c_1 can be selected as $\min_i c_i$. Thus, the number of cuts necessary for the initial division is reduced compared to the naive protocol in [19]. $X^+(X^-)$ might consist of multiple disconnected pieces. In this case, the disconnected pieces are collected to make one piece. X^+ and X^- might contain both positive and negative portions for the other players.

The assignment of X^+ uses the protocol in [15]. The protocol is shown in Fig. 3, in which the Selfridge-Conway protocol is modified. Initially, P_1 cuts X^+ into three pieces. If both of P_2 and P_3 think at most one piece has a non-negative utility, an envy-free assignment is easily obtained. If P_2 or P_3 thinks that at least two pieces have a non-negative utility, the Selfridge-Conway protocol can be executed because P_1 thinks any portion of X^+ has a non-negative utility.

Theorem 1 [15]. *The assignment result of X^+ by the protocol in Fig. 3 is envy-free.*

Proof. First, consider the case when both of P_2 and P_3 consider that at most one piece among X_1^+, X_2^+, and X_3^+ has a non-negative utility. Consider the subcase when both of P_2 and P_3 think the same piece, say X_1^+, has a non-negative utility. P_2 and P_3 execute Divide-and-choose on X_1^+. Let P_2 and P_3 obtain X_{12}^+ and X_{13}^+, respectively. Since $X_1^+ = X_{12}^+ \cup X_{13}^+$ and any portion of X_1^+ has a non-negative utility for P_1, $\mu_1(X_{12}^+) \leq \mu_1(X_1^+) = \mu_1(X_2^+)$ and $\mu_1(X_{13}^+) \leq \mu_1(X_1^+) = \mu_1(X_2^+)$ hold. Since P_1 obtains X_2^+ and X_3^+, P_1 does not envy P_2 or P_3. P_2 and P_3 do not envy each other because of the envy-freeness of Divide-and-choose. P_2 does not envy P_1, since $\mu_2(X_2^+) < 0$ and $\mu_2(X_3^+) < 0$ hold. Similarly, P_3 does not envy P_1.

Next, consider the subcase when no piece has a non-negative utility for both of P_2 and P_3. In this case, P_2 and P_3 can obtain at most one piece whose utility is not negative for the player. P_1 obtains the remaining pieces, which have a negative utility for both of P_2 and P_3. Thus, every player does not envy the other players.

```
1  Begin
2    P₁ cuts into three pieces X₁⁺, X₂⁺, and X₃⁺ so that
         μ₁(X₁⁺) = μ₁(X₂⁺) = μ₁(X₃⁺).
3    If P₂ and P₃ consider at most one piece has a non-negative utility
       Then
4      If P₂ and P₃ consider the same piece (say, X₁⁺) has a non-negative
           utility Then
5        P₂ and P₃ execute Divide-and-choose on X₁⁺.
6        P₁ obtains X₂⁺ and X₃⁺.
7      Else
8        Each of P₂ and P₃ obtains at most one piece with a non-negative
             utility.
9        P₁ obtains the remaining piece(s).
10   Else
11     Let P₂ be a player who considers two pieces have some non-negative
           utility.
12     Rename the pieces so that μ₂(X₁⁺) ≥ μ₂(X₂⁺) ≥ μ₂(X₃⁺).
13     Execute the Selfridge-Conway protocol from Step 4 with the three
           pieces.
14 End.
```

Fig. 3. Three-player envy-free protocol for X^+ [15].

Next, consider the case when one player, say P_2, thinks two pieces have a non-negative utility. In this case, the Selfridge-Conway protocol can be executed. The reason is as follows. P_2 can cut L from X_1^+ if $\mu_2(X_1^+) > \mu_2(X_2^+)$ since both of these utilities are non-negative. Each player can select one piece among $X_1^{'+}$, X_2^+, and X_3^+. The assignment result is envy-free, since P_3 selects first, there are two equal utility pieces for P_2, and P_1 can obtain one full-size piece (Note that any portion of X^+ has non-negative utility for P_1, thus $\mu_1(X_1^{'+}) \leq \mu_1(X_1^+)$ holds). An envy-free assignment of L can also be realized. Even if the utility is positive or negative, P_a can cut L into three pieces with the same utility. P_a does not envy any other players since the three pieces have the same utility. P_b does not envy any other players since P_b first selects a piece. P_1 does not envy P_b since P_b does not obtain $1/3$ of X^+ (Note again P_1 thinks any portion of X^+ has a non-negative utility). P_1 does not envy P_a since P_1 selects a piece before P_a.   □

Next, X^- needs to be assigned. The protocol for X^- in [15] is not a discrete protocol. This paper shows a new discrete protocol. We modify the three-player envy-free chore division protocol shown in Fig. 2. The detailed protocol is shown in Fig. 4. The main differences between Oskui's protocol are these three points:

1. Any portion $x \subseteq X^-$ has a negative utility for P_1 by the definition.
2. At Step 5, when the best piece (X_1^-) is the same for P_2 and P_3, both players must have a negative utility for X_1^-.
3. At Step 13, when P_2 cuts E from X_2^- and F from X_3^-, E and F must be selected so that any portion of $E \cup F$ has a negative utility for P_2.

The reason for the necessity of the conditions is as follows: (1) P_1 must not envy for the assignment at Step 7, Step 10, Step 18, Step 29, and Step 33. The detail is shown in the proof. (2) At step 13, P_2 must be able to cut E from X_2^- and F from X_3^- so that $\mu_2(X_1^-) = \mu_2(X_2^- - E) = \mu_2(X_3^- - F)$, $\mu_2(X_1^-) < 0$, $\mu_2(X_2^-) < 0$, and $\mu_2(X_3^-) < 0$ are satisfied. For example, if $\mu_2(X_1^-) > 0$ and $\mu_2(X_2^-) < 0$, cutting E might not be able to be executed. (3) If E or F has a portion whose utility is positive for P_2, when P_3 cuts E' and F' at Step 20, the new $X_2^- - E'$ or $X_3^- - F'$ might become the best piece for P_2 and an envy-free assignment cannot be obtained at Step 15.

Theorem 2. *The assignment result of X^- by the protocol in Fig. 4 is envy-free.*

Proof. In the protocol, P_1 cuts X^- into three pieces X_1^-, X_2^-, and X_3^- so that $\mu_1(X_1^-) = \mu_2(X_2^-) = \mu_2(X_3^-) < 0$ is satisfied. First, P_2 and P_3 chooses the best piece. If the best pieces differ, an envy-free assignment is achieved when P_2 and P_3 selects its best piece and P_1 obtains the remaining piece. Note that even if P_2 or P_3 has more than one best piece, an envy-free assignment exists. For example, if P_2 has more than one best piece, P_3, P_2, and P_1 selects one piece in this order. After P_3 selects one piece, there is at least one remaining piece whose utility is the best for P_2. Thus, an envy-free assignment can be achieved.

Therefore, the remaining case to consider is P_2 and P_3 have the same best piece, say X_1^-. We assume that $\mu_2(X_1^-) < 0$ and $\mu_3(X_1^-) < 0$ are satisfied. Otherwise, X_1^- can be assigned to the players who have a non-negative utility by the Steps 6–11. If $\mu_2(X_1^-) \geq 0$ and $\mu_3(X_1^-) \geq 0$, X_1^- is divided between P_2 and P_3 using Divide-and-choose. If one of P_2 or P_3 has a non-negative utility to X_1^-, X_1^- is given to the player without envy. Then, the procedure is executed again for the remaining pieces.

Thus, we assume that $\mu_2(X_1^-) < 0$ and $\mu_3(X_1^-) < 0$. Since X_1^- is the best piece for P_2 and P_3, $\mu_2(X_2^-) \leq \mu_2(X_1^-) < 0$, $\mu_2(X_3^-) \leq \mu_2(X_1^-) < 0$, $\mu_3(X_2^-) \leq \mu_3(X_1^-) < 0$, and $\mu_3(X_3^-) \leq \mu_3(X_1^-) < 0$ are satisfied. Note that X^- might have some portions whose utility is positive for P_2 and/or P_3. P_2 cuts E from X_2^- and F from X_3^- so that $\mu_2(X_1^-) = \mu_2(X_2^- - E) = \mu_2(X_3^- - F)$ with the condition that any portion $x \subseteq E \cup F$ satisfies $\mu_2(x) < 0$. P_2 can execute this operation because $\mu_2(X_2^-) \leq \mu_2(X_1^-) < 0$ and $\mu_2(X_3^-) \leq \mu_2(X_1^-) < 0$. Note that E and F might not be a connected component. In that case, connect these pieces and treat E and F as a single piece. As the original Oskui's protocol, we consider the following three cases.

(Case 1) $\mu_3(X_2^- - E) \leq \mu_3(X_1^-)$ and $\mu_3(X_3^- - F) \leq \mu_3(X_1^-)$. In this case, P_1, P_3, and P_2 selects one piece in this order among X_1^-, $X_2^- - E$, and $X_3^- - F$. P_1 never selects X_1^- since every portion of $X_2^- \cup X_3^-$ has a negative utility for P_1. Without loss of generality, suppose that P_1 selects $X_2^- - E$. P_3 selects X_1^- since it is the best piece for P_3. Thus P_2 obtains $X_3^- - F$. This assignment is envy-free. P_1 does not envy since P_1 selects first. P_2 does not envy since P_2 thinks the three pieces have the same utility.

Last, E and F need to be assigned. P_2 cuts E and F into three pieces E_1, E_2, E_3 and F_1, F_2, F_3 so that $\mu_2(E_1) = \mu_2(E_2) = \mu_2(E_3)$ and $\mu_2(F_1) = \mu_2(F_2) =$

```
 1  Begin
 2  P₁ cuts X⁻ into three pieces X₁⁻, X₂⁻, and X₃⁻ so that
```
$$\mu_1(X_1^-) = \mu_2(X_2^-) = \mu_2(X_3^-) \text{ is satisfied.}$$
```
 3  If the best piece for P₂ and P₃ differs Then
 4     P₂ and P₃ selects the best piece. P₁ obtains the remaining piece.
 5  Else /* Let X₁⁻ be the best piece for P₂ and P₃. */
 6     If μ₂(X₁⁻) ≥ 0 and μ₃(X₁⁻) ≥ 0 Then
 7        Execute Divide-and-choose on X₁⁻ between P₂ and P₃.
 8        Let X⁻ = X₂⁻ ∪ X₃⁻ and goto 2:
 9     Else if μ₂(X₁⁻) ≥ 0 or μ₃(X₁⁻) ≥ 0 Then
10        Assign X₁⁻ to the player who thinks μ(X₁⁻) ≥ 0.
11        Let X⁻ = X₂⁻ ∪ X₃⁻ and goto 2:
12     Else /* μ₂(X₁⁻) < 0 and μ₃(X₁⁻) < 0. */
13        P₂ cuts E from X₂⁻ and F from X₃⁻ so that
```
$$\mu_2(X_1^-) = \mu_2(X_2^- - E) = \mu_2(X_3^- - F) \text{ is satisfied with the}$$
condition that any portion $x \subset E \cup F$ satisfies $\mu_2(x) < 0$.
```
14        If μ₃(X₂⁻ - E) ≤ μ₃(X₁⁻) and μ₃(X₃⁻ - F) ≤ μ₃(X₁⁻) Then
15           P₁, P₃, and P₂ select one piece in this order among X₁⁻, X₂⁻ - E,
             and X₃⁻ - F.
16           Wlog P₁ selects X₂⁻ - E. P₃ selects X₁⁻. P₂ obtains X₃⁻ - F.
17           P₂ cuts E and F into three pieces E₁, E₂, E₃ and F₁, F₂, F₃ so
             that μ₂(E₁) = μ₂(E₂) = μ₂(E₃) and μ₂(F₁) = μ₂(F₂) = μ₂(F₃) are
             satisfied.
18           P₃, P₁, and P₂ select one piece among Es and Fs in this order.
19        Else if μ₃(X₁⁻) ≤ μ₃(X₂⁻ - E) and μ₃(X₁⁻) ≤ μ₃(X₃⁻ - F) Then
20           P₃ cuts E' ⊆ E and F' ⊆ F so that
```
$$\mu_3(X_2^- - E') = \mu_3(X_3^- - F') = \mu_3(X_1^-) \text{ are satisfied.}$$
```
21           Execute Step 15-18 by changing the roles of P₂ and P₃ and
             renaming (E', F') to (E, F).
22        Else /* μ₃(X₁⁻) is between μ₃(X₂⁻ - E) and μ₃(X₃⁻ - F). */
23           Wlog μ₃(X₂⁻ - E) ≤ μ₃(X₁⁻) ≤ μ₃(X₃⁻ - F) holds.
24           P₃ cuts F' ⊆ F so that μ₃(X₃⁻ - F') = μ₃(X₁⁻) is satisfied.
25           P₁ selects the best piece between X₂⁻ - E and X₃⁻ - F'.
26           If P₁ selects X₂⁻ - E Then
27              P₃ obtains X₃⁻ - F'. P₂ obtains X₁⁻.
28              P₃ cuts E and F' into three pieces E₁, E₂, E₃ and F₁', F₂', F₃' so
                that μ₃(E₁) = μ₃(E₂) = μ₃(E₃) and μ₃(F₁') = μ₃(F₂') = μ₃(F₃')
                are satisfied.
29              P₂, P₁, and P₃ select one piece among Es and F's in this order
30           Else /* P₁ selects X₃⁻ - F'. */
31              P₂ obtains X₂⁻ - E. P₃ obtains X₁⁻.
32              P₂ cuts E and F' into three pieces E₁, E₂, E₃ and F₁', F₂', F₃' so
                that μ₂(E₁) = μ₂(E₂) = μ₂(E₃) and μ₂(F₁') = μ₂(F₂') = μ₂(F₃')
                are satisfied.
33              P₃, P₁, and P₂ select one piece among Es and F's in this order
34  End.
```

Fig. 4. Three-player envy-free division protocol for X^-.

$\mu_2(F_3)$ are satisfied. P_3, P_1 and P_2 select one piece among Es and Fs in this order. P_3 does not envy the other players since P_3 selects first. P_2 does not envy the other players since P_2 thinks the utilities of three pieces are the same.

P_1 does not envy P_2 since P_1 selects earlier than P_2. The reason why P_1 does not envy P_3 is as follows: $\mu_1(E) \leq \mu_1(F)$ is satisfied since P_1 selects $X_2^- - E$. Thus, by the selection of a piece of E and F, P_1 obtains even in the worst case $1/2(\mu_1(E)+\mu_1(F)) \geq \mu_1(E)$, since every portion of X^- has a negative utility for P_1. Thus, P_1 obtains in the worst case $\mu_1(X_2^- - E)+\mu_1(E) = \mu_1(X_2^-) = \mu_1(X_1^-)$. Therefore, P_1 does not envy P_3 who obtains X_1^- and some pieces of E and F. Note again the utilities of any portion of E and F are negative for P_1.

(Case 2) $\mu_3(X_1^-) \leq \mu_3(X_2^- - E)$ and $\mu_3(X_1^-) \leq \mu_3(X_3^- - F)$.
P_3 cuts $E' \subseteq E$ and $F' \subseteq F$ that satisfy $\mu_3(X_2^- - E') = \mu_3(X_1^-)$ and $\mu_3(X_3^- - F') = \mu_3(X_1^-)$. Such a cut is possible since $\mu_3(X_2^-) \leq \mu_3(X_1^-) < 0$ and $\mu_3(X_2^-) \leq \mu_3(X_1^-) < 0$ are satisfied. Since any portion of $E \cup F$ has a negative utility for P_2, $\mu_2(X_1^-) \geq \mu_2(X_2^- - E')$ and $\mu_2(X_1^-) \geq \mu_2(X_3^- - F')$ are satisfied. Now, rename E' to E and F' to F. Then, the condition of (Case 1) is satisfied by P_2. Thus, by changing the roles of P_2 and P_3, the procedure of (Case 1) can be executed and an envy-free assignment can be obtained.

(Case 3) $\mu_3(X_1^-)$ is between $\mu_3(X_2^- - E)$ and $\mu_3(X_3^- - F)$.
Without loss of generality, suppose that $\mu_3(X_2^- - E) \leq \mu_3(X_1^-) \leq \mu_3(X_3^- - F)$ holds. In this case, P_3 cuts $F' \subseteq F$ that satisfies $\mu_3(X_3^- - F') = \mu_3(X_1^-)$. This operation is possible for P_3 since $\mu_3(X_3^-) \leq \mu_3(X_1^-) < 0$ is satisfied. P_1 selects the best piece between $X_2^- - E$ and $X_3^- - F'$. Note that X_1^- cannot be the best piece for P_1 since $\mu_1(X_1^-) = \mu_1(X_2^-) = \mu_1(X_3^-)$.

(Case 3-1) P_1 selects $X_2^- - E$.
In this subcase, P_3 obtains $X_3^- - F'$. P_2 obtains X_1^-. P_1 does not envy the other players since P_1 selects first. P_3 does not envy the other players since $\mu_3(X_3^- - F') = \mu_3(X_1^-) \geq \mu_3(X_2^- - E)$ holds. P_2 does not envy the other players since $\mu_2(X_1^-) = \mu_2(X_2^- - E) \geq \mu_2(X_3^- - F')$ is satisfied.

Last, E and F' need to be assigned. P_3 cuts E and F' into three pieces E_1, E_2, E_3 and F_1', F_2', F_3' so that $\mu_3(E_1) = \mu_3(E_2) = \mu_3(E_3)$ and $\mu_3(F_1') = \mu_3(F_2') = \mu_3(F_3')$ are satisfied. P_2, P_1, and P_3 select one piece among Es and F's in this order.

Envy-freeness for P_3 and P_2 are the same as the reason of (Case 1). The reason why P_1 does not envy P_2 is as follows: $\mu_1(E) \leq \mu_1(F')$ is satisfied since P_1 selects $X_2^- - E$. Thus, by the selection of a piece of E and F', P_1 obtains even in the worst case $1/2(\mu_1(E) + \mu_1(F')) \geq \mu_1(E)$. Thus, P_1 obtains in the worst case $\mu_1(X_2^- - E) + \mu_1(E) = \mu_1(X_2^-) = \mu_1(X_1^-)$. Therefore, P_1 does not envy P_2 who obtains X_1^- and some pieces of E and F'.

(Case 3-2) P_1 selects $X_3^- - F'$
In this subcase, P_2 obtains $X_2^- - E$. P_3 obtains X_1^-. P_1 does not envy the other players since P_1 selects first. P_3 does not envy to the other players since $\mu_3(X_3^- - F') = \mu_3(X_1^-) \geq \mu_3(X_2^- - E)$ holds. P_2 does not envy the other players since $\mu_2(X_1^-) = \mu_2(X_2^- - E) \geq \mu_2(X_3^- - F')$ is satisfied.

Last, E and F' need to be assigned. P_2 cuts E and F' into three pieces E_1, E_2, E_3 and F_1', F_2', F_3' so that $\mu_2(E_1) = \mu_2(E_2) = \mu_2(E_3)$ and $\mu_2(F_1') = \mu_2(F_2') = \mu_2(F_3')$ are satisfied. P_3, P_1 and P_2 select one piece among Es and F's in this order. Envy-freeness for P_3 and P_2 are the same as the reason of (Case 1).

The reason why P_1 does not envy P_3 is as follows: $\mu_1(E) \geq \mu_1(F')$ is satisfied since P_1 selects $X_3^- - F'$. Thus, by the selection of a piece of E and F', P_1 obtains even in the worst case $1/2(\mu_1(E) + \mu_1(F')) \geq \mu_1(F')$. Thus, P_1 obtains in the worst case $\mu_1(X_3^- - F') + \mu_1(F') = \mu_1(X_3^-) = \mu_1(X_1^-)$. Therefore, P_1 does not envy P_3 who obtains X_1^- and some pieces of E and F'.   □

5   Conclusion

This paper showed a three-player discrete envy-free division protocol for mixed manna. This protocol reduces the initial division by the naive protocol. Note that the initial division still needs $\min_i c_i$ cuts, thus elimination of the initial division is the most important open problem. Also, each player's role in the protocol differs among the players and meta-envy [13] exists. A meta-envy-free protocol is necessary for ideal fairness.

References

1. Aleksandrov, M.: Jealousy-freeness and other common properties in fair division of mixed manna. arXiv preprint arXiv:2004.11469 (2020)
2. Aleksandrov, M., Walsh, T.: Two algorithms for additive and fair division of mixed manna. In: Schmid, U., Klügl, F., Wolter, D. (eds.) KI 2020. LNCS (LNAI), vol. 12325, pp. 3–17. Springer, Cham (2020). https://doi.org/10.1007/978-3-030-58285-2_1
3. Aziz, H., Caragiannis, I., Igarashi, A., Walsh, T.: Fair allocation of combinations of indivisible goods and chores. arXiv preprint arXiv:1807.10684 (2018)
4. Aziz, H., Mackenzie, S.: A discrete and bounded envy-free cake cutting protocol for any number of agents. In: 2016 IEEE 57th Annual Symposium on Foundations of Computer Science (FOCS), pp. 416–427. IEEE (2016)
5. Bogomolnaia, A., Moulin, H., Sandomirskiy, F., Yanovskaya, E.: Dividing goods and bads under additive utilities. Higher School of Economics Research Paper No. WP BRP **153** (2016)
6. Bogomolnaia, A., Moulin, H., Sandomirskiy, F., Yanovskaya, E., et al.: Competitive division of a mixed manna. Econometrica **85**(6), 1847–1871 (2017)
7. Brams, S.J., Taylor, A.D.: Fair Division: From Cake-Cutting to Dispute Resolution. Cambridge University Press, Cambridge (1996)
8. Brandt, F., Conitzer, V., Endriss, U., Lang, J., Procaccia, A.D.: Handbook of Computational Social Choice. Cambridge University Press, Cambridge (2016)
9. Dehghani, S., Farhadi, A., HajiAghayi, M., Yami, H.: Envy-free chore division for an arbitrary number of agents. In: Proceedings of the Twenty-Ninth Annual ACM-SIAM Symposium on Discrete Algorithms, pp. 2564–2583. SIAM (2018)
10. Farhadi, A., Hajiaghayi, M.T.: On the complexity of chore division. In: Proceedings of the 27th International Joint Conference on Artificial Intelligence, pp. 226–232. AAAI Press (2018)
11. Garg, J., McGlaughlin, P.: Computing competitive equilibria with mixed manna. In: Proceedings of the 19th International Conference on Autonomous Agents and MultiAgent Systems, pp. 420–428 (2020)
12. Heydrich, S., van Stee, R.: Dividing connected chores fairly. Theor. Comput. Sci. **593**, 51–61 (2015)

13. Manabe, Y., Okamoto, T.: Meta-envy-free cake-cutting and pie-cutting protocols. J. Inf. Process. **20**(3), 686–693 (2012)
14. Moulin, H.: Fair division in the age of internet. Annu. Rev. Econ. **11**, 407–441 (2019)
15. Okano, Y., Manabe, Y.: A three-player envy-free division protocol for mixed manna. In: Proceedings of International Conference on Information Technology and Computer Science (ICITCS 2018) (2018)
16. Peterson, E., Su, F.E.: Four-person envy-free chore division. Math. Mag. **75**(2), 117–122 (2002)
17. Procaccia, A.D.: Cake cutting: not just child's play. Commun. ACM **56**(7), 78–87 (2013)
18. Robertson, J., Webb, W.: Cake-Cutting Algorithms: Be Fair if You Can. AK Peters/CRC Press, Boca Raton (1998)
19. Segal-Halevi, E.: Fairly dividing a cake after some parts were burnt in the oven. In: Proceedings of the 17th International Conference on Autonomous Agents and MultiAgent Systems, pp. 1276–1284. International Foundation for Autonomous Agents and Multiagent Systems (2018)

Convolutional Variational Autoencoders for Audio Feature Representation in Speech Recognition Systems

Olga Yakovenko[1,2(✉)] and Ivan Bondarenko[1]

[1] NSU, Novosibirsk, Russia
o.iakovenko@g.nsu.ru, i.yu.bondarenko@gmail.com
[2] Zolotaya Korona, Saint Petersburg, Russia

Abstract. For many Automatic Speech Recognition (ASR) tasks audio features as spectrograms show better results than Mel-frequency Cepstral Coefficients (MFCC), but in practice they are hard to use due to a complex dimensionality of a feature space. The following paper presents an alternative approach towards generating compressed spectrogram representation, based on Convolutional Variational Autoencoders (VAE). A Convolutional VAE model was trained on a subsample of the LibriSpeech dataset to reconstruct short fragments of audio spectrograms (25 ms) from a 13-dimensional embedding. The trained model for a 40-dimensional (300 ms) embedding was used to generate features for corpus of spoken commands on the GoogleSpeechCommands dataset. Using the generated features an ASR system was built and compared to the model with MFCC features.

Keywords: Variational Autoencoder · Speech recognition · Audio feature representation

1 Introduction

Automatic recognition of the spoken language has already became a part of a daily life for many people in the modern world. Although algorithms for automatic speech recognition have progressed greatly throughout the last years, most of the applications still utilize a basic set of features – Mel-frequency cepstral coefficients. These kind of features are processed rapidly and can produce good results, but recent research [1] has proven that raw FFT spectrograms give better accuracy on ASR tasks when combined with Deep Neural Networks (DNN) for feature-extracting.

The drawback of using spectrograms as the inputs to a recognition system is that a lot of computational power has to be used to process a single audio. With the increase of length of the audio increases the time spent computing an optimal path from first to last sound. Embeddings, generated by VAE, can be used as a compressed version of the general FFT spectrogram features for

© Springer Nature Switzerland AG 2020
C. Martín-Vide et al. (Eds.): TPNC 2020, LNCS 12494, pp. 54–66, 2020.
https://doi.org/10.1007/978-3-030-63000-3_5

both traditional Gaussian Mixture Models and modern DNNs. Moreover, this approach can be used for dimensionality reduction of input data [2] that can subsequently be used for visualization of audio data or for reduction of occupied space on a hard drive.

Traditionally VAE is used as a generative model, similar to Generative Adversarial Networks (GAN). For the past several years there has been going a lot of research on the topic of audio generation with VAEs, including the fascinating DeepMind's VQ-VAE [3], which is a successor of WaveNet [4]. The main features of those two systems is that having the train samples of some audio clips the system learns the probability distributions over observed features, making it possible to generate new samples by selecting other values from these distributions.

VAE was found out to be a good tool for dimensionality reduction using the bottleneck features of the hidden layer. For example, authors of [2] prove in their paper that VAE is a natural evolution of the robust PCA algorithm. Basic Autoencoders (AE) are also known to be able to reduce the dimensionality of the data, but the resulting embedding does not serve as a good generalization, because the hidden representations of the intermediate layer are poorly structured due to non-probabilistic nature of AE.

Over the past few years, there has also been attempts to perform construction of audio embeddings. The main goal of this approach is to be able to compare many utterances to some etalon utterance or to compare different utterances against each other and present all of them in some feature space. This approach could be found to be used in the spoken term recognition by example [5], for speaker identification or verification using Siamese Neural Networks [6] and for semantic embedding construction based on context based on Recurrent Neural Networks (RNN) and skipgram/cbow architectures [7].

It is important to notice, that most of the presented approaches use recurrent structures for analyzing variable-length audio data. Recurrent structures enable good quality of automatically determining features, relevant to the task, having approximately same length. The drawback here is that if the system was trained on samples of length from 4 s to 10 s, it will produce unexpected results for samples much longer than 10 s. Researcher is forced to either adapt his data to fit the model, or to build his own model that would fit his data. These drawbacks can be avoided by using fixed-length features, such as MFCC or VAE-based features, presented in the following paper.

Thus, in this paper an approach towards feature generation for audio data is presented. The first part is dedicated to the feature generation itself and the ability to reconstruct the signal from the resulting embedding, while the second part describes the experiments with the embeddings for an ASR task.

2   Traditional Audio Features for ASR/TTS Tasks

Audio wave is a sequence of positive and negative values, the values represent the amplitudes of the fluctuation of a sound device. The frequency and the amount of the fluctuation defines different sounds (Fig. 1).

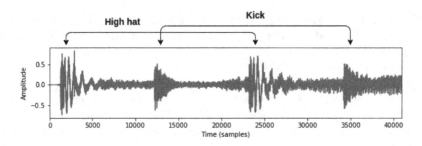

Fig. 1. Amplitude audio representation.

2.1 Raw Wave

Sometimes raw signal is used for speech recognition or generation tasks. The only preprocessing that the sound may undergo is discretization of an analog sound when it is being recorded. It is possible to analyse a discrete signal, if the task itself is not too complex (e.g. recognition of loud noises, of sound patterns) but also if the system consists of an end-to-end structure that besides solving the main tasks is also capable to detect frequencies in a signal. Some of those end-to-end architectures include 1D Convolutions or PixelCNNs.

2.2 Spectrogram

A traditional approach towards deep analysis of speech and sounds is mostly realized through spectrograms using a Short-Time Fourier Transform (STFT). Spectrograms are quite useful for manual analysis: for example, for detection of formants in human's speech. Generally, spectrograms are very good means of learning information from audio data, since sounds, that are produced by the vocal cord and, more importantly, speech, are characterized by cooccurrence of different harmonics and their change through time. STFT is applied to a discrete signal, so the data is broken up into overlapping chunks. Each chunk is Fourier transformed, and the result is added to a matrix, which records magnitude and phase for each point in time and frequency. This can be expressed as:

$$\mathbf{STFT}\{x[n]\}(m, \omega) \equiv X(m, \omega) =$$
$$\sum_{n=-\infty}^{\infty} x[n]w[n-m]e^{-j\omega n} \tag{1}$$

with signal $x[n]$ and window $w[n]$.

The magnitude squared of the STFT yields the spectrogram representation of the Power Spectral Density of the function (Fig. 2):

$$\text{spectrogram}\{x[n]\}(m, \omega) \equiv |X(m, \omega)|^2 \tag{2}$$

The described spectrogram was generated for the LibriSpeech dataset during the experiments with VAE.

One of the commonly used modifications of STFT spectrograms are mel-spectrograms. During this modification each of the time frames in a spectrogram are passed through series of triangular filters (mel-scaled filters). Mel filters are based on a hand-crafted mel-scale, which represents the extent to which humans can distinguish sounds of different frequencies.

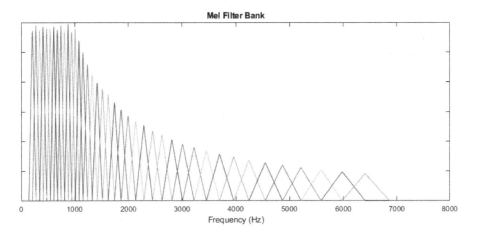

Fig. 2. Mel-scaled filterbanks.

All of the aforementioned approaches have led us to the traditional approach for creation of audio features: Mel-Frequency Cepstral Coefficients (MFCC).

2.3   MFCC

Once we have the mel-spectrograms, we can then proceed to the computation of the Mel-Frequency Cepstral Coefficient (MFCC). It consists of three simple steps:

1. Compute elementwise square of each value in the mel-spectrogram;
2. Compute elementwise logarithm of each element;
3. Apply discrete cosine transform to the list of mel log powers, as if it were a signal.

The final result will also be a matrix, quite unreadable by a human eye, but surprisingly effective when used for both Speech to Text (STT) and Text to Speech (TTS). To this day MFCC features are used mostly in all speech-related technologies.

Mel-spectrogram and MFCC are means towards compressing audio data without erasing the information relevant to speech, since these features are further used in applications, connected to speech.

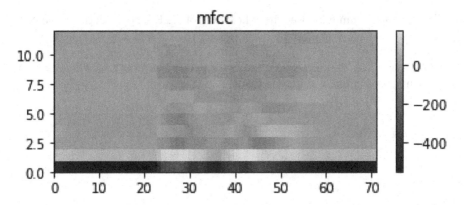

Fig. 3. MFCC of the LibriSpeech sample 1779-142733-0000.wav.

Here we determine the goal of this study: we believe that it is possible to compress audio in analogous way, but with the help of neural network, specifically, a Variational Autoencoder. We are going to cover the architecture in the next chapter.

3   Audio VAE

As was mentioned in the introduction, Variational Autoencoders can be successfully used not just as a generative network, but also as a dimensionality reduction tool. This is the one of the main reasons for selecting this architecture. The other reason for selecting a VAE for audio compression is the assumption that a VAE that is trained on a big clean corpus of speech will then be able to extract features from a spectrogram that are relevant only to the speech. Therefore, the encoder of the resulting VAE will be able to conduct denoising, selection of relevant frequencies and compression simultaneously. As an interesting additional feature, this kind of network may be used for generating sounds that sound close to the true signal, that way acting as a option for augmentation.

It is also important to specify that encoder and decoder of the VAE include convolutional layers instead of fully-connected layers to evade a big amount of parameters to optimize and improve the recognition of formants of various frequencies and scales.

3.1   Architecture

VAE architecture was inspired by traditional VAE for image generation and segmentation. The VAE neural network is symmetric, where encoder and decoder parts include 2 convolution layers with kernel sizes 8 and stride 2. The encoder and decoder part are connected by a bottleneck which consists of 2D global average pooling layer, then followed by mean and variance layers of the VAE and finally the sampling layer (Fig. 4).

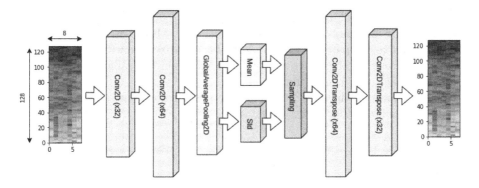

Fig. 4. VAE architecture.

As for any other VAE, special loss function had to be defined that consists of two parts: reconstruction loss and regularisation. In our case reconstruction loss is Mean Squared Error (MSE) between the true values and predicted values and regularisation is estimated by Kullback-Leibler divergence between the distribution that is present in the data and the distribution that has been modeled by our encoder.

$$\mathcal{L}(\boldsymbol{\phi}, \boldsymbol{\theta}, \mathbf{x}, \mathbf{x}') =$$
$$\|\mathbf{x} - \mathbf{x}'\|^2 + \tag{3}$$
$$-0.0005 * D_{\mathrm{KL}}(q_{\phi}(\mathbf{h}|\mathbf{x}) \| p_{\theta}(\mathbf{h}))$$

where $p_{\theta}(\mathbf{x}|\mathbf{h})$ is the directed graphical model that we want to approximate, encoder is learning an approximation of this model $q_{\phi}(\mathbf{h}|\mathbf{x})$ to the Gaussian multivatiate (in our case) distribution $p_{\theta}(\mathbf{h}|\mathbf{x})$ where ϕ and θ denote the parameters of the encoder (recognition model) and decoder (generative model) respectively.

3.2 Dataset

Training of the system was carried out on a subset of the LibriSpeech dataset [8]. LibriSpeech flac files were transformed to mono-channel wav, sampling rate 16 kHz, signed PCM little endian with bit rate 256 kB/s and bit depth 16. The subset was formed as follows:

– Dataset was split into train and test with 2097 audiofiles representing train and 87 representing test.
– Train set included utterances from 1031 speakers, test set – 40 speakers.
– Spectrograms were calculated from the audio data.
– Each utterance was split into fragments of 0.025 s with stride of 0.01 s.

That left us with 1047736 samples for training and 30548 samples for testing. One input sample had the shape of 8 timestamps by 128 wave frequency stamps.

The choice for making such a small window (a small 25 ms window) was determined by different ASR systems, which use MFCC as their features. Later we want to compare the performance of an ASR system with VAE features and MFCC features, thus it is important to maintain the same conditions for feature generation for clear comparison.

The dynamics for the training of the VAE audio features are shown on Fig. 5 for the train set and Fig. 6 for the test set.

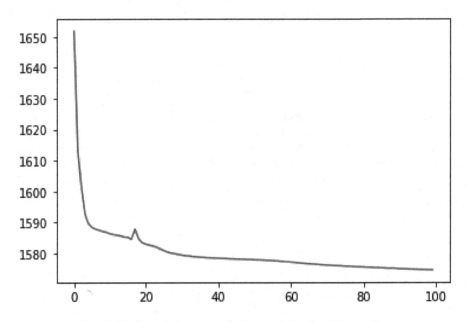

Fig. 5. Train loss dynamics during training for 100 epochs.

3.3 Reconstruction

The system described earlier was used for the encoding and reconstruction of the audio. Once we have trained the VAE, we can compress and decompress some samples from the dataset, some examples of the original and reconstructed samples can be seen in Fig. 7.

We can see from the pictures, that despite a big compression rate from 1024 elements of the spectrogram to just 13 elements of the latent vector, the information about the energised parts of the spectrum is still preserved. Moreover, the system seems to have learned the common localisation of the human speech (lower frequencies) and the way it can change over time.

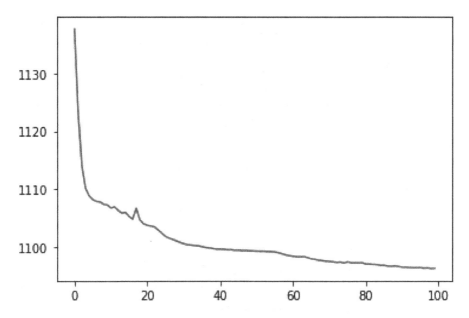

Fig. 6. Test loss dynamics during training for 100 epochs.

The next step would be to visually compare the VAE features that we have achieved with MFCC features. MFCC for a file from the LibriSpeech dataset we have calculated earlier, see Fig. 3, and now we can see the analoguous features for the VAE generated encoding on Fig. 8. It is evident from the pictures, that VAE has a better ability to code necessary segments of audio where human speech takes place, and seems to ignore the any kind of other sounds, that may sound on the background. On the other hand, MFCC features seem to detect some of the activity in the background, which may not reflect on ASR systems too well.

3.4 Generation

Since the trained encoder of the VAE is an approximation to a Gaussian multivariate distribution and the decoder is a directed graphical model, we can sample examples of spectrograms from the distribution and visualize them using our decoder.

For every component in the latent representation 4 evenly spaced numbers are chosen in the interval $[-1, 1]$. Then the resulting 4 vectors that differ by one value are transformed into spectrograms. Examples for some components are presented in Fig. 9.

It can be seen from the figures, that the VAE has learned how human speech may sound and has successfully encapsulated that knowledge in a multivariate Gaussian distribution.

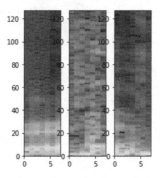

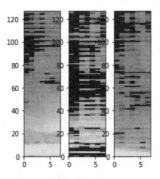

Fig. 7. Examples of reconstruction (lower) of the samples from the 13-dimensional hidden representation of the real sample (upper). The dark purple segments in the reconstructed pictures are the elements of matrix, that are equal to 0.

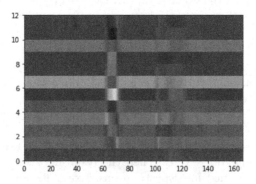

Fig. 8. Example of VAE encoding of the LibriSpeech sample 1779-142733-0000.wav.

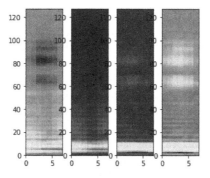

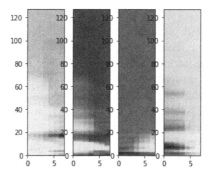

Fig. 9. Samples from the multivariate (13 variables) Gaussian distribution, modeled by VAE, alternation of the 2-nd (top) and 5-th (bottom) variable, while the other are kept as mean values for the distribution.

4   Experiments

It is essential to compare developed approach with the existing. Therefore, experiments were carried out to evaluate the performance of resulting embeddings in a speech recognition task in comparison to MFCC features. Although the previous part was dedicated to reconstructing 25 ms feature frames, in this part 300 ms feature frames are regarded. The experiment with 25 ms frames and comparison with MFCC features in a Kaldi environment is planned for the nearest future.

4.1   Dataset

The GoogleSpeechCommands [9] dataset was used for training and testing. Dataset includes audio fragments of 30 different commands, spoken in noisy conditions. The choice of this dataset was mainly determined by the relative simplicity to test it for both VAE and MFCC features: it is fixed-length audio while containing one of the 30 commands in a single audio. One of the other main reasons was that we have mentioned earlier, that VAE has a great potential for smoothing audio and performing general noise reduction, and it was interesting to test the system on noisy audio. Training was performed on 46619 samples, testing on 11635 samples from the dataset. Audio data had the same format as LibriSpeech: mono-channel wav, sampling rate 16 kHz, signed PCM little endian with bit rate 256 kB/s and bit depth 16.

VAE features were generated in a window 0.3 s with 0.1 overlap. The resulting vectors were then concatenated to serve as a representation of the feature vector of a spoken command.

For the MFCC features an analysis window of length 0.025 s was used with a step of 0.01 s and 26 filterbanks. For one window 13-dimensional cepstrum vector was generated.

4.2   Architecture

With this type of dataset it is possible to solve a simple multiclass task, since all the audios are of the same length and one audio only belongs to one class simultaneously. The ASR system architecture was a basic Multi-Layered Perceptron (MLP) of the following structure: 2 fully-connected layers of 100 hidden units with 0.2 dropout rate and ReLU activation followed by a softmax layer (Fig. 10).

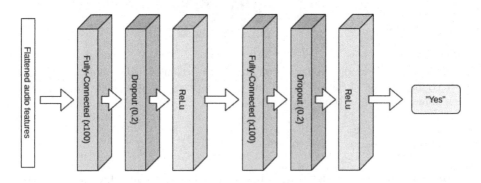

Fig. 10. ASR Neural Network structure.

Although we are solving such a simple ASR task (command recognition), that is quite far away from many practical ASR systems, still solving this task may give us the understanding the potential of the VAE features in comparison to MFCC.

4.3   Results

The results of the experiments are shown in the Table 1 below.

Table 1. Speech recognition results

Results	VAE	MFCC
Train accuracy	**0.45**	0.41
Test accuracy	**0.49**	**0.49**
MLP training time	**42 s**	63 s
Best epoch	**12**	17
Train size	**204 MB**	668 MB

What we can see from the results in the table is that VAE does not concede to the MFCC features, while generally taking up less space. That means that being 3x smaller, VAE features carry approximately the same amount of acoustic information as the MFCC features. This can be very useful in the cases when the audio information has to be stored somewhere (e.g. etalon voice samples, database of speech segments). Furthermore, when the input to the neural network is smaller, as in the case of VAE features in comparison to MFCC, then the amount of parameters in a network also becomes smaller and this leads to faster convergence of the neural network (as it is also highlighted in the results table).

5 Conclusions

This research has shown that convolutional VAEs are capable of reconstructing audio data in the form of spectrograms. They succeed at representing fixed-length audio data fragments for the ASR tasks. As a result, convolutional VAEs feature extracting have shown relatively good results in a recognition task on a noisy dataset, in comparison to traditional MFCC features. Finally, the embeddings, generated by VAE occupy 3 times less space in comparison to MFCC, despite being as informative. The resulting algorithms, scripts and models are available on GitHub for any researcher that would be interested.

The further work that has to be done is to test the 13-dimensional latent features of the VAE as an input for a proper ASR system (e.g. Kaldi, DeepSpeech). It is planned to carry out the experiment using Kaldi in the nearest future. This will be done for English and Russian languages, for the Voxforge dataset.

References

1. Amodei, D., et al.: Deep speech 2: end-to-end speech recognition in English and Mandarin. In: ICML (2016)
2. Dai, B. et al.: Hidden Talents of the Variational Autoencoder (2017)
3. van den Oord, A., et al.: Neural Discrete Representation Learning. In: NIPS (2017)
4. van den Oord, A., et al.: WaveNet: a generative model for raw audio. In: SSW (2016)

5. Zhu, Z., et al.: Siamese recurrent auto-encoder representation for query-by-example spoken term detection. In: Interspeech (2018)
6. Milde, B., Biemann, C.: Unspeech: unsupervised speech context embeddings. In: Interspeech (2018)
7. Chung, Y.-A., Glass, J.R.: Speech2Vec: a sequence-to-sequence framework for learning word embeddings from speech. In: Interspeech (2018)
8. LibriSpeech. http://www.openslr.org/12/
9. GoogleSpeechCommands. https://ai.googleblog.com/2017/08/launching-speech-commands-dataset.html
10. Audio_vae. https://github.com/nsu-ai-team/audio_vae

Quantum Computing
and Unconventional Computing

Quantum Candies and Quantum Cryptography

Junan Lin[1]($\boxtimes$)(iD) and Tal Mor[2]

[1] Institute for Quantum Computing, Department of Physics and Astronomy, University of Waterloo, Waterloo, ON N2L 3G1, Canada
j242lin@uwaterloo.ca
[2] Computer Science Department, Technion – Israel Institute of Technology, Technion City, Haifa 3200003, Israel
talmo@cs.technion.ac.il

Abstract. The field of quantum information is becoming more known to the general public. However, effectively demonstrating the concepts underneath quantum science and technology to the general public can be a challenging job. We investigate, extend, and much expand here "quantum candies" (invented by Jacobs), a pedagogical model for intuitively describing some basic concepts in quantum information, including quantum bits, complementarity, the no-cloning principle, and entanglement. Following Jacob's quantum candies description of the well known quantum key distribution protocol BB84, we explicitly demonstrate various additional quantum cryptography protocols using quantum candies in an approachable manner. The model we investigate can be a valuable tool for science and engineering educators who would like to help the general public to gain more insights about quantum science and technology: most parts of this paper, including many protocols for quantum cryptography, are expected to be easily understandable by a layperson without any previous knowledge of mathematics, physics, or cryptography.

Keywords: Quantum Information · Quantum Cryptography · Quantum Candy · Physics Education

1 Introduction

Quantum information science and technology is a growing field that provides interesting concepts such as quantum computers, quantum teleportation, and quantum cryptography. Its development has proved fruitful in both theoretical and experimental aspects, leading to various demonstrations in research labs. More recently the hi-tech became majorly involved, with companies such as IBM, Google, Intel, Microsoft, and Alibaba (plus many startup companies) investing in quantum devices for computing and/or communication and cryptography.

The relevant "quantum concepts", in their simplest forms, can be demonstrated with simple information units known as quantum binary digits (a binary digit gets one of two values, zero or one), named quantum bits or qubits.

C. Martín-Vide et al. (Eds.): TPNC 2020, LNCS 12494, pp. 69–81, 2020.
https://doi.org/10.1007/978-3-030-63000-3_6

Many applications of quantum cryptography, including quantum key distribution (QKD) protocols [4,5,8], can be explained using qubits. While the basic ideas behind quantum information in general, and especially behind these QKD protocols, are not very complicated for an "insider", they can be abstruse for someone without the necessary physics or mathematics background. This hinders general audiences from correctly understanding these concepts. An intuitive description of such concepts will potentially be beneficial not only for the general public, but also for researchers in other fields to understand and visualize protocols.

In this work, we follow—and much expand—a simple but powerful model of "quantum candies" (or in short, "qandies") originally suggested by Jacobs [9], who proposed a new type of very special candies plus weird machines that produce those special candies. The non-conventional properties of the quantum candies and those machines—plus our wide and wild expansions—are used here as explanatory tools for various quantum concepts and technologies.

The model had originally been developed in two (independent) steps: Karl Svozil presented "chocolate balls" in several papers (e.g. [14]), including using these on an actual stage to demonstrate a pseudo-quantum model that resembles quantum cryptography. Kayla Jacobs, independently [9], invented an intuitive and much-closer-to-quantum variant based on properties of hypothetical candies having two different colors and two different tastes. To the best of our knowledge, Jacobs' model was presented in seminars (at MIT and at the Technion, and mainly to high-school students) but has never been officially published.

The paper is structured as follows. In Sect. 2 we review Svozil's and Jacobs' demonstrations of the most well-known QKD protocol: the BB84 protocol [5]. We then propose several straightforward and more sophisticated extensions (including the famous B92 protocol [4] and more). In Sect. 3 we expand the quantum candies model to explain various quantum concepts including entanglement, and an attack on "quantum bit commitment" in Sect. 3.2. We end with some brief closing remarks in Sect. 4.

2   Quantum Cryptography, Chocolate Balls, Quantum Candies, the BB84 Protocol, and Beyond

Suppose that two users, Alice and Bob, would like to communicate secretly. They may do so if they share a secret random and sufficiently long key (typically, a string of bits). Thus, the remaining problem is how to distribute an identical random and secure key.

Quantum key distribution (QKD) protocols solve the key distribution problem by utilizing quantum objects that, due to the rules of quantum theory, cannot be copied, and any attempt to copy them or even slightly obtain information from them enables Alice and Bob to detect the presence of the eavesdropper. Thus an eavesdropper can block the communication but cannot learn the secrets.

The BB84 QKD protocol proposed by Bennett and Brassard in 1984 [5], is simple and it also can serve as an excellent tool for understanding the basics of quantum theory. Svozil and Jacobs found simple *and sweet* ways to describe the BB84 protocol in somewhat-classical ways.

2.1   Chocolate Balls and Generalized Urn Model

Svozil [14] described a simple way to stage the BB84 protocol using real-life chocolate balls, based on the so-called generalized urn (GU) model by Wright [16]. In this model, the qubits are represented by chocolate balls wrapped in black foil with two binary numbers printed on the surface, one binary digit (0 or 1) in red color and the other binary digit (0 or 1) in green. If we denote the case of a zero written in red and a zero written in green as {0,0}[red,green], then the four types of balls include also {0,1}[red,green], {1,0}[red,green] and {1,1}[red,green].

Any user can view the numbers on the chocolate balls, but *must obey* the restriction that he/she must put on red-filtering or green-filtering glasses first, so that only one binary number can be seen every time a person looks at a ball.

The chocolate balls are drawn from a large urn containing an equal number of the four types of balls. To send a string of random bits to Bob, Alice wears a pair of colored glasses, randomly draws a single ball from the urn, and records the number she sees so she keeps the data regarding both the digit and its color. The ball is then sent to Bob who, before obtaining it, randomly picks a glasses color and wears the glasses. Only then Bob is allowed to observe it, and then to record the color and number (as Alice did).

After repeating these steps as many times as they wish, each time again randomly picking a new pair of colored glasses, Alice and Bob then announce their choices of colors publicly, and keep the bits obtained only in the cases where they picked the same color of glasses, which guarantees that they will obtain the same bit string. About half the data is thrown away, in case all previous choices were made at random.

If the transmission between Alice and Bob for the chocolate balls is not eavesdropped, or if eavesdropped by an eavesdropper that *follows the rules*, then the distributed key can be trusted. However, a cheating eavesdropper (we call her Eve) can obtain *all* the transmitted information by simply not obeying the imposed law of wearing colored glasses. Moreover, her observations do not change the chocolate balls. Svozil [15] analyzed various urn models and their connections to quantum physics, and of course was aware that this demonstration of BB84 only partially illustrates the BB84 protocol, as it does not illustrate its true quantumness or the resulting security.

2.2   Jacobs' Quantum Candies Model

We now consider Jacobs' model, where, instead of chocolate balls, there exists candies to which we gradually assign "quantumness". We call the resulting sweets "quantum candy" (or, *qandy*, or Jacob's qandies). The model was originally presented by Kayla Jacobs [9] as an easy way to present quantum bits and QKD to the general audience.

Jacobs considered candies that have two different *general properties*, color and taste. The color of a candy can be red (R) or green (G), while the taste can be chocolate (C) or vanilla (V).

At first, the above general properties of color and taste and specific properties (red, green, chocolate, vanilla) show much similarity to Svozil's sweets, and may actually even found to be fully equivalent! Here are the four options of chocolate balls versus four options of candies, with an obvious one-to-one correspondence:

$$\{0,0\}[\text{red,green}] \longleftrightarrow \{C,R\}[\text{taste,color}]$$
$$\{0,1\}[\text{red,green}] \longleftrightarrow \{C,G\}[\text{taste,color}]$$
$$\{1,0\}[\text{red,green}] \longleftrightarrow \{V,R\}[\text{taste,color}]$$
$$\{1,1\}[\text{red,green}] \longleftrightarrow \{V,G\}[\text{taste,color}]$$

It is trivial to see that this translation from the generalized urn model is exact thus far, hence if an eavesdropper (on BB84) could *both* look and taste, the candies protocol becomes as insecure as the generalized urn model once Eve does not obey the rules.

As described in Fig. 1, we impose some unusual rules onto these candies that make them *"qandies"*. First, each qandy has only a single specific property:

$$\{C\}[\text{taste}], \ \{V\}[\text{taste}], \ \{R\}[\text{color}], \ \{G\}[\text{color}]$$

What are the implications from this rule in terms of generating the qandies and in terms of "observing" them? First, a user can *only* learn about one general property of a qandy, but not both. Namely, if one looks at a qandy, it will appear as red or green, but one cannot taste it anymore (its taste is destroyed by looking at it); if one tastes a qandy, he/she would taste either chocolate or vanilla, but one cannot learn anything about its color anymore (its color is destroyed). Second, a qandy-making machine has four buttons, one for choosing C, one for choosing V, one for choosing R and one for choosing G. Third, if the machine generates (as an example) a chocolate qandy (C), one can taste and know it is chocolate, but if one looks, a random color is seen (R or G) and the taste is destroyed.

The key feature of these qandies is that each single qandy **really** has only a single specific property. This is one form of what is known as the complementarity principle[1] in quantum physics: if color is defined, taste cannot be defined, and if taste is defined color cannot be defined. The rule of complementarity applies both to the person (i.e. person/machine) preparing the qandies, and to anyone observing the qandy.

But maybe an extremely sophisticated (having some future technology) eavesdropper can somehow know both the color and taste? Surprisingly, Einstein's view of quantum physics, e.g. his famous sentence "God does not play dice" and also the EPR paradox [7], is also in complete correspondence to the

---

[1] Other forms of the principle exist, e.g., that elementary particles like electrons or photons have both particle characteristics and wave characteristics.

above. In his view quantum physics is incomplete: it has "hidden varaibles" and a deeper theory (not yet known to Science, but maybe known to that futuristic Eve) may unveil the hidden variables and hence will provide both the color and the taste of these candies.

If we try to use our "classical imagination" to *build* the machine, we might think as Einstein did: imagine a futuristic machine which produces standard classical candies that are wrapped with an identical piece of edible but opaque candy paper, such that none of the candy's properties can be known by only looking at a freshly prepared candy. The machine is a black box to all users, who can only interact with the machine through four external buttons: $\{C\}, \{V\}, \{R\}, \{G\}$. If Alice presses $\{R\}$ or $\{G\}$ to prepare a candy with definite color, that candy does not have a defined taste, and *vice versa*—when one general property is well defined, the other general property becomes *random*. So any user cannot fix or learn both the color and taste of a candy. And indeed, if Alice's produces a candy with a specific color, say $\{R\}$, and Bob tastes that candy, he will taste a random taste ($\{C\}$ or $\{V\}$). And similarly, looking at a candy having a specific taste will result in seeing a random color ($\{R\}$ or $\{G\}$).

Einstein believed that even if one general property must be randomized, its actually not—its specific property is still *there*, but well-hidden. Hence a *deeper theory* (beyond quantum) could reveal both general properties with their explicit specific properties, so the candies eventually will follow (in the eyes of a futuristic scientist) classical intuition and eventually—will be identical to Svozil's chocolate balls.

Today—due to a theorem known as Bell's theorem [3], and various confirming experiments (the first done by Aspect [1,2])—the modern view is that we do not follow Einstein's belief anymore. As understood today, when Alice asks for a qandy with a definite taste, the machine would produce one with Alice's desired taste, but with NO DEFINED COLOR, and if Alice wants a qandy with a definite color, the machine would produce one with Alice's desired color, but with NO DEFINED TASTE! The complementarity rule is so deeply inherent in Jacobs' qandies model that we may say the other general property does not exist at all (it is not even random), and it only becomes random if an observation is made.

Finally, the qandy model illustrates that an observation alters the qandies' properties, leading to a no cloning principle and to secure QKD.

2.3   Orthogonality, and No-Cloning

We now discuss an important implication of these qandies, which will be useful in explaining the BB84 protocol. Here, the key concept is *orthogonality*: we say that two qandy states are orthogonal to each other when they are different states of the same general property: $\{R\}$ and $\{G\}$ are orthogonal states, and $\{C\}$ and $\{V\}$ are also orthogonal states. Crucially, orthogonal states can be *perfectly distinguished* if an observation is made to distinguish them. I.e., if Alice sends to Bob a color qandy, and tells bob it is a colored qandy, then Bob can distinguish whether the qandy is red or green by looking at it. On the other hand, if Bob

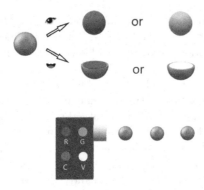

Fig. 1. Top: illustrative figures of qandies with two general properties, color and taste. Before any choice of observation, all qandies appear identical. If one looks at a qandy, it will appear as red or green, but one cannot taste it again; if one tastes a qandy, he/she would taste either chocolate or vanilla, but one cannot then learn anything about its color. Bottom: a qandy-producing machine. The user can press one of the four buttons on the machine and generate the corresponding qandy. Only one general property can be fixed for every qandy produced, while the other general property would be randomly assigned by the machine (if we follow Einstein) or have the other property non-existing at all (if we follow modern understanding and Jacob's qandies). (Color figure online)

is given randomly a red or chocolate qandy, then no observation can determine, with 100% chance of being correct, the specific property of that qandy.

The ability of identifying a particular state directly translates to the ability of copying (cloning) a qandy. Thus, the existence of non-orthogonal states results in the impossibility to copy a random qandy that can be in arbitrary states. This is named the no-cloning principle and is central to the safety of many quantum cryptography protocols, as we will now see.

2.4   BB84 QKD with Qandies

We now demonstrate how Alice and Bob may utilize qandies to achieve the task of secure key distribution, using the BB84 protocol. First, prior to sending anything, they determine a set of rules that assign binary values to states of each specific property; for example, they may assign 0 to red color and chocolate taste, and 1 to green color and vanilla taste. This would allow their communication to result in a string of bits. Then, when they are later separated and would like to exchange a key to encrypt their message, they repeatedly perform the following: Alice randomly presses one of the four buttons on her qandy machine, records her choice, and has the qandy delivered to Bob. Upon receiving, Bob randomly decides what he would like to do with it: he can either "look" and record its color, or "taste" and record its taste. He then translates the result into 0 or 1 and records the bit value *as well as* his action.

After this has been repeated for a sufficient number of times, Alice and Bob will communicate through the classical channel to compare their preparation and observation *methods* for every qandy[2]. Specifically, Alice tells Bob whether she prepared a qandy with definite color or a definite taste, and Bob tells Alice whether he tasted or looked. Note that they do not reveal their bit values to each other. They keep the result if the two methods match, and discard otherwise[3]. For example, if for qandy number 17 Alice generated a qandy with definite color (say $\{R\}$), and Bob measured a general property of a color, they will share an identical knowledge (unless natural noise or an eavesdropper destroyed it and input an error). This establishes a string of random bits between the two parties.

The safety of this protocol can be understood from the no-cloning principle. Let us analyze a specific eavesdropping attack—the "measure-resend attack": Suppose Eve gambles and looks at qandy number 17. She will see R and hence get full information. She then creates a new copy of Alice's red qandy and sends to Bob, and Bob observes red as he is supposed to. However, we know that, in general, learning or cloning is impossible as discussed earlier; indeed, if Eve gambles badly and decides to taste qandy number 17, she will learn an irrelevant information (a random taste) and resend a definite taste, hence "corrupt" the original bit that Alice intended to send. With a probability of 50% Bob will see G instead of R, i.e., Eve generated noise.

From Table 1 we see that overall, Eve's measure-resend attack will result in about 25% mismatched bits among those shared between Alice and Bob, which shall be revealed to them by comparing a sufficiently long subset of their bits through the classical (insecure yet unjammable) channel. In this case, Alice and Bob can discard their shared bits, and re-start this procedure again (via a different qandies channel) to obtain a new bit string, and verify (as we saw) that no eavesdropper is present. It has been proven that a secret key can be obtained via post-processing of the data, as long as the error-rate is smaller than around 10% [13].

Table 1. Agreement probability between Alice and Bob due to the measure-resend attack. The table entries indicate actions taken by the eavesdropper as well as their occurring probabilities. A green cell implies agreement between Alice and Bob, whereas a red cell implies a disagreement. In 25% of the cases, their bits do not agree.

Bob \ Alice	Color	Taste
Look	Look, 50% / Taste, 25% Taste, 25%	Discard
Taste	Discard	Look, 25% Look, 25% / Taste, 50%

---

[2] The classical channel is assumed to be insecure yet unjammable.

[3] If Bob can keep the qandies un-measured in a qandies' memory, the bit rate can be doubled, as he will taste or look only after learning Alice's preparation method.

2.5 A Few Direct Extensions

Two simple variants of BB84 are presented to show that making the properties somewhat more classical is possible, while keeping the goal of secure communication. If qandies had only the color property and not the taste (or vice versa—if had only the taste), a classical description would be immediate, cloning would be possible, and all parties, the sender the receiver and any potential eavesdropper will see everything—the green or the red. One variant of BB84 that is somewhat close to be classical works when taste exists but qandies with taste are only rarely used. Such a protocol can still be proven secure [10]. Another variant suggested the possibility that the tastes exist, but the machine used by the sender can only generate two colors (red and green) and just one taste (say, chocolate). As long as the receiver can detect both colors and both tastes, this protocol is secure [12]. This protocol had later led on to many protocols in which one party can only be aware of colors, and still—such protocols (named semi-quantum key distribution) are secure.

A much more famous and well known protocol, the B92 protocol (when adjusted to qandies), uses just a single color and a single taste. In the B92 protocol [4], Alice only prepares two types of qandies: red and chocolate, which she and Bob agreed to stand for bits 0 and 1 respectively. When Bob receives a qandy, he randomly chooses to taste or look, but does not reveal his choice to Alice as in BB84. Instead, he publicly announces to Alice whether he *succeeds* or *fails* for every qandy, where the success condition is defined as *tasting vanilla* or *seeing green*. He then associates seeing green with the bit 1 because Alice never prepared green and red could not lead to seeing green (only chocolate could); and he associates vanilla with 0 because Alice never prepared vanilla and chocolate could not lead to tasting vanilla (only red could). After sending many qandies, as in BB84, they compare a subset of the bits to determine whether an eavesdropper is present, and final post-processing is used to generate a final key.

We can easily extend the qandies model to have more than two colors and tastes leading to additional key distribution protocols; some of those are actually "beyond quantum" in one sense or another.

For example, if instead of trying to imitate quantum bits–qubits, we try to imitate quantum trits–qutrits, we simply add one additional color (say, blue) and one additional taste (say, peanut butter). Interestingly, if we follow restrictions imposed by quantum theory, we must have the same number of colors and tastes. Of course Alice and Bob are not forced to use all three colors and tastes in such a case, but once we define the candies to be analogous to qutrits, the eavesdropper can make use of that extended qandies space.

Another fascinating extension is to go back to just two colors and two tastes, but add a third property, say texture, to yield "the six-state protocol"[4]. The six-state protocol is a generalization of the BB84 protocol, where 3 pairs of orthogonal states (each pair belonging to one general property) of qandies are

---

[4] Interestingly having just two specific properties (two colors etc.) and having four general properties—e.g. color, taste, texture, and smell, is not consistent with the rules of quantum theory.

used; this requires a slightly more general machine that is capable of preparing qandies with 3 general properties, a color, a taste, and a texture—the texture of a qandy can be, for example, soft or crunchy. As in BB84, the machine can only prepare a qandy with one definite specific property, and one can only learn about one general property of a qandy. And if a qandy is prepared with one specific property (say the taste of vanilla) an attempt to look at it or to "feel" its texture must yield a random outcome, and the person eating it feels no softness or crunchiness. The resulting QKD protocol is (in some sense) more secure than BB84: if we assume Eve applies an observation and sends according to her outcome, then among the bits intercepted by Eve, for which Alice and Bob used the same general property, 1/3 of them would result in an inconsistency between Alice and Bob. This is higher than in the BB84 protocol, meaning that there exists a level of natural error such that BB84 cannot be made secure while the six-state protocol can be made secure. Of course, this comes at some cost— increasing the total number of qandies that Alice must share with Bob, due to the increased number (i.e. 2/3) of discarded cases.

3 Multi-Qandies and Pseudo-Entanglement

We have demonstrated the principle of complementarity using the qandy picture, and illustrated why the BB84 protocol is safe. We now exploit other quantum-inspired concepts that can be demonstrated by going far beyond Jacobs' qandy model. Specifically we shall consider here multi-qandy state, and qandies-correlations (i.e. pseudo-entanglement), closely related to quantum entanglement.

It is easy to imagine a system of multiple qandies: for example, a system of a chocolate qandy and a green qandy can be described as $\{C\}_1\{G\}_2$, where the subscript denotes the qandy's number. The two qandies live in different "spaces", denoted by the separation of the two states $\{\ \}_1\{\ \}_2$. As we will see, we can define new types of multi-qandy system that goes beyond a group of independent qandies. In some sense, this demonstrates another complementarity principle, as we clarify by the end of this section.

3.1 Correlated Qandies and Pseudo-Entanglement

Quantum entanglement is a phenomenon often called "spooky action at a distance". In its simplest form, it describes the behavior of two spatially separated systems where measurement outcomes on both systems are correlated in a weird (non-classical) way. We can partially mimic it using two qandies.

To demonstrate this, we need to imagine a qandy-producing machine of a new type, which generates (in addition to the previously described single qandies) four types of correlated pairs of qandies. One type of correlated pairs, denoted as $\{\phi_+\}$, has the property that if the same test-action is performed on both qandies, the outcomes are always random but identical. If both are looked at, then the outcome would always be either (red, red) or (green, green), each occurring with

50% probability; similarly, if both are tasted, then the outcome would always be either (chocolate, chocolate) or (vanilla, vanilla), each occurring with 50% probability. On the other hand, if one qandy is tasted while the other is looked at, each outcome is random on its own, and there are no correlations between the two outcomes. These correlated qandies are different than the qandies of the earlier sections in the sense that each qandy in the pair can no longer be assigned a definite taste or color, and only the correlations are now defined.

We define the other correlated qandy pairs similarly as follows:

- $\{\phi_+\}$ as above;
- $\{\psi_+\}$: If both candies are looked at, they present opposite colors, but whenever they are tasted, they present identical tastes;
- $\{\phi_-\}$: If both candies are looked at, they present identical colors, but whenever they are tasted, they present opposite tastes;
- $\{\psi_-\}$: If both candies are looked at, they present opposite colors, and whenever they are tasted, they present opposite tastes.

As before, in all these cases, if one qandy is tasted while the other is looked at, there are no correlations between the outcomes, and the outcomes are totally random. These qandies possess what we call pseudo-entanglement.

We can easily mimic a variant of BB84 using such a machine. This, in its quantum version, is called the EPR scheme [6,8]. Here, Alice prepares a correlated pair $\{\phi_+\}$. She then sends one qandy to Bob and keeps the other one. Each of them chooses whether to taste the qandy or look at it. They expect the same result if both performed the same action, and they expect random and uncorrelated results if they performed different actions. After repeating a sufficient number of times, they compare their actions and keep only the results from the cases which they performed the same action.

In all the cases where Alice and Bob performed the same action, their result is identical, random, and secure against Eve. This ensures the safety of the protocol. Importantly, even if Eve prepares the qandy pairs (instead of Alice), she does not know what answer Alice and Bob would get.

3.2 Quantum Bit Commitment

With correlated qandies, we can show another interesting quantum cryptographic protocol; unfortunately, the protocol is actually insecure, and the simplest and most typical attack showing its insecurity can be fully described using pseudo-entangled qandies. We first consider a goal called bit commitment, where Alice would like to first deliver a bit to Bob, and reveal the bit at a later time. However, the two parties may not trust each other: for example, Bob may suspect that Alice could change her bit after it has been sent, and Alice may suspect that Bob could somehow know the bit before she decides to reveal it. We divide the protocol into a commit stage and a reveal stage.

One quantum scheme (along with a proof of its insecurity!) was proposed by Bennett and Brassard in 1984 [5]. Their scheme works as follows: In the commit stage, Alice prepares n qandies with definite colors (each randomly chosen to be red or green) if she wants to commit a bit 0, or n qandies with a definite taste (randomly chocolate or vanilla) if she wants to commit 1. She keeps a record of what she has prepared (a list of red, chocolate, green, etc., for example), and delivers the n qandies to Bob, without telling him how she had prepared them.

At the reveal stage, she tells Bob her choice of preparation of all n qandies, which effectively uncovers the bit. Bob, who is assumed to have a memory where he keeps the qandies[5], can verify that she did not cheat (i.e., changed the bit she originally intended to send) by asking Alice what he should get for each qandy.

The safety consideration of the protocol is as follows. Clearly, if Bob randomly looks at or tastes the qandies, the result is completely random and meaningless, as the information is fully encoded in Alice's preparation method. Thus, the best strategy for Bob is to do nothing at the commit stage, and then he can fully verify Alice's opening at the reveal stage. So Alice can be sure that Bob does not have any information on her bit. On the other hand, since Alice cannot change the qandies once they're in Bob's hand, if Alice did cheat by telling Bob the opposite method, she would need to guess Bob's random results, which has a success probability of 2^{-n}. Therefore, cheating can be prevented with arbitrarily high probability if Bob requires Alice to verify a longer and longer bit string.

However, the above argument does not hold if Alice is capable of preparing pseudo-entangled qandies. Alice can cheat by doing the following—she prepares n pairs of qandies in $\{\phi_+\}$, sends one of each pair to Bob and keeps the other one until she wants to reveal. At the reveal stage, she can tell Bob any bit she "was commiting" (either color or taste), and when Bob would like to verify, she can taste or look at (according to her choice at the last minute) every qandy, and tell Bob the results to verify on the other member of each pseudo-entangled pair. Because of the perfect correlation in both color and taste for $\{\phi_+\}$, Bob would always be convinced, while Alice has the complete freedom to cheat and decide what she wants to send long after the committing stage. Therefore, the protocol is no longer safe when pseudo-entangled qandies are available to Alice; a similar insecurity argument is true in the quantum scenario, and is even generalized to any possible quantum bit-commitment protocol [11].

This protocol and the attack demonstrate nicely the spooky action at a distance! Alice controls Bob's qandies, exactly to the desired level, even though she has no access to them at the stage when she decides on how to control them.

4   Conclusion

In this work, we have introduced and extended the quantum candy model proposed by Jacobs, and used it to demonstrate some of the most important concepts in quantum information science and quantum cryptography in an approachable manner. Our work is meant to be a useful tool for introducing quantum science to the general public. We emphasize that the qandy model

---

[5] There is a similar protocol if Bob has no memory, with a slightly different analysis.

does not always need to follow quantum theory and can be extended in many ways. We leave this to the full paper, as well as the well established connection to quantum theory, which mainly contains quantum superposition and unitary transformations.

Acknowledgments. J.L. and T.M. thank the Schwartz/Reisman Foundation. J.L. is supported by NSERC Canada. T.M. was also partially supported by Israeli MOD.

References

1. Aspect, A., Dalibard, J., Roger, G.: Experimental test of Bell's inequalities using time-varying analyzers. Phys. Rev. Lett. **49**(25), 1804–1807 (1982). https://doi.org/10.1103/PhysRevLett.49.1804
2. Aspect, A., Grangier, P., Roger, G.: Experimental realization of Einstein-Podolsky-Rosen-Bohm Gedankenexperiment : a new violation of Bell's inequalities. Phys. Rev. Lett. **49**(2), 91–94 (1982). https://doi.org/10.1103/PhysRevLett.49.91
3. Bell, J.S.: On the Einstein Podolsky Rosen paradox. Physics Physique Fizika **1**(3), 195–200 (1964). https://doi.org/10.1103/PhysicsPhysiqueFizika.1.195
4. Bennett, C.H.: Quantum cryptography using any two nonorthogonal states. Phys. Rev. Lett. **68**(21), 3121–3124 (1992). https://doi.org/10.1103/PhysRevLett.68.3121
5. Bennett, C.H., Brassard, G.: Quantum cryptography: public key distribution and coin tossing. In: International Conference on Computers, Systems and Signal Processing, Bangalore, India, pp. 175–179 (1984)
6. Bennett, C.H., Brassard, G., Mermin, N.D.: Quantum cryptography without Bell's theorem. Phys. Rev. Lett. **68**(5), 557–559 (1992). https://doi.org/10.1103/PhysRevLett.68.557
7. Einstein, A., Podolsky, B., Rosen, N.: Can quantum-mechanical description of physical reality be considered complete? Phys. Rev. **47**(10), 777–780 (1935). https://doi.org/10.1103/PhysRev.47.777
8. Ekert, A.K.: Quantum cryptography based on Bell's theorem. Phys. Rev. Lett. **67**(6), 661–663 (1991). https://doi.org/10.1103/PhysRevLett.67.661
9. Jacobs, K.: Private communication (2009)
10. Lo, H.-K., Chau, H.F., Ardehali, M.: Efficient quantum key distribution scheme and a proof of its unconditional security. J. Cryptol. **18**(2), 133–165 (2004). https://doi.org/10.1007/s00145-004-0142-y
11. Mayers, D.: Unconditionally secure quantum bit commitment is impossible. Phys. Rev. Lett. **78**(17), 3414–3417 (1997). https://doi.org/10.1103/PhysRevLett.78.3414
12. Mor, T.: No cloning of orthogonal states in composite systems. Phys. Rev. Lett. **80**(14), 3137–3140 (1998). https://doi.org/10.1103/PhysRevLett.80.3137
13. Shor, P.W., Preskill, J.: Simple proof of security of the BB84 quantum key distribution protocol. Phys. Rev. Lett. **85**(2), 441–444 (2000). https://doi.org/10.1103/PhysRevLett.85.441
14. Svozil, K.: Staging quantum cryptography with chocolate balls. Am. J. Phys. **74**(9), 800–803 (2006). https://doi.org/10.1119/1.2205879

15. Svozil, K.: Non-contextual chocolate balls versus value indefinite quantum cryptography. Theoret. Comput. Sci. **560**(P1), 82–90 (2014). https://doi.org/10.1016/j.tcs.2014.09.019
16. Wright, R.: Generalized urn models. Found. Phys. **20**(7), 881–903 (1990). https://doi.org/10.1007/BF01889696

From Practice to Theory: The "Bright Illumination" Attack on Quantum Key Distribution Systems

Rotem Liss[(⊠)] and Tal Mor

Computer Science Department, Technion – Israel Institute of Technology,
Technion City, Haifa 3200003, Israel
{rotemliss,talmo}@cs.technion.ac.il

Abstract. The "Bright Illumination" attack [Lydersen et al., Nat. Photon. 4, 686–689 (2010)] is a practical attack, fully implementable against quantum key distribution systems. In contrast to almost all developments in quantum information processing (for example, Shor's factorization algorithm, quantum teleportation, Bennett-Brassard (BB84) quantum key distribution, the "Photon-Number Splitting" attack, and many other examples), for which theory has been proposed decades before a proper implementation, the "Bright Illumination" attack preceded any sign or hint of a theoretical prediction. Here we explain how the "Reversed-Space" methodology of attacks, complementary to the notion of "quantum side-channel attacks" (which is analogous to a similar term in "classical"—namely, non-quantum—computer security), has missed the opportunity of predicting the "Bright Illumination" attack.

Keywords: Quantum Cryptography · QKD · Security · Reversed-Space Attacks · Bright Illumination · Practice · Theory · Side-Channel Attacks

1 Introduction

In the area of quantum information processing, theory usually precedes experiment. For example, the BB84 protocol for quantum key distribution (QKD) was suggested in 1984 [2], five years before it was implemented [1], and it still cannot be implemented in a perfectly secure way even today [16,25]. The "Photon-Number Splitting" attack was suggested in 2000 [5,6], but it is not implementable today. Quantum computing was suggested in the 1980s (see, e.g., [7]), but no useful and universal quantum computer (with a large number of clean qubits) has been implemented until today [22]. The same applies to Shor's factorization algorithm [27,28], to quantum teleportation [3] (at least to some extent; see also [21]), and to many other examples.

In contrast to the above examples, the "Bright Illumination" attack against practical QKD systems was presented and fully implemented in 2010 [18], *prior* to any theoretical prediction of the possibility of such an attack. Here we ask the question: could the "Bright Illumination" attack have been theoretically predicted?

The work of T.M. and R.L. was partly supported by the Israeli MOD Research and Technology Unit, and by the Gerald Schwartz & Heather Reisman Foundation.

C. Martín-Vide et al. (Eds.): TPNC 2020, LNCS 12494, pp. 82–94, 2020.
https://doi.org/10.1007/978-3-030-63000-3_7

Quantum key distribution (QKD) makes it possible for two parties, Alice and Bob, to agree on a shared secret key. This task, that is impossible for two parties using only classical communication, is made possible by taking advantage of quantum phenomena: Alice and Bob use an insecure quantum channel and an authenticated (unjammable) classical channel. The resulting key is secure even against an adversary (Eve) that may use the most general attacks allowed by quantum physics, and remains secret indefinitely, even if Eve has unlimited computing power.

For example, in the BB84 QKD protocol [2], Alice sends to Bob N qubits, each of them randomly chosen from the set of quantum states $\{|0\rangle, |1\rangle, |+\rangle \triangleq \frac{|0\rangle + |1\rangle}{\sqrt{2}}, |-\rangle \triangleq \frac{|0\rangle - |1\rangle}{\sqrt{2}}\}$, and Bob measures each of them either in the computational basis $\{|0\rangle, |1\rangle\}$ or in the Hadamard basis $\{|+\rangle, |-\rangle\}$, chosen randomly. Thereafter, Alice and Bob postprocess the results by using the classical channel. If Alice and Bob use matching bases, they share a bit (unless there is some noise or eavesdropping); if they use mismatching bases, Bob's results are random. Alice and Bob reveal their basis choices, and discard the bits for which they used mismatching bases. After that, they publicly reveal a random subset of their bits in order to estimate the error rate (then discarding those exposed test bits), aborting the protocol if the error rate is too high; and they perform error correction and privacy amplification processes, obtaining a completely secret, identical final key.

The security promises of QKD are true in theory, but its *practical* security is far from being guaranteed. The practical implementations of QKD use realistic photons; therefore, they deviate from the theoretical protocols, which use ideal qubits. These deviations make possible various attacks [16,24], related to the idea of "side-channel attacks" in classical (i.e., non-quantum) computer security.

For example, the "Photon-Number Splitting" (PNS) attack [5,6] (see Subsect. 2.1) takes advantage of some specific imperfections: while the quantum state sent by Alice *should* be encoded in a single photon, Eve exploits the fact that in most implementations, Alice sometimes sends to Bob more than one photon (e.g., two photons). The PNS attack was found using more realistic notations—the Fock space notations; the main insight of [5,6] is that using proper notations is vital, both when theoretically searching for possible loopholes and attacks against QKD, and when attempting to prove its security.

The "Bright Illumination" practical attack [18] uses a weakness of Bob's measurement devices that allows Eve to "blind" them and fully control Bob's measurement results. Eve can then get full information on the secret key, without inducing any error.

In Sect. 2 we explain experimental QKD systems and their weaknesses: we introduce the Fock space notations, the "Photon-Number Splitting" (PNS) attack, and two imperfections of Bob's detection process. In Sects. 3 and 4 we describe the practical "Bright Illumination" attack and the "Reversed-Space" methodology of attacks [4,10,11], respectively, and in Sect. 6 we bring together all the above notions for explaining the theory underlying the "Bright Illumination" attack. As an important side issue, in Sect. 5 we describe the notion of "quantum side-channel attacks", partially related to all the above. We conclude that while the "Bright Illumination" attack is not a "side-channel" attack, it can be modeled as a "Reversed-Space" attack [11]:

this attack and similar attacks could and should have been proposed or anticipated by theoreticians.

2 Experimental QKD, Imperfections, and the Fock Space Notations

The BB84 protocol may be experimentally implemented in a "polarization-based" implementation, that we can model as follows: Alice's quantum states, that are sent to Bob, are single photons whose polarizations encode the quantum states. The four possible states to be sent by Alice are $|0\rangle$, $|1\rangle$, $|+\rangle$, and $|-\rangle$, where $|0\rangle = |\leftrightarrow\rangle$ (a single photon in the horizontal polarization) and $|1\rangle = |\updownarrow\rangle$ (a single photon in the vertical polarization). The states $|+\rangle = |\nearrow\rangle$ and $|-\rangle = |\nwarrow\rangle$ correspond to orthogonal diagonal polarizations.

For measuring the incoming photons, Bob uses a polarizing beam splitter (PBS) and two detectors. Bob actively configures the PBS for choosing his random measurement basis (the computational basis $\{|0\rangle, |1\rangle\}$ or the Hadamard basis $\{|+\rangle, |-\rangle\}$). If the PBS is configured for measurement in the computational basis, it sends any *horizontally* polarized photon to one arm and sends any *vertically* polarized photon to the other arm. In the end of each arm, a detector is placed, which clicks whenever it detects a photon. Therefore, the detector in the first arm clicks *only* if the $|0\rangle$ qubit state is detected, and the detector in the second arm clicks *only* if the $|1\rangle$ qubit state is detected. A *diagonally* polarized photon (i.e., $|+\rangle = |\nearrow\rangle$ or $|-\rangle = |\nwarrow\rangle$) would cause exactly one of the detectors (uniformly random) to click. Similarly, if the PBS is configured for measurement in the Hadamard basis, it distinguishes $|+\rangle$ from $|-\rangle$. This implementation may be slow, because Bob needs to randomly choose a basis for each arriving photon.

A more practical—yet imperfect—variant of this implementation uses a "passive" basis choice (e.g., [15]). This variant uses one polarization-independent beam splitter, two PBSs, and *four* detectors. In this variant, the polarization-independent beam splitter randomly sends each photon to one arm or to another. A photon going to the first arm is then measured (as described above) in the computational basis, while a photon going to the second arm is measured (as described above) in the Hadamard basis. This "passive" variant is exposed to various attacks; see Sect. 4.

2.1 The Fock Space Notations and the "Photon-Number Splitting" (PNS) Attack

We use the Fock space notations for describing practical QKD systems:

- In the simplest case, there are $k \geq 0$ photons, and all these photons belong to *one* photonic mode. The Fock state $|k\rangle$ represents k photons in this single mode: for example, $|0\rangle$ is the vacuum state, representing no photons in that mode; $|1\rangle$ represents one photon in that mode; $|2\rangle$ represents two photons in that mode; and so on.
- For describing several different *pulses* of photons (for example, photons traveling on different arms or at different time bins, or any other *external* degree of freedom), we need several photonic *modes*. For example, if we assume a single photon in two

pulses (and, thus, in two modes), we can describe a qubit[1]: for the computational basis $\{|o\rangle, |1\rangle\}$ of a single qubit, we write $|o\rangle = |0\rangle \otimes |1\rangle \equiv |0\rangle|1\rangle$ and $|1\rangle = |1\rangle \otimes |0\rangle \equiv |1\rangle|0\rangle$. (Those two modes are mathematically described using a tensor product, but we omit the $\otimes$ sign for brevity.) A superposition, too, describes a single photon in those two pulses: for example, the Hadamard basis states are $|\pm\rangle = \frac{|0\rangle|1\rangle \pm |1\rangle|0\rangle}{\sqrt{2}}$.

- More generally, if we have $k = k_1 + k_0$ photons in two different pulses (two modes), where k_1 photons are in one pulse and k_0 photons are in the other pulse, we write $|k_1\rangle|k_0\rangle$. Subscripts are added for specifying the types of pulses—for example, $|k_1\rangle_{t_1}|k_0\rangle_{t_0}$ for the two time bins t_1, t_0, or $|k_1\rangle_A|k_0\rangle_B$ for the two arms A, B.
- For describing more than two pulses (namely, more than two modes), we use generalized notations: for example, $k = k_2 + k_1 + k_0$ photons in three time bins are denoted $|k_2\rangle_{t_2}|k_1\rangle_{t_1}|k_0\rangle_{t_0}$. In particular, the vacuum state (absence of photons) is denoted $|0\rangle$ for one mode, $|0\rangle|0\rangle$ for two modes, $|0\rangle|0\rangle|0\rangle$ for three modes, and so on.

The above notations assume the photon *polarizations* (which are an *internal* degree of freedom) to be identical for all k photons. However, a single photon in a single pulse generally has two orthogonal polarizations: horizontal $\leftrightarrow$ and vertical $\updownarrow$. For each pulse, the two polarizations are described as two modes; therefore, m pulses mean $2m$ modes.

In this paper, we denote *polarization* modes of $k = k_1 + k_0$ photons by $|k_1, k_0\rangle$ (without any subscript), and denote only *pulse* modes by $|k_1\rangle|k_0\rangle$ (always with subscripts). Thus:

- For a *single* pulse, the two *polarization* modes describe a qubit if there is exactly *one photon* in the pulse. The computational basis states are $|o\rangle = |0, 1\rangle$ (representing *one* photon in the horizontal polarization mode and *zero* photons in the vertical polarization mode) and $|1\rangle = |1, 0\rangle$ (where the single photon is in the vertical mode).
- Similarly to the above, we can also describe: (a) superpositions; (b) the state $|k_1, k_0\rangle$ of $k = k_1 + k_0$ photons in those two polarization modes (k_1 photons in the vertical mode and k_0 photons in the horizontal mode); and (c) the vacuum state $|0, 0\rangle$.

We have seen that the Fock space notations extend *much* beyond the ideal single-qubit world, which is represented by the two-dimensional space $\text{Span}\{|o\rangle, |1\rangle\}$. Ideally, in BB84, Alice should send a qubit in this two-dimensional space; however, in practice, Alice sometimes sends states in a higher-dimensional Fock space.

The "Photon-Number Splitting" (PNS) attack [5,6] (which showed all QKD experiments done until around 2000 to be insecure) is based on analyzing the *six*-dimensional Hilbert space $\text{Span}\{|0, 0\rangle, |0, 1\rangle, |1, 0\rangle, |0, 2\rangle, |2, 0\rangle, |1, 1\rangle\}$, which represents all typical pulses with two polarizations if we can neglect the case of three or more photons—namely, if we assume $k_1 + k_0 \leq 2$. The PNS attack is based on three observations [5,6]: (a) Alice sometimes sends *two-photon pulses* in one of the four allowed polarizations; (b) Eve can, in principle, distinguish a two-photon pulse from a single-photon pulse without influencing the polarizations; and (c) Eve can, in principle, split such a two-photon pulse into two pulses, each containing a single photon, without influencing the polarizations. Thus, Eve can "steal" a single photon from each such two-photon pulse (without influencing the other photon), save it, and, after learning the basis, get full

---

[1] The notations $|o\rangle, |1\rangle, |\pm\rangle$ are used for the standard qubit (in a two-dimensional Hilbert space).

information about this pulse without being noticed. This attack could have been detrimental to the security of QKD, but counter-measures [13,17,23,30] have been found later.

2.2 Imperfections of Bob's Detectors

Two important examples of imperfections (see [10]) are highly relevant to various "Reversed-Space" attacks. As we show in this paper, those two imperfections must be *combined* for understanding the "Bright Illumination" attack.

Imperfection 1: Our realistic assumption, which is true for standard detectors in QKD implementations, is that Bob's detectors cannot *count* the number of photons in a pulse. Thus, they cannot distinguish *all* Fock states $|k\rangle$ from one another, but can only distinguish the Fock state $|0\rangle$ (a lack of photons) from the Fock states $\{|k\rangle : k \geq 1\}$. Namely, standard detectors can only decide whether the mode is empty ($k = 0$) or has at least one photon ($k > 0$). In contrast, we assume that Eve can (in principle) do anything allowed by the laws of quantum physics; in particular, Eve may have such "photon counters".

In particular, let us assume that there are *two* pulses, each of them consisting of a single mode. Bob cannot know whether a pulse contains one photon or two photons; therefore, he cannot distinguish between $|1\rangle|0\rangle$ and $|2\rangle|0\rangle$ (and, similarly, he cannot distinguish between $|0\rangle|1\rangle$ and $|0\rangle|2\rangle$). For example, assume that Alice sends the $|1\rangle|0\rangle$ state (a qubit) to Bob, and Eve replaces Alice's state by $|2\rangle|0\rangle$ and sends it to Bob instead (or, similarly, assume that Eve replaces $|0\rangle|1\rangle$ by $|0\rangle|2\rangle$). In this case, Bob cannot notice the change, and no error can occur; still, Bob got a state he had not expected to get. It may be possible for Eve to take advantage of this fact in a fully-designed attack.

Imperfection 2: Our realistic assumption is that Bob cannot know exactly *when* the photon he measured arrived. For example (in a polarization-based implementation):

– Alice's ideal qubit arrives at time t (states denoted $|0,1\rangle_t|0,0\rangle_{t+\delta}$, $|1,0\rangle_t|0,0\rangle_{t+\delta}$).
– Eve's photon may arrive at time $t + \delta$ (states denoted $|0,0\rangle_t|0,1\rangle_{t+\delta}$, $|0,0\rangle_t|1,0\rangle_{t+\delta}$).

Again, Eve may take advantage of this fact in a fully-designed attack.

Similar imperfections can be found if Bob cannot know exactly what the *wavelength* of the photon is, or *where* the photon arrives.

The conceptual difference between the two imperfections is in whether Bob can (ideally) avoid measuring the extra states sent by Eve, or not:

– In Imperfection 1, Eve may send more than one photon, and Bob must measure the state (while he cannot count the number of photons using current technology).
– In Imperfection 2, Eve sends states in two separate subsystems. Bob can, in principle, ignore the "wrong" subsystem in case he knows for sure it has not been sent by Alice.

3   The "Bright Illumination" Attack

The "Bright Illumination" blinding attack [18] works against QKD systems that use Avalanche Photodiodes (APDs) as Bob's detectors. As an example, we describe below the implementation of this attack against a system implementing the BB84 protocol in a polarization-based scheme, but it is important to note that the attack can be adapted to most QKD protocols and implementations that use APDs [18].

The APDs can be operated in two "modes of operation": the "linear mode" that detects only a light beam above a specific power threshold, and "Geiger mode" that detects even a single photon (but cannot count the number of photons). In this attack, the adversary Eve sends a continuous strong light beam towards Bob's detectors, causing them to operate *only* in the linear mode (thus "blinding" the detectors).

After Bob's detectors have been blinded (and in parallel to sending the continuous strong beam, making sure they are kept blind), Eve performs a "measure-resend" attack: she detects the qubit (single photon) sent by Alice, measures it in one of the two bases (exactly as Bob would do), and sends to Bob a *strong* light beam depending on the state she measured, a little above the power threshold of the detectors. For example, if Eve measures the state $|1,0\rangle$, she sends to Bob the state $|k,0\rangle$ for $k \gg 1$. Now, if Bob chooses the same basis as Eve, he will measure the same result as Eve; and if Bob chooses a different basis, he will measure nothing, because the strong light beam will get split between the two detectors. This means that Bob will always either measure the same result as Eve or lose the bit.

In the end, Bob and Eve have exactly the same information, so Eve can copy Bob's classical post-processing and get the same final key as Alice and Bob do. Moreover, Eve's attack causes no detectable disturbance, because Bob does not know that his detectors have operated in the wrong mode of operation; the only effect is a loss rate of 50% (that is not problematic: the loss rate for the single photons sent by Alice is usually much higher, so Eve can cause Bob to get the same loss rate he expects to get).

This attack was both developed and experimentally demonstrated against commercial QKD systems by [18]. See [18] for more details and for diagrams.

4   "Reversed-Space" Attacks

The "Reversed-Space" methodology, described in [8, 10, 11], is a theoretical framework of attacks exploiting the imperfections of Bob. This methodology is a special case (easier to analyze) of the more general methodology of "Quantum Space" attacks [8, 9], that exploits the imperfections of *both* Alice and Bob; the "Reversed-Space" methodology assumes Alice to be ideal and only exploits Bob's imperfections [4, 8, 10, 11]. (Another special case of a "Quantum Space" attack is the PNS attack [5, 6] described above.)

In the ideal QKD protocol, Bob expects to get from Alice a state in the Hilbert space $\mathscr{H}^{A}$; however, in the "Reversed-Space" attack, Bob gets from Eve an unexpected state, residing in a larger Hilbert space called the "space of the protocol" and denoted by $\mathscr{H}^{P}$. In principle, Eve could have used a huge space $\mathscr{H}^{I}$ such that $\mathscr{H}^{A} \subseteq \mathscr{H}^{P} \subseteq \mathscr{H}^{I}$: the huge Hilbert space $\mathscr{H}^{I}$ consists of *all* the quantum states that Eve *can possibly* send to Bob, but it is too large, and most of it is irrelevant.

Because "Reversed-Space" attacks assume a "perfect Alice" (sending prefect qubits), it is usually easy to find the *relevant* subspace $\mathscr{H}^{\mathrm{P}}$, as we demonstrate by three examples below; $\mathscr{H}^{\mathrm{P}}$ is only enlarged (relative to the ideal space $\mathscr{H}^{\mathrm{A}}$) by Bob's imperfections. Therefore, $\mathscr{H}^{\mathrm{P}}$ is the space that includes all the states that may be useful for Eve to send to Bob. The space $\mathscr{H}^{\mathrm{P}}$ is defined by taking all the possible measurement results of Bob and reversing them in time; more precisely, it is the span of all the states in $\mathscr{H}^{\mathrm{A}}$ *and* all the states that Eve can send to Bob so that he gets the measurement results she desires.

Whether Bob is aware of it or not, his experimental setting treats not only the states in $\mathscr{H}^{\mathrm{A}}$, but all the possible inputs in the "space of the protocol" $\mathscr{H}^{\mathrm{P}}$. Bob then classifies them into three classes: (1) valid states from Alice, (2) losses, and (3) invalid states. *Valid states* are always treated in conventional security analysis: a random subset is compared with Alice for estimating the error rate, and then the final key is obtained using the error correction and privacy amplification processes. *Losses* are expected, and they are not counted as noise. *Invalid states* are usually counted as errors (noise), but they do not appear in ideal analyses of ideal protocols. We note that loss rate and error rate are computed separately: the error rate must be small (e.g., around 10%) for the protocol not to be aborted by Alice and Bob, while the loss rate can be much higher (even higher than 99%). Any "Reversed-Space" attack takes advantage of the possibility that Bob treats some states in $\mathscr{H}^{\mathrm{P}}$ in the wrong way, because he does not expect to get those states.

Eve's attack is called "Reversed-Space" because Eve can devise her attack by looking at Bob's possible measurement results: Eve finds a measurement result she wants to be obtained by Bob (because he interprets it in a way desired by her) and reverses the measurement result in time for finding the state in $\mathscr{H}^{\mathrm{P}}$ she should send to Bob. In particular, if Bob applies the unitary operation $\mathscr{U}_{\mathrm{B}}$ on his state prior to his measurement, Eve should apply the inverted operation $\mathscr{U}_{\mathrm{B}}^{-1} = \mathscr{U}_{\mathrm{B}}^{\dagger}$ to each state corresponding to each possible measurement outcome of Bob.

We present three examples of "Reversed-Space" attacks. For simplicity, we only consider BB84 implemented in a polarization-based scheme (as described in Sect. 2), but the attacks may be generalized to other implementations, too. We emphasize that all three examples have been chosen to satisfy two conditions, also satisfied by the "Bright Illumination" attack: (a) Eve performs a "measure-resend" attack in a basis she chooses randomly, and (b) it is possible for Eve to get full information without inducing noise.

Example 1 (a special case of the "Trojan Pony" attack [12]): This example exploits Imperfection 1 and assumes Bob uses an "active" basis choice (see Sect. 2 for both).

In this attack, Eve performs a "measure-resend" attack—namely, she measures each qubit state sent from Alice to Bob in a random basis, and resends "it" towards Bob. However, instead of resending it as a single photon, she resends a huge number of photons towards Bob: she sends many *identical* photons, all with the same polarization as the state she measured ($|0\rangle$, $|1\rangle$, $|+\rangle$, or $|-\rangle$). If Bob chooses the same basis as Eve, he will get the same result as her, because Imperfection 1 causes his system to treat the incoming states $|0,k\rangle$ and $|k,0\rangle$ (for any $k \geq 1$) as if they were $|0,1\rangle$ and $|1,0\rangle$, respectively; but if he chooses a different basis from Eve, both of his detectors will (almost surely) click. If Bob decides to treat this *invalid* event (a two-detector click) as an "error", the error rate will be around 50%, so Alice and Bob will abort the protocol; but if he naively decides to treat this event as a "loss", Eve can get full information without inducing errors.

Alice sends an ideal qubit (a single photon), while Eve may send any number of photons. Therefore, using the Fock space notations, $\mathscr{H}^{A} = \mathscr{H}_2 \triangleq \text{Span}\{|0,1\rangle, |1,0\rangle\}$ and $\mathscr{H}^{P} = \text{Span}\{|m_1, m_0\rangle : m_1, m_0 \geq 0\}$.

Example 2 (a special case of the "Faked States" attack [8, 19, 20]): This attack exploits Imperfection 2 (Sect. 2). We assume that Bob has four detectors (namely, that he uses the "passive" basis choice variant of the polarization-based encoding; see Sect. 2), and that his detectors have different (but overlapping) *time gates* during which they are sensitive: given the three different times $t_0 < t_{1/2} < t_1$, the detectors for the computational basis are sensitive only to pulses sent at t_0 or $t_{1/2}$ (or in between), and the detectors for the Hadamard basis are sensitive only to pulses sent at $t_{1/2}$ or t_1 (or in between). Alice normally sends her pulses at $t_{1/2}$ (when both detectors are sensitive), but Eve may send her pulses at t_0, $t_{1/2}$, or t_1.

Eve performs a "measure-resend" attack by measuring Alice's state in a random basis, and resending it towards Bob as follows: if Eve measures in the computational basis, she resends the state at time t_0; and if she measures in the Hadamard basis, she resends the state at time t_1. Therefore, Bob gets the same result as Eve if he measures in the same basis as hers, but he gets a loss otherwise (because Bob's detectors for the other basis are not sensitive at that timing). This means that Eve gets full information without inducing any error.

Using the same notations as in Imperfection 2, the state $|m_1, m_0\rangle_{t_0} |n_1, n_0\rangle_{t_{1/2}} |o_1, o_0\rangle_{t_1}$ consists of the Fock states $|m_1, m_0\rangle$ sent at time t_0, $|n_1, n_0\rangle$ sent at time $t_{1/2}$, and $|o_1, o_0\rangle$ sent at time t_1. Alice sends an ideal qubit (a single photon at time $t_{1/2}$), while Eve may send a single photon at any of the times t_0, $t_{1/2}$, or t_1, or a superposition.

Therefore, $\mathscr{H}^{A} = \mathscr{H}_2 \triangleq \text{Span}\{|0,0\rangle_{t_0}|0,1\rangle_{t_{1/2}}|0,0\rangle_{t_1} , |0,0\rangle_{t_0}|1,0\rangle_{t_{1/2}}|0,0\rangle_{t_1}\}$ and $\mathscr{H}^{P} = \text{Span}\{|0,1\rangle_{t_0}|0,0\rangle_{t_{1/2}}|0,0\rangle_{t_1} , |1,0\rangle_{t_0}|0,0\rangle_{t_{1/2}}|0,0\rangle_{t_1} , |0,0\rangle_{t_0}|0,1\rangle_{t_{1/2}}|0,0\rangle_{t_1} ,$ $|0,0\rangle_{t_0}|1,0\rangle_{t_{1/2}}|0,0\rangle_{t_1} , |0,0\rangle_{t_0}|0,0\rangle_{t_{1/2}}|0,1\rangle_{t_1} , |0,0\rangle_{t_0}|0,0\rangle_{t_{1/2}}|1,0\rangle_{t_1}\}$.

Example 3 (the "Fixed Apparatus" attack [4]) can be applied by Eve if Bob uses a "passive" basis choice (Sect. 2). In this attack, Eve sends to Bob an unexpected state, and this state "forces" Bob to obtain the basis Eve wants. This attack makes it possible for Eve to force Bob choose the same basis as her (and, therefore, get the same outcome as her), thus stealing the whole key without inducing any errors or losses. The attack is only possible if Eve has a one-time access to Bob's laboratory, because it requires Eve to first compromise Bob's device (otherwise, she cannot send him that unexpected state).

Assume that Bob uses a polarization-independent beam splitter that splits the incoming beam into two different output arms (as described in Sect. 2). This beam splitter has two input arms: a *regular arm*, through which the standard incoming beam comes, and a *blocked arm*, where the incoming state is always assumed to be the zero-photon beam $|0,0\rangle$ (the vacuum state of two polarizations). If Eve can drill a small hole in Bob's device, exactly where the blocked arm gets its input from, then she can send a beam to the blocked arm and not only to the standard arm. It is proved [4] that Eve can then cause the beam splitter to choose an output arm to her desire, instead of choosing a "random" arm. The state $|m_1, m_0\rangle_r |n_1, n_0\rangle_b$ consists of the Fock state $|m_1, m_0\rangle$ sent through the *regular arm* of the beam splitter and the Fock state $|n_1, n_0\rangle$ sent through the *blocked arm*. Alice sends an ideal qubit (a single photon through the regular arm), while Eve may send a single photon through any of the two arms or a superposition. Therefore, $\mathscr{H}^A = \mathscr{H}_2 \triangleq \mathrm{Span}\{|0,1\rangle_r |0,0\rangle_b \ , \ |1,0\rangle_r |0,0\rangle_b\}$ and $\mathscr{H}^P = \mathrm{Span}\{|0,1\rangle_r |0,0\rangle_b \ , \ |1,0\rangle_r |0,0\rangle_b \ , \ |0,0\rangle_r |0,1\rangle_b \ , \ |0,0\rangle_r |1,0\rangle_b\}$.

5   Quantum Side-Channel Attacks

Shamir's "Quantum Side-Channel Attack" on Polarization-Based QKD: The following attack was proposed by Adi Shamir in a meeting with one of the authors (T.M.) around 1996–1999 [26], and it may have never been published (but see similar attacks below). Shamir's attack only applies to QKD implementations that use "*active*" basis choice (as opposed to the "passive" basis choice, which leads to the "Fixed Apparatus" attack described in Example 3 of Sect. 4). The attack is related to Imperfection 2 described in Sect. 2: Bob's apparatus must be fully or partially ready to receive Alice's photon before it arrives. For example, if the photon is supposed to arrive at time t, then Bob's setup is already partially ready at time $t - \delta$; in particular, Bob decides the *basis choice* and configures the polarizing beam splitter accordingly before time $t - \delta$. The attack also assumes that the detectors themselves are still inactive (blocked) at time $t - \delta$, and are activated just before time t. Therefore, at time $t - \delta$, the polarizing beam splitter is already configured to match the required basis (the computational basis or the Hadamard basis), while the detectors are still blocked.

Eve's attack is sending a strong pulse at time $t - \delta$, that hits the polarizing beam splitter (but not the blocked detectors) and gets reflected back to Eve, containing full or partial information on the direction of the polarizing beam splitter—and, thus, on the basis choice. Assuming Eve gets the information on Bob's basis choice *before* she receives Alice's pulse, Eve could employ the following full attack: Eve measures the photon coming from Alice *in the same basis chosen by Bob*, learns the qubit's value, and resends to Bob the resulting state (in the same basis), obtaining full information while inducing no errors and no losses.

One can suggest two ways to possibly prevent the attack: (a) opening the detection window (activating the detectors) *shortly* after the polarizing beam splitter is configured according to the basis choice (if the time difference is sufficiently short, Eve cannot find Bob's basis choice on time for employing the full attack); or (b) blocking access to the polarizing beam splitter until the detectors are activated (although this solution may be hard to implement).

As we explain in Sect. 6, the "Bright Illumination" attack could have been predicted by adding Imperfection 1 described in Sect. 2 (namely, detection of multi-photon pulses) to the above idea of a strong pulse sent at time $t - \delta$ towards Bob (i.e., Imperfection 2, as already discussed here) and using the Fock space notations.

"Conventional Optical Eavesdropping" and "Quantum Side-Channel Attacks": Other attacks, similar to Shamir's attack, have been independently developed—for example, the "Large Pulse" attack [29], which attacks both Alice's and Bob's set-ups. As written in [29]: "This [large pulse] attack is one of the possible methods of conventional optical eavesdropping, a new strategy of eavesdropping on quantum cryptosystems, which eliminates the need of immediate interaction with transmitted quantum states. It allows the eavesdropper to avoid inducing transmission errors that disclose her presence to the legal users."

Instead of restricting ourselves to "conventional optical eavesdropping on quantum cryptosystems", we make use of a different sentence from [29]—"eavesdropping on quantum cryptosystems which eliminates the need of immediate interaction with transmitted quantum states"—and we define "quantum side-channel attacks" as follows:

A *quantum side-channel attack* is any eavesdropping strategy which eliminates the need of any immediate interaction with the transmitted quantum states.

According to the above definition, both Shamir's attack and the "Large Pulse" attack are "quantum side-channel attacks", because they attack the devices and not the quantum states themselves. On the other hand, the "Reversed-Space" attacks and the "Quantum Space" attacks (see Sect. 4) can be fully described using a proper description of the QKD protocol, which uses the Fock space notations; therefore, they should *not* be considered as "quantum side-channel attacks". In fact, we can say they are *complementary* to "quantum side-channel attacks", and we name them "*state*-channel attacks".

In a classical communication world, the notion of "side-channel attacks" makes use of any information leaked by the *physical* execution of the algorithm (see, for example, [14]). Accordingly, other researchers (e.g., [24]) have chosen to adopt a wide definition of "quantum side-channels", which also includes the "Photon-Number Splitting" attack and many other practical attacks. However, we prefer to take a narrower view of "quantum side-channel attacks", as explained above.

6 From Practice to Theory: The Possibility of Predicting the "Bright Illumination" Attack

The "Bright Illumination" attack could have been predicted, because it simply combines Imperfections 1 and 2 that were described in Sect. 2: namely, detecting many photons at time $t - \delta$, while the single "information" photon should have arrived at time t. In some sense, it seems to merge a "Reversed-Space" attack and a "quantum side-channel attack", because it attacks both the transmitted quantum states and the detectors themselves. However, because Bob's detectors are fully exposed to Eve at both times t and $t - \delta$ (unlike the "Large Pulse" attack [29], where the detectors are not exposed at time $t - \delta$), we see the "Bright Illumination" attack as a special (and fascinating) case of "Reversed-Space" attack, and not as a "quantum side-channel attack".

The "Bright Illumination" attack is made possible by a *lack of information* on the "space of the protocol" $\mathscr{H}^{\mathrm{P}}$: Eve sends many photons (as in Imperfection 1) at time $t - \delta$ (as in Imperfection 2), and Bob does not notice her disruption because he cannot *count* the number of photons and cannot *block* the detectors at time $t - \delta$.

For preventing all the possible attacks and proving full security, it must be known how Bob's detectors treat *any* number k of photons sent to him by Eve, and it must also be known how Bob's detectors treat multiple pulses. In particular, a detector definitely cannot operate properly in the hypothetical scenario where an infinite number of photons (with infinite energy) arrives as its input. A potentially secure system must have an estimated threshold N, such that if $k \lesssim N$ photons arrive, they are correctly measured by the detectors (treated as one photon), and if $k \gtrsim N$ photons arrive, the measurement result is clearly invalid and is known to Bob (for example, smoke comes out of the detectors, or the detectors are burned). N is estimated, so there is a small unknown range near it.

Prior to the "Bright Illumination" attack, it seems that no systematic effort has been invested in finding or approximating the threshold N and characterizing the detectors' behavior on *all* possible inputs (any number of photons k). A proper "Reversed-Space" analysis would have suggested that experimentalists *must* check what N is and fully analyze the behavior of Bob's detectors on each quantum state; such an analysis would then have found the "space of the protocol" $\mathcal{H}^P$ which is available for Eve's attack.

A careful "Reversed-Space" analysis—if it had been carried out—would then have found that instead of *one* estimated threshold N (with some small unknown range around it), there are *two* estimated thresholds N_1, N_2, such that $N_1 < N_2$, with a some small unknown range around each of them, and a *large* difference between them. Therefore, there are three main ranges of the numbers of photons k: (a) for $k \lesssim N_1$ photons, Bob's detectors work well (and click if at least one photon arrives); (b) for $N_1 \lesssim k \lesssim N_2$ photons, it would have become *known* that some strange phenomena happen—for example, that Bob's detectors switch to the "linear mode"; and (c) for $k \gtrsim N_2$ photons, Bob's detectors malfunction (e.g., the detectors are burned).

Thus, surprisingly, even if the experimentalist had not known about the two modes of operation ("Geiger mode" and the "linear mode") existing for each detector, he or she could still have discovered the two different thresholds N_1, N_2 and then investigated the detectors' behavior in the middle range $N_1 \lesssim k \lesssim N_2$. This would have allowed him or her to discover the "linear mode" and realize that there is also a need to check *multiple* pulses for finding the correct "space of the protocol" and for analyzing the security against "Reversed-Space" attacks. Namely, the "Reversed-Space" approach makes it possible to discover attacks even if the detectors are treated as *a black box* whose internal behavior is unknown. By theoretically trying to prove security against any theoretical "Reversed-Space" attack, it would have been possible to find the practical "Bright Illumination" attack; it would have even been possible to study the operation of a "*black-box*" detector and discover, for example, that it has a "linear mode" of operation (even if this mode of operation had not been already known for realistic detectors).

7   Conclusion

We have seen a rare example (in quantum information processing) where experiment preceded theory. We can see now that this experimental attack could have been theoretically predicted: for a system to be secure, Bob must be sure that Eve cannot attack by sending an unexpected number of photons, and he must know what happens to his detectors for any number of photons. Otherwise—Eve can attack; and we could have known that this may be possible. We have also defined the general notion of "quantum side-channel attacks", distinguishing "state-channel attacks" (including "Reversed-Space" and "Quantum Space" attacks) that interact with the transmitted (prepared or measured) quantum states, from "quantum side-channel attacks" that *do not interact* with the transmitted quantum states.

References

1. Bennett, C.H., Bessette, F., Brassard, G., Salvail, L., Smolin, J.: Experimental quantum cryptography. J. Cryptol. **5**(1), 3–28 (1992). https://doi.org/10.1007/BF00191318
2. Bennett, C.H., Brassard, G.: Quantum cryptography: public key distribution and coin tossing. In: International Conference on Computers, Systems & Signal Processing, pp. 175–179 (1984)
3. Bennett, C.H., Brassard, G., Crépeau, C., Jozsa, R., Peres, A., Wootters, W.K.: Teleporting an unknown quantum state via dual classical and Einstein-Podolsky-Rosen channels. Phys. Rev. Lett. **70**, 1895–1899 (1993). https://doi.org/10.1103/PhysRevLett.70.1895
4. Boyer, M., Gelles, R., Mor, T.: Attacks on fixed-apparatus quantum-key-distribution schemes. Phys. Rev. A **90**, 012329 (2014). https://doi.org/10.1103/PhysRevA.90.012329
5. Brassard, G., Lütkenhaus, N., Mor, T., Sanders, B.C.: Limitations on practical quantum cryptography. Phys. Rev. Lett. **85**, 1330–1333 (2000). https://doi.org/10.1103/PhysRevLett.85.1330
6. Brassard, G., Lütkenhaus, N., Mor, T., Sanders, B.C.: Security aspects of practical quantum cryptography. In: Preneel, B. (ed.) EUROCRYPT 2000. LNCS, vol. 1807, pp. 289–299. Springer, Heidelberg (2000). https://doi.org/10.1007/3-540-45539-6_20
7. Deutsch, D.: Quantum theory, the Church-Turing principle and the universal quantum computer. P. Roy. Soc. Lond. A Mat. **400**, 97–117 (1985). https://doi.org/10.1098/rspa.1985.0070
8. Gelles, R.: On the security of theoretical and realistic quantum key distribution schemes. Master's thesis, Technion - Israel Institute of Technology, Haifa, Israel (2008)
9. Gelles, R., Mor, T.: Quantum-space attacks. arXiv preprint arXiv:0711.3019 (2007)
10. Gelles, R., Mor, T.: Reversed space attacks. arXiv preprint arXiv:1110.6573 (2011)
11. Gelles, R., Mor, T.: On the security of interferometric quantum key distribution. In: Dediu, A.-H., Martín-Vide, C., Truthe, B. (eds.) TPNC 2012. LNCS, vol. 7505, pp. 133–146. Springer, Heidelberg (2012). https://doi.org/10.1007/978-3-642-33860-1_12
12. Gottesman, D., Lo, H.K., Lütkenhaus, N., Preskill, J.: Security of quantum key distribution with imperfect devices. Quantum Inf. Comput. **4**, 325–360 (2004)
13. Hwang, W.Y.: Quantum key distribution with high loss: toward global secure communication. Phys. Rev. Lett. **91**, 057901 (2003). https://doi.org/10.1103/PhysRevLett.91.057901
14. Köpf, B., Basin, D.: An information-theoretic model for adaptive side-channel attacks. In: Proceedings of the 14th ACM Conference on Computer and Communications Security, CCS 2007, pp. 286–296 (2007)
15. Kurtsiefer, C., et al.: A step towards global key distribution. Nature **419**, 450 (2002). https://doi.org/10.1038/419450a
16. Lo, H.K., Curty, M., Tamaki, K.: Secure quantum key distribution. Nat. Photon. **8**, 595–604 (2014). https://doi.org/10.1038/nphoton.2014.14910.1038/nphoton.2014.149
17. Lo, H.K., Ma, X., Chen, K.: Decoy state quantum key distribution. Phys. Rev. Lett. **94**, 230504 (2005). https://doi.org/10.1103/PhysRevLett.94.230504

18. Lydersen, L., Wiechers, C., Wittmann, C., Elser, D., Skaar, J., Makarov, V.: Hacking commercial quantum cryptography systems by tailored bright illumination. Nat. Photon. **4**, 686–689 (2010). https://doi.org/10.1038/nphoton.2010.214

19. Makarov, V., Anisimov, A., Skaar, J.: Effects of detector efficiency mismatch on security of quantum cryptosystems. Phys. Rev. A **74**, 022313 (2006). https://doi.org/10.1103/PhysRevA.74.022313

20. Makarov, V., Hjelme, D.R.: Faked states attack on quantum cryptosystems. J. Mod. Opt. **52**, 691–705 (2005). https://doi.org/10.1080/09500340410001730986

21. Pfaff, W., et al.: Unconditional quantum teleportation between distant solid-state quantum bits. Science **345**, 532–535 (2014). https://doi.org/10.1126/science.1253512

22. Preskill, J.: Quantum computing in the NISQ era and beyond. Quantum **2**, 79 (2018)

23. Scarani, V., Acín, A., Ribordy, G., Gisin, N.: Quantum cryptography protocols robust against photon number splitting attacks for weak laser pulse implementations. Phys. Rev. Lett. **92**, 057901 (2004). https://doi.org/10.1103/PhysRevLett.92.057901

24. Scarani, V., Bechmann-Pasquinucci, H., Cerf, N.J., Dušek, M., Lütkenhaus, N., Peev, M.: The security of practical quantum key distribution. Rev. Mod. Phys. **81**, 1301–1350 (2009). https://doi.org/10.1103/RevModPhys.81.1301

25. Scarani, V., Kurtsiefer, C.: The black paper of quantum cryptography: real implementation problems. Theor. Comput. Sci. **560**, 27–32 (2014). https://doi.org/10.1016/j.tcs.2014.09.015.10.1016/j.tcs.2014.09.015

26. Shamir, A.: Personal communication (around 1996–1999)

27. Shor, P.W.: Algorithms for quantum computation: discrete logarithms and factoring. In: Proceedings 35th Annual Symposium on Foundations of Computer Science, pp. 124–134 (1994)

28. Shor, P.W.: Polynomial-time algorithms for prime factorization and discrete logarithms on a quantum computer. SIAM Rev. **41**, 303–332 (1999). https://doi.org/10.1137/S0036144598347011

29. Vakhitov, A., Makarov, V., Hjelme, D.R.: Large pulse attack as a method of conventional optical eavesdropping in quantum cryptography. J. Mod. Opt. **48**, 2023–2038 (2001). https://doi.org/10.1080/09500340108240904

30. Wang, X.B.: Beating the photon-number-splitting attack in practical quantum cryptography. Phys. Rev. Lett. **94**, 230503 (2005). https://doi.org/10.1103/PhysRevLett.94.230503

Quantum-Inspired Algorithm
with Evolution Strategy

Anna Ouskova Leonteva[1]([🖂]) [ID], Ulviya Abdulkarimova[1,2],
Anne Jeannin-Girardon[1], Michel Risser[3], Pierre Parrend[1,4], and Pierre Collet[1]

[1] University of Strasbourg, ICUBE Lab CNRS UMR 7357, Strasbourg, France
anna.ouskova-leonteva@etu.unistra.fr
[2] Azerbaijan State Oil and Industry University, Baku, Azerbaijan
[3] Ubiblue Company, Strasbourg, France
[4] ECAM Strasbourg Europe, Schiltigheim, France

Abstract. Quantum-inspired algorithms are efficient for solving global
search optimization problems. Nevertheless, their application is limited
by two main requirements: a knowledge of a cost function and a big
computational effort. To address both limitations, this paper presents a
global optimization algorithm mixing a Quantum Diffusion Monte Carlo
(DMC) method and an Evolution Strategy (ES). The proposed approach
takes advantage of quantum models for efficiently finding solutions close
the global optimum by applying the DMC. However, the DMC needs to
be adapted to an optimization process. In order to improve relatively
slow convergence rate of the DMC, we integrate a step size control for a
diffusion displacement process of the DMC. Then, an (1+1)-ES is applied
to find the minimum value of the cost function. Experimentation shows
that the proposed approach can find global minima with fewer objective
function evaluations than Quantum Particle Swarm Optimization and
Quantum Annealing. Thus, it seems to be promising for solving black-box
problems, where a reliable trade-off between exploration and exploitation
is required.

Keywords: Quantum evolution · Single objective optimization ·
Black-box optimization · Global search optimization

1 Introduction

Global optimization problems become more and more difficult to solve due to
the development of scientific research and engineering technology. The goal of
global optimization is to find a d-dimensional solution $\boldsymbol{x} = (x_1, ..., x_d)$, that
corresponds to a global minimum (maximum) of a given cost function f, to be
optimized over the allowed range of its decision variables. The term "difficult"
is used to describe problems, where f is not specified in an analytic form and
must be evaluated by a simulation model which can therefore be considered as
black-box. Using a simulator also makes the evaluation of a potential solution

© Springer Nature Switzerland AG 2020
C. Martín-Vide et al. (Eds.): TPNC 2020, LNCS 12494, pp. 95–106, 2020.
https://doi.org/10.1007/978-3-030-63000-3_8

computationally intensive. Without any explicit knowledge of f, global search optimization algorithms have three main problems: (i) they get trapped into local optima; (ii) they need a very large number of f evaluation function calls; (iii) their computational complexity considerably depends on the number of dimensions d of the problem.

In this paper we focus on the first two issues. We consider a new method to improve the trade-off between global search capability and local search, targeted for black-box optimization problems in continuous search space.

Related Work. Among different approaches for global search optimization, algorithms based on an evolutionary simulation of quantum systems behavior are widely used in various domains [8]. The most well-known examples are Quantum Particle Swarm Optimization (QPSO) [11] and Quantum Annealing (QA) [10].

In order to explore the optimization problem landscape, QA applies a quantum fluctuation-based computation, where quantum fluctuation is a change in the amount of energy at a point in space for extremely short time lapses [1]. As classical Simulating Annealing, it is an adaptation of the Metropolis-Hastings algorithm, but it uses a quantum field instead of a thermal gradient. In practice, QA is more frequently used for discrete optimization problems [1], like travelling salesman problem, than for continuous optimization, due to a slow convergence rate.

In QPSO, all particles move under quantum-mechanical rules. A very important factor for QPSO performance is the choice of a shape for a potential well, that ensures bound states for particles moving in the quantum environment [8]. Usually, the shape of potential well has to be chosen as close as possible to f, which produces some difficulties in black-box optimization where f is unknown. Moreover, the quality of QPSO depends on the population size.

The above-mentioned weak points make QA and QPSO inefficient in cases of computationally intensive black-box problems.

Contributions. Our objective is to take advantage of the quantum model for providing effective global search capability in a relatively small number of f evaluations. To tackle this challenge, we propose a new algorithm, called QAES (Quantum-inspired Algorithm with Evolution Strategy), which combines the Diffusion Monte Carlo (DMC) [7] method with an evolutionary strategy (ES) [6]. First, we adapt the DMC method for solving black-box optimization problems in continuous search space and investigate its efficiency. Second, we improve the performance of DMC by using a (1+1)-ES strategy [2,6] in order to implement a pre-sampling. This ensures that the minimum value of f is achieved, after the ground state of the quantum model is found. Finally, the ES step size control [2,6] is used in order to adjust the variance in the diffusion displacement process.

The advantages of the proposed approach are following: (i) the DMC finds ground state, which ensures the best probability density of particles in the search space; (ii) the Branching process of the DMC allows the algorithm to "automatically" adjust the number of particles and thereby reduces the number of calls of

f; (iii) the integration of ES to the DMC helps to avoid local optima in a more efficient way than pure Quantum DMC.

The performance of the proposed algorithm, QAES, is evaluated on 24 test functions (in 2 and 5 d spaces) using the COCO framework [4]. QAES performance was compared against two quantum approaches: QPSO [11], QA [10], and two well-known classical approaches: BFGS [9] and BIPOP-CMAES [3]. The obtained results demonstrates the effectiveness of the proposed algorithm to find global optima for black-box optimization problem.

This paper is organized as follows: Sect. 2 covers the theoretical background, Sect. 3 details the proposed approach. In Sect. 4, the experimental study presents the obtained results on the Black-Box Optimization Benchmarks (BBOB) testbed. Finally, Sect. 5 outlines the conclusion.

2   Theoretical Background

2.1   Diffusion Monte Carlo Algorithm

The DMC method is used for investigating the quantum systems and for obtaining its ground state energy and wave function. The principle of the DMC method is to solve the Schrödinger equation in imaginary time $-i\tau$. This equation is defined as follows (units are dimensionless) [7]:

$$\frac{\partial\psi}{\partial\tau} = \frac{1}{2}\frac{\partial^2\psi}{\partial x^2} - (U(x) - E_{\mathrm{R}})\psi \tag{1}$$

where $U(x)$ is the potential energy, E_{R} is the reference energy, $\psi = \psi(x,\tau)$ is a wave function which depends on coordinate x and time τ, and may be interpreted as the density of diffusing particles ("walkers") and $U(x) - E_{\mathrm{R}}$ is a rate term describing a potential-dependent growth or reduction of the particle density.

Equation 1 is investigated by means of the Feynman Path Integral, using the Monte Carlo method. In this case, according to [7], the solution of Eq. 1 can be presented as:

$$\psi(x,\tau) = \lim_{N\to\infty} \int_{-\infty}^{\infty} \left(\prod_{j=0}^{N-1} dx_j\right) \prod_{n=1}^{N} W(x_n)P(x_n, x_{n-1})\psi(x_0, 0) \tag{2}$$

where $P(x_n, x_{n-1})$ and $W(x_n)$ are defined as:

$$P(x_n, x_{n-1}) = \sqrt{\frac{1}{2\pi\Delta\tau}} \exp\left(-\frac{(x_n - x_{n-1})^2}{2\Delta\tau}\right) \tag{3}$$

$$W(x_n) = \exp\left(-(U(x_n) - E_{\mathrm{R}})\Delta\tau\right) \tag{4}$$

and where $P(x_n, x_{n-1})$ is a Gaussian probability distribution centered around x_{n-1} with standard deviation $\sigma = \sqrt{\Delta\tau}$, $W(x_n)$ is a weight function, N is the current number of walkers, and a time step $\Delta\tau = \frac{\tau}{N}$. Equation 2 is solved by the

Initialize $\tau = 0$, $\Delta\tau > 0$
$N^{\tau=0} > 2$; $N_{max} > N^{\tau=0}$ - maximum possible number of walkers
$x_i^{\tau=0}$ - coordinate of i-walker ($i \in [0, N^{\tau}]$), is set randomly in $[x_{min}, x_{max}]$
$m_i = 0$ - empirical coefficient for x_i
$U_i^{\tau=0} = U(x_i^{\tau=0})$, $E_R^{\tau=0} = \sum_{i=0}^{N^{\tau=0}-1} U_i^{\tau=0}/N^{\tau=0}$
$\alpha > 0$, $\sigma = \sqrt{\Delta\tau}$, $T_{max} > 0$ - number of time steps to run simulations
repeat
    for $i = 0, ..., N^{\tau}$ **do**
        Diffusion displacement:
        $x_i^{\tau+1} = x_i^{\tau} + N(0, \sigma)$
        Branching:
        Compute the weight function $W(x_i^{\tau+1})$ (see Eq. 4)
        Update the number of walkers in ensemble:
        $m_i = \min(\text{int}(W(x_i^{\tau+1}) + \text{Uniform}(0, 1)), 3)$
        if $m_i == 0$ **then** $N^{\tau+1} = N^{\tau} - 1$ // walker x_i is removed from ensemble
        if $m_i > 1$ **then** $N^{\tau+1} = N^{\tau} + m_i - 1$ // $m_i - 1$ copies of walker x_i are
        made
    end
    Update: $E_R^{\tau+1} = E_R^{\tau} + \alpha \times (1 - N^{\tau+1}/N^{\tau})$
    $\tau = \tau + \Delta\tau$
until $\tau < T_{max}$;

Algorithm 1: QDMC - Quantum Diffusion Monte Carlo

DMC method, presented in Algorithm 1 (for one-dimensional x). Algorithm 1 is made up according to the mathematical description from the work [7].

For updating the E_R value, a "feedback" parameter α is chosen empirically to diminish unwanted correlations between the successive generations of x.

As a result of the described procedure, the ground state energy of the system is found from averaging the successive reference energies E_R.

2.2   Evolution Strategy

In this study, we use a (1+1)-ES with step size control strategy, described in [2]. (1+1)-ES is an elitist selection scheme with one parent and one offspring. The pseudo-code is given in Algorithm 2. At iteration $t \in \mathbb{N}_+$, the state of the (1+1)-ES is determined by sampling one candidate offspring $\boldsymbol{x}^t$ in d-dimensional search space from the Gaussian distribution, defined by the step size σ and an identity covariance matrix $\mathbf{I} \in \mathbb{R}^{d \times d}$. Using the identity matrix means that the variations of all variables are uncorrelated. The parent $\boldsymbol{p}^t$ is replaced by the offspring $\boldsymbol{x}^t$ if the offspring performs better than the parent.

The step size adaptation rule aims at maintaining a stable distribution of the success rate centered around $1/5$ [2]. The update of the step size depends on the empirical probability that the offspring has better value of cost functions than its parent: $\mathbb{E}\mathbb{1}_{f(\boldsymbol{x}^t)<f(\boldsymbol{p}^t)}$. According to this scheme, σ increases if the success probability is larger than $1/5$, and decreases if the success probability is smaller than $1/5$.

Given $d \in \mathbb{N}_+, d'_\sigma \approx \sqrt{n+1}$
Initialize $p^{t=0} \in \mathbb{R}^d, \sigma^{t=0} > 0$
repeat
> $x^t = p^t + \sigma^t N(\mathbf{0}, \mathbf{I})$ // Mutation operator
> $\sigma^{t+1} \leftarrow \sigma^t \exp\left(\frac{1}{d'_\sigma}(\mathbb{E}\mathbb{1}_{f(x^t) < f(p^t)} - 1/5)\right)$ // Step size update
> **if** $f(x^t) \le f(p^t)$ **then**
> > $p^{t+1} = x^t$ // Selection of x^t as the new parent if it is better than p^t
>
> **end**
> $t \leftarrow t+1$

until *stopping criterion is met*;

Algorithm 2: (1+1)-ES

3 Proposed Approach

3.1 Applying DMC to Optimization Process

We assume, that the random changes of decision variables x in the search space are similar to the diffusion displacement of particles coordinates in a quantum system. In the following, for ease of notation, we will call the decision variables of the optimization problem the "coordinates of particles" in dimension d and f the "potential energy". As described in Sect. 2.1, the procedure of solving the Schrödinger equation assumes a calculation of multidimensional integrals, using the Monte Carlo method, a Diffusion Displacement process and the Branching (Birth-Death) process of particles, distributed in the search space. As a result of the iterative process, the density of distribution of particles converges to a wave function of the ground state, where the minimum value of system energy is achieved.

According to the DMC (see Eq. 4), the difference between the potential energy and the reference energy routes the particles in the regions of the search space, where the wave function is increasing. Moreover, the Birth and Death processes of the DMC allow the algorithm to "automatically" adjust the number of walkers. At the beginning of the DMC process, the number of walkers is growing, in order to find the ground state; then the number of walkers is decreasing to the initial value, when the best probability density distribution of particles and the ground state of quantum system is found. Thereby the number of evaluations of the f function is reduced. Figure 1(a) visualises this adjustment process for the Sphere function on 5D, where the initial number of walkers is 20. We can see that the number of walkers is increasing while the ground state is not found. When the ground state energy is obtained (the value of reference energy stabilized around 83 in Fig. 1(b)), the number of walkers is decreasing to the initial number.

Theoretically, a challenge in applying the DMC to the global search process is going from the fact, that the ground state energy of the quantum system is not identical to the minimum of the potential. As it is shown in [7], in the case of one-dimensional harmonic oscillator model, the ground state energy $E_0 = 0.5$ and it is the minimal possible value of quantum system energy. Consequently, the particle can not achieve the bottom of potential well (where the potential energy $= 0$), because it contradicts the uncertainty principle of Heisenberg. For the above-mentioned reason, DMC can't achieve the global optimum of f, but can rapidly find the best probability density distribution, which is useful for finding global optimum of f. So, it can be applied for optimization, but its global search capability and its convergence rate need to be improved. Looking ahead, we plot in Fig. 1(b), the reference energy values (the light grey points), obtained by pure DMC and the potential energy values (the grey points), obtained by QAES (see Sect. 3.2).

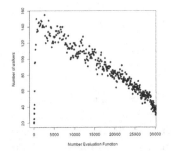 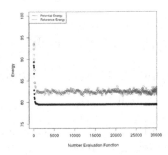

a)Number of walkers vs number of evaluations b) Energy vs number of evaluations

Fig. 1. Adjustment of the number of walkers according to energy changing in the DMC

3.2   Quantum-Inspired Algorithm with Evolution Strategy

In order to mitigate the above-mentioned issues of the DMC, we propose a Quantum-inspired Algorithm with Evolution Strategy (QAES), whose pseudo-code is provided in Algorithm 3. The notations are given in Table 1. As for the DMC, two iterative processes (Diffusion Displacement and Branching) are executed inside the simulation loop, but the following changes are incorporated: first, a (1+1)-ES is integrated into the Diffusion Displacement process. A new particle x^t is sampled from a probability distribution centered around x^{t-1}. Then the previous particle x^{t-1} is replaced by the current particle x^t, if the value of potential energy at least the same as the parents. The (1+1)-ES implements the pre-sampling, which ensures that the minimum value of f will be achieved, after the ground state energy is found. Second, we integrate the ES step control for the variance of Diffusion Displacement. As in the classical DMC, the weight function is calculated as an aggregate parameter for the Death and the Birth processes by Eq. 4. A quota of each process in this weight function is determined, according to the empirical coefficient m: if $m = 0$, the particle is removed, if $m = 1$ the number of particles remains unchanged, if $m > 1$ one particle is added. According to m value, the ES manages the variance of the Diffusion Displacement: if a particle is removed, the immediate adaptation of variance based on "failure" is applied; if the particle is added the "success" adaptation rule is used. Thereby the proposed algorithm avoids the local optima much faster than the classical DMC. Subsequently, we studied the impact of Cauchy and Gaussian distributions for the Diffusion Displacement. The obtained results let us to choose the Cauchy distribution, due to the fact that Cauchy is a very heavy tailed distribution, that has no finite mean. So it helps to make long jumps of particles coordinates in Diffusion Displacement and consequently, to improve the convergence rate.

Table 1. Notations used in Algorithm 3

Notation	Explication
x^t	Vector of coordinate of particle (decision variables of problem)
d	Coordinate dimension (number of decision variables)
N^t	Current number of walkers in DMC process
f	Potential energy (Cost function)
$flag(x^t)$	0 if particle x^t is deleted, otherwise 1
α	"Feedback" parameter
σ	Diffusion displacement step size

QAES has three hyper-parameters: α, $\sigma^{t=0}$ and $N^{t=0}$. In this paper we don't apply the hyper-parameter tuning methods and we don't adapt them to each function. The important limitation of QAES is the decreasing efficiency with growing of the dimension of optimisation problem. This limitation can be improved by the hyper-parameter adaptation to dimension.

4   Experimental Study

Our study investigates the following tasks: (i) the DMC efficiency for optimization process; (ii) an impact of different probability distributions in Diffusion Displacement on the performance; (iii) the performance of QAES; (iv) comparative results between DMC, QAES, QPSO [11], QA [10], and with two reference algorithms from the BBOB workshop: BFGS [9] and BIPOP-CMAES [3].

4.1   Experimental Setup

In order to test the statistical significance of results, we focus on the 24 functions from the (noiseless and single-objective) BBOB test suite [5]. BBOB is a very well-known testbed that is widely used in the community for comparison of algorithm performance in continuous search spaces. An overview of these functions is available in [5]. These functions are grouped into the following five categories: separable functions ($f1 - f5$), functions with low or moderate conditioning ($f6 - f9$), functions with high conditioning and uni-modal ($f10 - f14$), multi-modal functions with adequate global structure ($f15 - f19$), and multi-modal functions with weak global structure ($f20 - f24$). Each problem has 15

Given $d \in \mathbb{N}_+, f$
Initialize $N^{t=0} = d, \boldsymbol{x}^t \in \mathbb{R}^d, \sigma^{t=0} > 0, c_{succ} > 0, c_{fail} < 0, c_{succ}, c_{fail} \in \Omega(\frac{1}{d})$
$E_R^{t=0} = \sum_{i=0}^{N^{t=0}-1} f(\boldsymbol{x}_i^{t=0})/N^{t=0}, \alpha = d$
repeat
> **for** $i = 0, ..., N^t$ **do**
>> **Diffusion displacement with (1+1)-ES:**
>> $\boldsymbol{x}_i^{t+1} = \boldsymbol{x}_i^t + \sigma^t Cauchy(\mathbf{0}, \mathbf{I})$
>> **if** $f(\boldsymbol{x}_i^t) \leq f(\boldsymbol{x}_i^{t+1})$ **then**
>>> $\boldsymbol{x}_i^{t+1} = \boldsymbol{x}_i^t$
>>
>> **end**
>> **if** $f(\boldsymbol{x}_i^{t+1}) \leq f_{best}$ **then**
>>> $\boldsymbol{x}_{best} = \boldsymbol{x}_i^{t+1}$
>>> $f_{best} = f(\boldsymbol{x}_i^{t+1})$
>>
>> **end**
>> **Branching:**
>> $W(\boldsymbol{x}_i^{t+1}) = \exp(E_R^t - f(\boldsymbol{x}_i^{t+1}))$
>> $m_i = \min(\text{int}(W(\boldsymbol{x}_i^{t+1}) + \text{Uniform}(0, 1)), 2)$
>> **if** $m_i > 1$ **then**
>>> $N^{t+1} = N^t + 1; flag(\boldsymbol{x}_i^{t+1}) = 1; \sigma^{t+1} = \sigma^t \cdot \exp(c_{succ})$
>>
>> **end**
>> **else**
>>> $N^{t+1} = N^t - 1; flag(\boldsymbol{x}_i^{t+1}) = 0; \sigma^{t+1} = \sigma^t \cdot \exp(c_{fail})$
>>
>> **end**
>
> **end**
> **Update:** $E_R^{t+1} = E_R^t + \alpha \times (1 - N^{t+1}/N^t)$
> $t = t + 1$
until *stopping criterion is met;*

Algorithm 3: QAES

instances. For each instance, 15 runs were performed. We restrict our attention to the 2D and 5D variants. Thus, every test function was run 225 times for each d. The computational budget is set as $10000 \times d$ for all experiments. These settings strictly adhere to the standard benchmarking procedure of the GECCO BBOB workshops. The hyper-parameters are set is following: $\alpha = d$, $\sigma^{t=0} = 1/d$, $N^{t=0} = 20$.

Performance Metric and Presentation of Results. In order to ensure that the comparison between the proposed method and the comparative methods is fair, COCO [4] platform for comparing continuous optimizers in a black-box setting is used. In the COCO platform, the performance is measured in terms of Expected Run Time (ERT) - the number of evaluations (EF) conducted on a given problem until a given Target Value (TV) is hit. The TV is defined for each function as $\Delta f \in [10^2, 10^{-8}]$ [4]. The results are visualised in Fig. 2 and Fig. 3, where: x-axis is the number of needed EF in logarithmic scale; y-axis is the achieved TV precision, calculated as $function - \Delta f$ (in %). The results "best 2009" (shown as a thick line) in Figure 2 and Fig. 3 consists of the best solutions of multiple algorithms during the GECCO workshop 2009, and consequently, they are not used in this comparative study.

4.2   Experimental Results

Efficiency of DMC for Optimization Process. For the sake of simplicity, the DMC is tested only on 2D problems. Figure 2(a) shows a relative performance, where the mean value of EF over all 24 functions is plotted. We notice that the DMC works comparatively well on the first stage, because it quickly finds the ground state of the system. But after the first TV is found, it performs much slower than QPSO and does not achieve the last TV in many test cases. This result is predictable and proves the theoretical explanation in Sect. 3.1.

Impact of Probability Distribution on the Performance. In order to show the impact of the probability distribution choice on the performance of QAES, we investigate the Rastrigin function ($f4$) in 5D over 30 runs for each distribution (Gaussian and Cauchy). In Table 2, we compare the mean ERT with dispersion (in brackets) obtained for the different Δf with Cauchy and Gaussian distributions. With Cauchy, QAES obtains the highest accuracy ($\Delta f = 1e - 7$), because of the reasons explained in Sect. 3.2.

Table 2. QAES runtime with different probability distributions on $f4$ test function

Δf	$1e+1$	$1e+0$	$1e-1$	$1e-2$	$1e-3$	$1e-5$	$1e-7$
Cauchy	$2.3_{(0.5)}$	$76_{(10)}$	$75_{(52)}$	$76_{(40)}$	$76_{(120)}$	$76_{(60)}$	$77_{(23)}$
Gauss	$2.4_{(2)}$	$179_{(30)}$	$124_{(321)}$	∞	∞	∞	∞

Performance on 2D Problems. First, we compare the results of QAES and the DMC. Figure 2 shows that including ES significantly improved the performance of DMC. Aggregated results of ECDF for 24 functions in Fig. 2(a) show that QAES solves 100 % of the problems with the highest accuracy, whereas DMC (as well as QA) solves only 40 %. Second, we compare the performance of QAES and QPSO. As seen from Fig. 2(a) QAES slightly outperforms QPSO, which solves 90 % of the problems, due to the fact that QAES is more efficient on the multi-modal functions with weak global structure (see Fig. 2(f)). It is explained by ES step size control according to the type of the process (Birth or Death). On the rest of the functions, both algorithms work identically (see Fig. 2(b–e)). Finally, we notice that QAES is slower than BFGS and BIPOP-CMA in the middle stage (interval $[1.5, 4]$ of x-axis in Fig. 2(a–f)). However, as seen in Fig. 2(c, e, f) it performs better than BFGS on multi-modal and low and moderate conditional functions.

Performance on 5D Problems. First, we compare the results of quantum-inspired algorithms: QAES, QPSO and QA. From Figs. 3(a), which depicts the results of ECDF for 24 functions, we can conclude that QAES achieved in 1.4 × higher target precision than QPSO and in 4.5× than QA, by the same number of EF. It is explained by the fact that QAES does not need a large fixed population size during all the evolution process. QAES adjusts the number of particles on each iteration of MC: after finding the ground state, it has the minimum number of particles, which is enough for finding the global optimum thanks to the (1+1)-ES. Second, we compare the results of QAES, BFGS and BIPOP-CMA. According to Fig. 3(a), QAES is the second best method in terms of accuracy (82 % of solved problems), after BIPOP-CMA (98 %) and followed by BFGS (60 %). However, QAES solves 100 % of separable functions with the highest accuracy, and performs better than BIPOP-CMA (see Fig. 3 (b)). But QAES is quite slow on uni-modal, as well as multi-modal with adequate global structure functions (see Fig. 3(d, e)). And as in case of 2D problems, QAES is slower than BFGS and BIPOP-CMA in the middle stage. These facts can be explained by the inefficiency of the simple rule for step size control in ES. On the other side, QAES ensures a stable trade-off between exploration and exploitation on functions with low or moderate conditioning and multi-modal with weak global structure functions (see Fig. 3(c, f)).

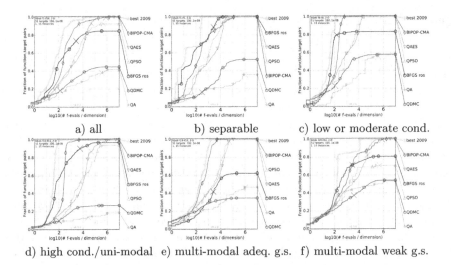

a) all   b) separable   c) low or moderate cond.

d) high cond./uni-modal   e) multi-modal adeq. g.s.   f) multi-modal weak g.s.

Fig. 2. Runtime distribution summary by function groups on 2D

The deep analysis of obtained results according to the structure of algorithm is the subject of our separate future work. In summary, the performance of QAES in terms of convergence rate and accuracy outperforms the results of the quantum algorithms (QPSO and QA). QAES has comparable results with

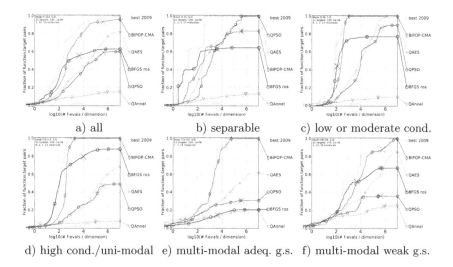

a) all   b) separable   c) low or moderate cond.

d) high cond./uni-modal   e) multi-modal adeq. g.s.   f) multi-modal weak g.s.

Fig. 3. Runtime distribution summary by function groups on 5D

BFGS and BIPOP-CMA on multi-modal functions and shows the best accuracy on separable functions.

But what is interesting is that the proposed algorithm can be transformed to a hybrid approach, when the ground state energy will be found on real quantum computer.

5   Conclusion

We analysed and modified a Quantum DMC algorithm to use it as a global search continuous optimizer. In particular, the main contribution of this paper regards the collaborative work between Quantum DMC and ES, which adjusts a number of particles in each MC cycle to the potential search space. The proposed algorithm doesn't need any knowledge about f and can be applied for solving black-box problems. We then evaluated the proposed approach on the 24 BBOB functions. Our observations in this study can be summarized as follows:

- DMC (without ES) is suitable for continuous optimization and shows the similar performance as QA;
- DMC can rapidly find the ground state of the quantum system, but cannot find the global minimum of f;
- ES significantly improves the accuracy and convergence rate of DMC.
- QAES (a combination of DMC and ES) solves 100% of problems on 2D, whereas DMC without ES solves only 40%;
- QAES achieved in 1.4 × higher target precision than QPSO and in 4.5× than QA for all functions on 5D problems;
- QAES is very efficient on separable functions: it solves 100% of the problems in 2D and 5D;

– QAES shows a slow convergence rate on uni-modal functions.

Further analysis is needed in order to integrate the mechanism of random distribution functions choice, which can provide an optimal sampling design. Further improvements have to be done for adaptation proposed approach to higher dimensions. The proposed algorithm was successfully applied in harmonic analysis and for optimization of an active magnetic regenerative refrigeration model. The results of these applications are a subject for separate consideration. In the future, the DMC part of the algorithm could be implemented in real quantum computer to find the ground state of the quantum system.

Acknowledgments. This work is funded through ANR project CoolMagEvo (ANR-17-CE05-0036). The ANR is gratefully acknowledged for its financial support. As well as Ubiblue Company for its collaboration.

References

1. de la Fuente Ruiz, A.: Quantum annealing. arXiv-1404 (2014)
2. Hansen, N., Arnold, D.V., Auger, A.: Evolution strategies. In: Kacprzyk, J., Pedrycz, W. (eds.) Springer Handbook of Computational Intelligence, pp. 871–898. Springer, Heidelberg (2015). https://doi.org/10.1007/978-3-662-43505-2_44
3. Hansen, N.: Benchmarking a BI-population CMA-ES on the BBOB-2009 function testbed. In: Proceedings of the 11th Annual Conference Companion on Genetic and Evolutionary Computation Conference: Late Breaking Papers, pp. 2389–2396 (2009)
4. Hansen, N., Auger, A., Ros, R., Mersmann, O., Tušar, T., Brockhoff, D.: COCO: a platform for comparing continuous optimizers in a black-box setting. Optim. Methods Softw. 1–31 (2020)
5. Hansen, N., Finck, S., Ros, R., Auger, A.: Real-parameter black-box optimization benchmarking 2009: Noiseless functions definitions. Research Report RR-6829, INRIA (2009)
6. Kern, S., Müller, S.D., Hansen, N., Büche, D., Ocenasek, J., Koumoutsakos, P.: Learning probability distributions in continuous evolutionary algorithms-a comparative review. Nat. Comput. **3**(1), 77–112 (2004). https://doi.org/10.1023/B:NACO.0000023416.59689.4e
7. Kosztin, I., Faber, B., Schulten, K.: Introduction to the diffusion monte Carlo method. Am. J. Phys. **64**(5), 633–644 (1996)
8. Mikki, S.M., Kishk, A.A.: Quantum particle swarm optimization for electromagnetics. IEEE Trans. Antennas Propag. **54**(10), 2764–2775 (2006)
9. Ros, R.: Benchmarking the BFGS algorithm on the BBOB-2009 function testbed. In: Proceedings of the 11th Annual Conference Companion on Genetic and Evolutionary Computation Conference: Late Breaking Papers, pp. 2409–2414 (2009)
10. Stella, L., Santoro, G.E., Tosatti, E.: Optimization by quantum annealing: lessons from simple cases. Phys. Rev. B **72**(1), 014303 (2005)
11. Sun, J., Xu, W., Feng, B.: A global search strategy of quantum-behaved particle swarm optimization. In: IEEE Conference on Cybernetics and Intelligent Systems, vol. 1, pp. 111–116. IEEE (2004)

How to Implement a Non-uniform or Non-closed Shuffle

Takahiro Saito[1]($\boxtimes$)(iD), Daiki Miyahara[1,3](iD), Yuta Abe[1](iD), Takaaki Mizuki[2](iD), and Hiroki Shizuya[1](iD)

[1] Graduate School of Information Sciences, Tohoku University,
6–3–09 Aramaki-Aza-Aoba, Aoba, Sendai 980–8579, Japan
`saito.takahiro.q7@dc.tohoku.ac.jp`
[2] Cyberscience Center, Tohoku University,
6–3 Aramaki-Aza-Aoba, Aoba, Sendai 980–8578, Japan
[3] National Institute of Advanced Industrial Science and Technology (AIST),
2–4–7 Aomi, Koto-ku, Tokyo 135–0064, Japan

Abstract. Card-based protocols allow to perform secure multiparty computations using a deck of physical cards, and rely on shuffle actions such as the (normal) shuffle, the random cut, and the random bisection cut. A shuffle action is mathematically defined by a pair of a permutation set (which is a subset of the symmetric group) and a probability distribution on it; while one can theoretically consider any shuffle action in mind, he or she may be unable to determine whether it can be easily implemented by human hands. As one of the most general results, Koch and Walzer showed that any uniform closed shuffle (meaning that its permutation set is a subgroup and its distribution is uniform) can be implemented by human hands with the help of additional cards. However, there are several existing protocols which use non-uniform and/or non-closed shuffles. To implement these specific shuffles, Nishimura et al. proposed an idea of using (special) physical cases that can store piles of cards as well as Koch and Walzer proposed an implementation of a specific non-closed shuffle with additional cards. Because their implementations handle a limited class of non-uniform and/or non-closed shuffles, it is still open to find a general method for implementing any shuffle. In this paper, we solve the above problem; we implement "any" shuffle with only additional cards, provided that every probability of its distribution is a rational number. Therefore, our implementation works for any non-closed or non-uniform shuffle (if the distribution is rational as above).

Keywords: Cryptography · Card-based protocols · Implementation of shuffle · Unconventional computation

1 Introduction

In 1989, den Boer [1] proposed the first *card-based protocol* called the "five-card trick." This protocol performs a secure computation of the logical AND using

© Springer Nature Switzerland AG 2020
C. Martín-Vide et al. (Eds.): TPNC 2020, LNCS 12494, pp. 107–118, 2020.
https://doi.org/10.1007/978-3-030-63000-3_9

two black cards ♣♣ and three red cards ♡♡♡, whose backsides have the same pattern ?. This paper begins by introducing the five-card trick.

1.1 Five-Card Trick

Assume that Alice has a private bit $a \in \{0,1\}$ and Bob has a private bit $b \in \{0,1\}$; the five-card trick takes a and b as inputs and outputs the value of $a \wedge b$ without revealing any information about a and b more than necessary, as follows.

1. Alice puts two face-down cards committing to her bit a according to the encoding: ♣♡ = 0, ♡♣ = 1. Bob puts two face-down cards similarly, and they put an additional red card in the middle. Then, swap the positions of Alice's two cards so that we have a negated value $\bar{a}$ as well as turn over the middle red card:

$$\underbrace{\boxed{?}\boxed{?}}_{a}\ \boxed{♡}\ \underbrace{\boxed{?}\boxed{?}}_{b} \rightarrow \underbrace{\boxed{?}\boxed{?}}_{\bar{a}}\ \boxed{?}\ \underbrace{\boxed{?}\boxed{?}}_{b}.$$

2. Apply a *random cut* (denoted by $\langle \cdot \rangle$) to the sequence of five cards:

$$\langle\, \boxed{?}\boxed{?}\boxed{?}\boxed{?}\boxed{?} \,\rangle \rightarrow \boxed{?}\boxed{?}\boxed{?}\boxed{?}\boxed{?}.$$

A random cut (RC), meaning a cyclic shuffling operation, uniformly and randomly shifts the positions of a sequence without changing its order. Mathematically, it uniformly chooses one permutation from the permutation set

$$\{\text{id}, (1\ 2\ 3\ 4\ 5), (1\ 2\ 3\ 4\ 5)^2, (1\ 2\ 3\ 4\ 5)^3, (1\ 2\ 3\ 4\ 5)^4\}, \tag{1}$$

and the chosen permutation is applied to the sequence of five cards (but nobody knows which permutation is applied), where id denotes the identity permutation and $(i_1\ i_2 \cdots i_\ell)$ represents a cyclic permutation.
3. Reveal the five cards. If the resulting sequence has three consecutive red cards ♡♡♡ (apart from cyclic rotation), then $a \wedge b = 1$. Otherwise, $a \wedge b = 0$.

To implement an RC, Alice (or Bob) quickly repeats cutting a sequence of cards until nobody (even including Alice) can trace the offsets. Note that this implementation was experimentally shown to be secure by Ueda et al. [22].

1.2 Unconventional Shuffles

As seen above, the five-card trick [1] elegantly performs a secure computation of AND by using an RC, which is implementable. On the other hand, this paper deals with unconventional shuffles: To understand them, let us consider the following permutation set, which is similar to the permutation set (1) that represents an RC used in the five-card trick:

$$\{\text{id}, (1\ 2\ 3\ 4\ 5), (1\ 2\ 3\ 4\ 5)^2, (1\ 2\ 3\ 4\ 5)^3\}; \tag{2}$$

namely, $(1\ 2\ 3\ 4\ 5)^4$ is excluded from (1). Compared to implementing an RC, it seems difficult for human hands to implement such a shuffle action of uniformly choosing one permutation from the above set and applying that permutation. This is because the permutation set (2) cannot be generated by a single element, i.e., it is not a cyclic group.

As another example, let us consider a shuffle action that divides a sequence of four cards into two halves and randomly swaps them. Mathematically, it uniformly and randomly chooses one permutation from the permutation set

$$\{\mathsf{id}, (1\ 3)(2\ 4)\},$$

and applies that permutation to the sequence. This kind of a shuffle is called a *random bisection cut* (RBC) and is used in several card-based protocols (e.g., [12,13,20]). Ueda et al. [21,22] showed the secure implementation of an RBC called the "spinning throw" as well as a more secure way using a polystyrene ball. Now, let us consider a "modified RBC" with a non-uniform probability distribution. For example, how could we implement a shuffle where id is chosen with a probability of $1/3$ and $(1\ 3)(2\ 4)$ is chosen with a probability of $2/3$? Surprisingly, such a non-uniform RBC is required for executing the card-based AND protocols with the minimal number of cards [7]. Implementing such a non-uniform shuffle seems difficult by only human hands.

Hereinafter, assume that, for a sequence of m (≥ 2) face-down cards, we want to apply a shuffle action. Formally, a *shuffle* is defined as a set of permutations $\Pi \subseteq S_m$ along with a probability distribution $\mathcal{F}$ on Π [10,11], where S_m denotes the symmetric group of degree m: We use the notation $(\mathsf{shuf}, \Pi, \mathcal{F})$ to mean that a permutation $\pi \in \Pi$ is drawn according to the distribution $\mathcal{F}$ and π is applied to the sequence of m cards.

There are three important categories of a shuffle.

Uniform shuffle. A shuffle $(\mathsf{shuf}, \Pi, \mathcal{F})$ is said to be *uniform* if the distribution $\mathcal{F}$ is uniform. That is, any $\pi \in \Pi$ is drawn with the equal probability. We sometimes write it as (shuf, Π) if $\mathcal{F}$ is uniform and $(\mathsf{shuf}, \mathcal{F})$ if $\mathcal{F}$ is non-uniform for simplicity.

Cyclic shuffle. A shuffle $(\mathsf{shuf}, \Pi, \mathcal{F})$ is said to be *cyclic* if the permutation set Π is a cyclic group, i.e., there exists a permutation π in Π such that $\Pi = \langle \pi \rangle = \{\pi^i \mid i \text{ is an integer}\}$.

Closed shuffle. A shuffle $(\mathsf{shuf}, \Pi, \mathcal{F})$ is said to be *closed* if Π is a subgroup of the symmetric group.

As shown in the above examples, one can consider any shuffle in mind although it is not so easy to determine whether such a (possibly, complex) shuffle is implementable by humans. One of the most general results is as follows: Koch and Walzer [6] in 2017 showed that any uniform closed shuffles can be implemented with additional cards whose back pattern is different from the pattern of cards to be shuffled.

For implementing a non-uniform and/or non-closed shuffle, there are two existing works, each of which proposed implementations of specific non-uniform and/or non-closed shuffles, as follows. Nishimura et al. [14] in 2018 proposed implementations of two kinds of shuffles:

$$(\text{shuf}, \{\text{id}, \pi\}, \mathcal{F}_1) \text{ and } (\text{shuf}, \Pi^{(s_1, s_2, \cdots, s_k)}, \mathcal{F}_2),$$

using (special) physical card cases that can store piles of cards. Here, π is any permutation in the symmetric group and $\Pi^{(s_1, s_2, \cdots, s_k)}$ is the permutation set obtained by dividing a sequence of cards into k piles, where the i-th pile consists of s_i cards, and arbitrarily shifting them. $\mathcal{F}_1$ and $\mathcal{F}_2$ are any distributions where each probability is a rational number. In 2017, Koch and Walzer [6] showed an implementation of the uniform non-closed shuffle

$$(\text{shuf}, \{\text{id}, (1\ 2\ 3\ 4\ 5)^3\})$$

using additional cards (and they mentioned that its formalization is possible). To summarize, their proposed implementations focus on a limited class of non-uniform and/or non-closed shuffles: How to implement any shuffle including non-uniform or non-closed shuffles remains an open problem.

1.3 Contribution

In this paper, we solve the above problem. That is, we propose implementations of any shuffle

$$(\text{shuf}, \{\pi_1, \pi_2, \ldots, \pi_k\}, \pi_1 \mapsto p_1, \pi_2 \mapsto p_2, \ldots, \pi_k \mapsto p_k),$$

for a positive integer $k\, (\geq 2)$, where π_i is a permutation in S_m and p_i is a rational number for every $i, 1 \leq i \leq k$. (Note that $\sum_{i=1}^{k} p_i = 1$.) Therefore, we can implement any shuffle even if it is non-uniform or non-closed (provided that the distribution is rational as above). Our proposed implementations require only additional cards (called "padding cards" in this paper), and hence, our result shows that the above problem can be solved without relying on any additional tool, such as special physical cases as proposed by Nishimura et al. [14].

Specifically, we propose two implementations. In Sect. 3, we show the first one that is specialized for $k = 2$: We implement a non-uniform RBC with padding cards and combine our implementation and the idea by Koch and Walzer [6]. In Sect. 4, we show the second one that is for any k. It is based on another idea where we regard a permutation as a sequence of number cards.

One might think that this paper considered a narrow problem and our proposed methods would have less applications. We note that our proposed techniques can be applied to the problem of uniformly generating a hidden random permutation without fixed points (also known as Secret Santa) [2] although we omit the details due to the page limit length.

1.4 Related Work

The mainstream in the field of card-based protocols was to use a uniform and cyclic shuffle. In 2015, Koch et al. [7] first studied non-uniform and/or non-closed shuffles and proposed card-minimal AND protocols using such unconventional shuffles. In 2015, Nishimura et al. [15] showed that a non-closed shuffle can be used to construct a COPY protocol with the minimal number of cards (and the general one was proposed in [16]). In 2017, Kaster et al. [3] showed that using non-uniform and/or non-closed shuffles is related to the necessary and sufficient numbers of cards for constructing an AND protocol. In 2018, Ruangwises and Itoh [17] and Koch [4] independently showed a card-minimal AND protocol with non-closed shuffles. In 2018, Hashimoto et al. [2] showed that a non-uniform shuffle is useful for uniformly generating a random permutation without fixed points.

Recently, Koch et al. [5] proposed a card-minimal AND protocol with a standard deck of cards using an RC in 2019. Miyahara et al. [8] proposed efficient implementations of Yao's millionaire protocol using an RC in 2020. A uniform closed shuffle called a pile-scramble shuffle has been often used when constructing zero-knowledge proof protocols for puzzles [9,18] and secure ranking protocols [19].

2 Preliminaries

In this section, we formally explain a deck of cards and introduce the shuffle action called a pile-shifting scramble used in our implementations.

Card. In Sect. 1.1, we introduced the five-card trick that uses a deck of cards, each of whose front side is ♣ or ♡ and each of whose backside is ?. Our implementations use such a two-colored deck of cards as well as *number cards* having numbers written on the front side:

$$\boxed{1}\boxed{2}\cdots\boxed{n}$$

for some natural number n. Those cards satisfy the following two conditions.

- All cards are of the same size and weight, and we cannot distinguish them from the backsides, e.g., there is no scratch on the backsides.
- The pattern on the backside is vertically asymmetric such as ?¿.

The first condition is necessary for ensuring the security of card-based protocols: If this condition does not hold, a player may identify each face-down card and information about it will be leaked. The second is necessary when we use a two-colored deck of cards as padding cards in our proposed methods, as seen later.

Pile-Shifting Scramble. Nishimura et al. [14] showed the notion of a pile-shifting scramble and use it for their implementation. It is a shuffle action denoted by $\langle \cdot | \cdot | \cdots | \cdot \rangle$ that randomly shifts a sequence of piles of cards $(A_1, \ldots, A_k)$:

$$\langle \underbrace{\boxed{?}\boxed{?}\cdots\boxed{?}}_{A_1} | \underbrace{\boxed{?}\boxed{?}\cdots\boxed{?}}_{A_2} | \cdots | \underbrace{\boxed{?}\boxed{?}\cdots\boxed{?}}_{A_k} \rangle,$$

where each pile consists of the same number of cards. We demonstrate that it can be implemented by using the vertically asymmetric property, as proposed by Ueda et al. [21].

1. Make the first card of each pile A_i upside down for every $i, 1 \le i \le k$:

$$A_i : \boxed{?}\boxed{?} \cdots \boxed{?}.$$

2. Apply an RC to the sequence of piles:

$$\langle\ \boxed{?}\boxed{?}\boxed{?} \cdots \boxed{?}\boxed{?}\boxed{?}\boxed{?} \cdots \boxed{?} \cdots \boxed{?}\boxed{?}\boxed{?} \cdots \boxed{?}\ \rangle.$$

Then, shift the sequence so that an arbitrary upside down card becomes the first one.

3   Our Implementation for Two-State Shuffles

In this section, we show our implementation that performs (shuf, $\{\pi_1, \pi_2\}, \mathcal{F})$ with padding cards, where $\mathcal{F}$ is rational. Note that our implementation does not require any additional tool such as the special physical cases used in [14]. We first show the idea behind our implementation in Sect. 3.1. Then, we present our methods in the succeeding subsections.

3.1   Idea

Assume a sequence of m face-down cards (to be shuffled). To implement

$$(\text{shuf}, \{\pi_1, \pi_2\}, \mathcal{F}),$$

let us first transform it as follows.

1. To "virtually" transform π_1 to id, we apply a permutation π_1 (to a sequence of m cards), i.e., apply (perm, π_1), before applying the shuffle. Hence, we derive (shuf, $\{\text{id}, \pi_2\pi_1^{-1}\}, \mathcal{F})$.
2. To see $\pi_2\pi_1^{-1}$ in a different angle, we use the well-known fact that any permutation can be uniquely expressed as the product of disjoint cyclic permutations. That is, $\pi_2\pi_1^{-1}$ can be expressed as $\sigma_1\sigma_2\cdots\sigma_\ell$ for some natural number ℓ where σ_i is a cyclic permutation and any pair of σ_i and σ_j, $i \ne j$, is disjoint; we derive (shuf, $\{\text{id}, \sigma_1\sigma_2\cdots\sigma_\ell\}, \mathcal{F})$.
3. To make $\sigma_1\sigma_2\cdots\sigma_\ell$ simple, we use another well-known fact that any permutation π can be expressed as a conjugate $\tau\rho\tau^{-1}$ for some permutation τ where ρ is of the same type of π. Using this fact, for example, we can transform $(1\,3\,5\,7\,9)(2\,4\,6\,8\,10)$ to $\tau(1\,2\,3\,4\,5)(6\,7\,8\,9\,10)\tau^{-1}$ where $\tau = (2\,6\,8\,9\,5\,3)(4\,7)$. In this way, we transform $\sigma_1\sigma_2\cdots\sigma_\ell$ to $\tau\rho_1\rho_2\cdots\rho_\ell\tau^{-1}$ where

$$\rho_i = (1+\Sigma_{j=1}^{i-1}|\rho_j| \quad 2+\Sigma_{j=1}^{i-1}|\rho_j| \quad \cdots \quad \Sigma_{j=1}^{i}|\rho_j|), \tag{3}$$

and $|\pi|$ denotes the length of a cyclic permutation π. Note that ρ_i has the same length of σ_i.

To summarize, we transform $(\mathsf{shuf}, \{\pi_1, \pi_2\}, \mathcal{F})$ into a series of four actions:

$$(\mathsf{perm}, \pi_1)$$
$$(\mathsf{perm}, \tau^{-1})$$
$$(\mathsf{shuf}, \{\mathsf{id}, \rho_1\rho_2\cdots\rho_\ell\}, \mathcal{F})$$
$$(\mathsf{perm}, \tau).$$

To implement $(\mathsf{shuf}, \{\mathsf{id}, \rho_1\rho_2\cdots\rho_\ell\}, \mathcal{F})$, we first show an implementation of a uniform shuffle $(\mathsf{shuf}, \{\mathsf{id}, \rho_1\rho_2\cdots\rho_\ell\})$ (which might formalize the implementation proposed by Koch and Walzer [6, Appendix B]) using the RC and RBC. Then, by implementating a non-uniform RBC with padding cards, we show our implementation of $(\mathsf{shuf}, \{\mathsf{id}, \rho_1\rho_2\cdots\rho_\ell\}, \mathcal{F})$.

3.2 Uniform and Single Cycle Case

As mentioned before, Koch and Walzer [6] showed an implementation of $(\mathsf{shuf}, \{\mathsf{id}, (1\,2\,3\,4\,5)^3\})$ and stated that its formalization is possible. Let us show that given a single cycle ρ_i in (3), implementing $(\mathsf{shuf}, \{\mathsf{id}, \rho_i\})$ is possible, which is almost the same as the implementation in [6], as follows.

1. Suppose that we have a sequence of $|\rho_i|$ face-down cards (to which we want to apply the shuffle). Place a sequence of additional $|\rho_i|$ face-down cards as padding cards below the sequence:

$$
\begin{matrix}
{\scriptstyle 1} & {\scriptstyle 2} & & {\scriptstyle |\rho_i|} \\
\boxed{?}\,\boxed{?} & \cdots & \boxed{?} \\
\boxed{?}\,\boxed{?} & \cdots & \boxed{?}\,. \\
\heartsuit\;\;\clubsuit & & \clubsuit
\end{matrix}
$$

The first card in the additional sequence is $\heartsuit$ and the remaining cards are $\clubsuit$s.

2. Apply an RBC as follows:

$$
\begin{matrix}
\boxed{?}\;\boxed{?}\cdots\boxed{?} \\
[\boxed{?}|\boxed{?}]\cdots\boxed{?}
\end{matrix}
\;\to\;
\begin{matrix}
\boxed{?}\boxed{?}\cdots\boxed{?} \\
\boxed{?}\boxed{?}\cdots\boxed{?}\,.
\end{matrix}
$$

That is, $\heartsuit$ is either in the first or the second with the equal probability in the resulting sequence.

3. Considering the cards in the same column as a pile, apply a pile-shifting scramble to the sequence of piles:

$$
\left\langle
\begin{matrix}\boxed{?}\\\boxed{?}\end{matrix}\;
\begin{matrix}\boxed{?}\\\boxed{?}\end{matrix}\;
\cdots\;
\begin{matrix}\boxed{?}\\\boxed{?}\end{matrix}
\right\rangle
\;\to\;
\begin{matrix}
\boxed{?}\boxed{?}\cdots\boxed{?} \\
\boxed{?}\boxed{?}\cdots\boxed{?}\,.
\end{matrix}
$$

Remember that this shuffle can be reduced to an RC as shown in Sect. 2.
4. Reveal the sequence of padding cards; one $\heartsuit$ should appear.
5. Shift the sequence of piles so that the revealed $\heartsuit$ becomes in the first position. The resulting upper sequence is either the original one or the shifted one to the right with a probability of $1/2$, i.e., the desired shuffle has been applied.

3.3 Uniform and Multiple Cycles Case

The previous subsection implies that applying $(\mathsf{shuf}, \{\mathsf{id}, \rho_i\})$ and $(\mathsf{shuf}, \{\mathsf{id}, \rho_j\})$, $i \neq j$, sequentially is possible. We now show that $(\mathsf{shuf}, \{\mathsf{id}, \rho_i\rho_j\})$ is possible by performing an RBC once. (Remember that ρ_i and ρ_j are disjoint.)

1. Suppose that we have a sequence of $|\rho_i|$ face-down cards and a sequence of $|\rho_j|$ ones. Place a sequence of $|\rho_i|$ padding cards and a sequence of $|\rho_j|$ padding ones below the two sequences, as follows:

   The first card in each sequence is $\heartsuit$ and the remaining cards are $\clubsuit$s.
2. Apply an RBC as follows:

   That is, $\heartsuit$ is either in the first or the second with a probability of $1/2$ in each of the resulting sequences.
3. The remaining steps are exactly the same as the implementation described in the previous subsection. That is, we apply a pile-shifting scramble to each sequence of piles, reveal every additional sequence, and then shift each sequence according to the positions of each of revealed $\heartsuit$s.

Similarly, $(\mathsf{shuf}, \{\mathsf{id}, \rho_1\rho_2 \cdots \rho_\ell\})$ is possible by performing an RBC and pile-shifting scrambles.

3.4 Non-uniform Case

Here, we consider non-uniform shuffles $(\mathsf{shuf}, \mathsf{id} \mapsto p/q, \ \rho_1\rho_2 \cdots \rho_\ell \mapsto 1 - p/q)$. Extending the above discussion, it suffices to deal with a non-uniform RBC:

$$(\mathsf{shuf}, \mathsf{id} \mapsto p/q, \ (1 \ \ell+1)(2 \ \ell+2) \cdots (\ell \ 2\ell) \mapsto 1 - p/q),$$

where the probability p/q is a non-zero rational number and p is relatively prime to q. We show that it can be implemented with $2q$ padding cards, as follows.

1. Suppose that we have a sequence of $m = 2\ell$ face-down cards ⟦?⟧ ⟦?⟧ (to be shuffled), each of which consists of ℓ cards. Place q padding cards in the middle of the sequence and also q padding cards next to the resulting sequence, as follows:

   Then, turn over all the face-up cards.

2. Apply an RBC to the sequence:

$$[\,\boxed{?}\|\boxed{?}\,\cdots\,\boxed{?}\,|\,\boxed{?}\|\boxed{?}\,\cdots\,\boxed{?}\,]\,.$$

3. Apply an RC to the left padding cards:

$$\boxed{?}\|\,\langle\,\boxed{?}\,\cdots\,\boxed{?}\,\rangle\,\boxed{?}\|\boxed{?}\,\cdots\,\boxed{?}\,\rightarrow\,\boxed{?}\|\boxed{?}\,\cdots\,\boxed{?}\,\boxed{?}\|\boxed{?}\,\cdots\,\boxed{?}\,.$$

Note that if the two halves were not swapped by the RBC in step 2, the first card in the left padding cards is ♣ with a probability of p/q. If the two halves were swapped, the first card in the left additional cards is ♣ with a probability of $1 - p/q$.

4. Reveal the first card of the left padding cards. If it is ♣, do nothing; otherwise, swap the two halves.[1]

4   Our Implementation for General Case

In this section, let us implement a shuffle

$$(\mathsf{shuf}, \pi_1 \mapsto p_1/q, \pi_2 \mapsto p_2/q, \ldots, \pi_k \mapsto p_k/q), \tag{4}$$

where each probability is a non-zero rational number and the greatest common divisor of $(p_1, \ldots, p_k)$ is relatively prime to q. Note that $\sum_{i=1}^{k} p_i = q$. The following implementation generalizes our implementation of a non-uniform RBC proposed in Sect. 3.

4.1   Applying a Permutation with Number Cards

Hereinafter, we express a permutation π by a sequence of number cards. For example, using five number cards, express $\pi = (3\ 4\ 1\ 2\ 5)$ as follows:

$$\pi : \boxed{3}\boxed{4}\boxed{1}\boxed{2}\boxed{5}.$$

We show that applying π to a sequence of cards is possible without revealing any information about π using the above sequence, as follows [2]:

1. Place the sequence representing π below to a sequence to which we want to apply π:

$$\boxed{?}\boxed{?}\boxed{?}\boxed{?}\boxed{?}$$
$$\pi : \boxed{?}\boxed{?}\boxed{?}\boxed{?}\boxed{?}.$$

2. Considering the cards in the two same column as a pile, apply a pile-shifting scramble to the sequence of piles:

$$\left\langle\,\frac{\boxed{?}}{\boxed{?}}\,\Big|\,\frac{\boxed{?}}{\boxed{?}}\,\Big|\,\cdots\,\Big|\,\frac{\boxed{?}}{\boxed{?}}\,\right\rangle \rightarrow \frac{\boxed{?}\boxed{?}\cdots\,\boxed{?}}{\boxed{?}\boxed{?}\cdots\,\boxed{?}}.$$

---

[1] After swapping them, the padding $2q$ cards are discarded.

3. Reveal all the cards in the second row. Then, rearrange the two sequences together so that the second row becomes id.

$$
\begin{array}{ccccc} 1 & 2 & 3 & 4 & 5 \\ \boxed{?} & \boxed{?} & \boxed{?} & \boxed{?} & \boxed{?} \end{array} \rightarrow \begin{array}{ccccc} 5 & 1 & 2 & 3 & 4 \\ \boxed{?} & \boxed{?} & \boxed{?} & \boxed{?} & \boxed{?} \end{array}
$$

$$
\boxed{2}\boxed{3}\boxed{4}\boxed{5}\boxed{1} \rightarrow \boxed{1}\boxed{2}\boxed{3}\boxed{4}\boxed{5}.
$$

Thus, to implement the shuffle (4), it suffices to choose a sequence of number cards representing π_i with a probability of p_i/q.

4.2 Description

We are now ready to show our implementation for the general case.

1. Let n be the greatest number among $|\pi_1|, \ldots, |\pi_k|$. Place a sequence of face-down (number) cards that represents π_i, $1 \le i \le k$; we denote it by A_i: $\boxed{?}$:

$$
\pi_i : \overbrace{\boxed{?}\boxed{?}\cdots\boxed{?}}^{n \text{ cards}} \rightarrow A_i : \boxed{?}.
$$

2. Place q additional cards next to A_i according to the probability of π_i as follows:

$$
A_i : \boxed{?} \underbrace{\boxed{1}\boxed{1}\cdots\boxed{1}}_{p_{i+1 \bmod k}} \underbrace{\boxed{2}\boxed{2}\cdots\boxed{2}}_{p_{i+2 \bmod k}} \cdots \underbrace{\boxed{k}\boxed{k}\cdots\boxed{k}}_{p_{i+k \bmod k}} \rightarrow A'_i : \boxed{?}.
$$

Regard A_i and the q additional cards as a pile denoted by A'_i.

3. Apply a pile-shifting scramble to the sequence of piles $A'_1, A'_2, \ldots, A'_k$:

$$
\langle \boxed{?} | \boxed{?} | \cdots | \boxed{?} \rangle \rightarrow \boxed{?}\boxed{?}\cdots\boxed{?}.
$$

4. Take one pile among the resulting piles; we denote it by A'_j. Apply an RC to its additional cards:

$$
A'_j : \boxed{?} \langle \boxed{?}\boxed{?}\cdots\boxed{?} \rangle.
$$

5. Reveal any card of the resulting additional cards. Let the revealed card be $\boxed{\ell}$. Then $A'_{j+\ell \bmod k}$ is the desired sequence. That is, the ℓ-th pile to the right of A'_j (up to rotation) is chosen with the desired probability.

5   Conclusion

In this paper, we proposed implementations of any shuffles (including non-uniform and non-cyclic shuffle) $(\mathsf{shuf}, \{\pi_1, \pi_2, \ldots, \pi_k\}, \mathcal{F})$ for a positive integer $k \, (\ge 2)$, where π_i is a permutation and $\mathcal{F}$ is any distribution where every probability is a rational number. For $k = 2$, the main idea is to implement a non-uniform RBC. For $k > 2$, the main idea is to introduce number cards corresponding to permutations, among which we choose one according the distribution.

It is an interesting open problem to deal with non-uniform shuffles whose probabilities are not rational numbers. (This might be impossible.) Also, for $k > 2$, a large number of cards are required depending on the probability distribution in our implementation. To improve upon this would be an intriguing future work.

Acknowledgments. This work was supported in part by JSPS KAKENHI Grant Numbers JP19J21153 and JP19K11956. We thank the anonymous referees, whose comments have helped us to improve the presentation of the paper.

References

1. Boer, B.: More efficient match-making and satisfiability *the five card trick*. In: Quisquater, J.-J., Vandewalle, J. (eds.) EUROCRYPT 1989. LNCS, vol. 434, pp. 208–217. Springer, Heidelberg (1990). https://doi.org/10.1007/3-540-46885-4_23
2. Hshimoto, Y., Nuida, K., Shinagawa, K., Inamura, M., Hanaoka, G.: Toward finite-runtime card-based protocol for generating a hidden random permutation without fixed points. In: IEICE Transactions on Fundamentals of Electronics, Communications and Computer Sciences. 2018. Lecture Notes in Computer Science, vol. E101.A , no. 9, pp. 1503–1511 (2018). https://doi.org/10.1587/transfun.E101.A.1503
3. Kastner, J., et al.: The minimum number of cards in practical card-based protocols. In: Takagi, T., Peyrin, T. (eds.) ASIACRYPT 2017. LNCS, vol. 10626, pp. 126–155. Springer, Cham (2017). https://doi.org/10.1007/978-3-319-70700-6_5
4. Koch, A.: The landscape of optimal card-based protocols (2018). https://eprint.iacr.org/2018/951
5. Koch, A., Schrempp, M., Kirsten, M.: Card-based cryptography meets formal verification. In: Galbraith, S.D., Moriai, S. (eds.) Advances in Cryptology - ASIACRYPT 2019. Lecture Notes in Computer Science, vol. 11921, pp. 488–517. Springer International Publishing, Cham (2019). https://doi.org/10.1007/978-3-030-34578-5_18
6. Koch, A., Walzer, S.: Foundations for actively secure card-based cryptography. Cryptology ePrint Archive, Report 2017/422 (2017)
7. Koch, A., Walzer, S., Härtel, K.: Card-based cryptographic protocols using a minimal number of cards. In: Iwata, T., Cheon, J.H. (eds.) ASIACRYPT 2015. LNCS, vol. 9452, pp. 783–807. Springer, Heidelberg (2015). https://doi.org/10.1007/978-3-662-48797-6_32
8. Miyahara, D., Hayashi, Y., Mizuki, T., Sone, H.: Practical card-based implementations of Yao's millionaire protocol. Theoret. Comput. Sci. **803**, 207–221 (2020). https://doi.org/10.1016/j.tcs.2019.11.005
9. Miyahara, D., et al.: Card-based ZKP protocols for Takuzu and Juosan. In: Farach-Colton, M., Prencipe, G., Uehara, R. (eds.) 10th International Conference on Fun with Algorithms (FUN 2020). Leibniz International Proceedings in Informatics (LIPIcs), vol. 157, pp. 20:1–20:21. Schloss Dagstuhl-Leibniz-Zentrum für Informatik, Dagstuhl, Germany (2020). https://drops.dagstuhl.de/opus/volltexte/2020/12781
10. Mizuki, T., Shizuya, H.: A formalization of card-based cryptographic protocols via abstract machine. Int. J. Inf. Secur. **13**, 15–23 (2014). https://doi.org/10.1007/s10207-013-0219-4

11. Mizuki, T., Shizuya, H.: Computational model of card-based cryptographic protocols and its applications. In: IEICE Transactions on Fundamentals of Electronics, Communications and Computer Sciences, vol. E100.A, no. 1, pp. 3–11 (2017). https://doi.org/10.1587/transfun.E100.A.3

12. Mizuki, T., Sone, H.: Six-card secure AND and four-card secure XOR. In: Deng, X., Hopcroft, J.E., Xue, J. (eds.) FAW 2009. LNCS, vol. 5598, pp. 358–369. Springer, Heidelberg (2009). https://doi.org/10.1007/978-3-642-02270-8_36

13. Nishida, T., Mizuki, T., Sone, H.: Securely computing the three-input majority function with eight cards. In: Dediu, A., Martín-Vide, C., Truthe, B., Vega-Rodríguez, A.M. (eds.) Theory and Practice of Natural Computing. TPNC 2013. Lecture Notes in Computer Science, vol. 8273, pp. 193–204. Springer, Heidelberg (2013). https://doi.org/10.1007/978-3-642-45008-2_16

14. Nishimura, A., Hayashi, Y., Mizuki, T., Sone, H.: Pile-shifting scramble for card-based protocols. IEICE Trans. Fundam. Electron. Commun. Comput. Sci. **E101-A**, 1494–1502 (2017). https://doi.org/10.1587/transfun.E101.A.1494

15. Nishimura, A., Nishida, T., Hayashi, Y., Mizuki, T., Sone, H.: Five-card secure computations using unequal division shuffle. In: Dediu, A., Magdalena, L., Martín-Vide, C. (eds.) Theory and Practice of Natural Computing. TPNC 2015. Lecture Notes in Computer Science, vol. 9477, pp. 109–120. Springer, Cham (2015). https://doi.org/10.1007/978-3-319-26841-5_9

16. Nishimura, A., Nishida, T., Hayashi, Y., Mizuki, T., Sone, H.: Card-based protocols using unequal division shuffles. Soft Comput. **22**, 361–371 (2018). https://doi.org/10.1007/s00500-017-2858-2

17. Ruangwises, S., Itoh, T.: AND protocols using only uniform shuffles. In: van Bevern, R., Kucherov, G. (eds.) Computer Science - Theory and Applications. CSR 2019. Lecture Notes in Computer Science, vol. 11532, pp. 349–358. Springer, Cham (2019). https://doi.org/10.1007/978-3-030-19955-5_30

18. Sasaki, T., Miyahara, D., Mizuki, T., Sone, H.: Efficient card-based zero-knowledge proof for Sudoku. Theoret. Comput. Sci. **839**, 135–142 (2020). https://doi.org/10.1016/j.tcs.2020.05.036

19. Takashima, K., et al.: Card-based secure ranking computations. In: Li, Y., Cardei, M., Huang, Y. (eds.) Combinatorial Optimization and Applications. COCOA 2019. Lecture Notes in Computer Science, vol. 11949, pp. 461–472. Springer, Cham (2019). https://doi.org/10.1007/978-3-030-36412-0_37

20. Takashima, K., Miyahara, D., Mizuki, T., Sone, H.: Card-based protocol against actively revealing card attack. In: Martín-Vide, C., Pond, G., Vega-Rodríguez, M. (eds.) Theory and Practice of Natural Computing. TPNC 2019. Lecture Notes in Computer Science, vol. 11934, pp. 95–106. Springer, Cham (2019). https://doi.org/10.1007/978-3-030-34500-6_6

21. Ueda, I., Miyahara, D., Nishimura, A., Hayashi, Y., Mizuki, T., Sone, H.: Secure implementations of a random bisection cut. Int. J. Inf. Secur. **19**, 445–452 (2020). https://doi.org/10.1007/s10207-019-00463-w

22. Ueda, I., Nishimura, A., Hayashi, Y., Mizuki, T., Sone, H.: How to implement a random bisection cut. In: Martín-Vide, C., Mizuki, T., Vega-Rodríguez, M.A. (eds.) TPNC 2016. LNCS, vol. 10071, pp. 58–69. Springer, Cham (2016). https://doi.org/10.1007/978-3-319-49001-4_5

Swarm Intelligence, Evolutionary Algorithms, and DNA Computing

A Study on Efficient Asynchronous Parallel Multi-objective Evolutionary Algorithm with Waiting Time Limitation

Tomohiro Harada$^{(\boxtimes)}$ ⓘ

Faculty of System Design, Tokyo Metropolitan University, Hino, Japan
harada@tmu.ac.jp
http://comp.sd.tmu.ac.jp/tomohiro-harada/index_en.html

Abstract. This paper attempts a new scheme of a semi-asynchronous parallel evolutionary algorithm (PEA), named time-limitation asynchronous PEA (TLAPEA). TLAPEA takes a balance between the search capability and the computational efficiency of PEA by synchronizing the solution evaluations within a particular waiting time before generating solutions. To reduce the idling time to wait for the slower evaluation of solutions, TLAPEA waits for a while for other solutions after the evaluation of a solution completes. The waiting time is decided from the average evaluation time of solutions and a new asynchrony parameter. This paper conducts an experiment to compare the proposed method with the full synchronous and asynchronous parallel evolutionary algorithm on multi-objective optimization problems. The experiment uses a state-of-the-art indicator-based multi-objective evolutionary algorithm, $I_{\mathrm{SDE}}+$. Our experiment examines several variances of evaluation time on a parallel computing simulation. The experimental result reveals that TLAPEA with shorter time limitation obtains a high quality of solutions quicker than the synchronous and asynchronous ones regardless of the variance of the evaluation time.

Keywords: Asynchronous evolutionary algorithm · Parallel evolutionary algorithm · Multi-objective optimization · Waiting time

1 Introduction

Evolutionary algorithms (EAs), typified by genetic algorithm (GA) [7] and genetic programming (GP) [13], have been applied to a wide range of real-world applications because of their high search capability without any problem-specific knowledge. When applying EAs to real-world applications, solution evaluations may take much computational time because of, for example, physical simulation to evaluate solutions or measurement of actual consumption time.

This work was supported by Japan Society for the Promotion of Science Grant-in-Aid for Young Scientists Grant Number JP19K20362.

C. Martín-Vide et al. (Eds.): TPNC 2020, LNCS 12494, pp. 121–132, 2020.
https://doi.org/10.1007/978-3-030-63000-3_10

Parallel EAs (PEAs) are a possible attempt to speed-up the optimization process by evaluating solution fitness in parallel. Although several PEAs have been proposed in the last decades [1,3,6,20], conventional PEAs waste much idle time waiting to the most expensive fitness evaluation of solution if evaluation times of solutions differ. This is because conventional PEAs generate a new population after evaluating all newly generated solutions.

Asynchronous evolution approaches have been proposed to overcome this problem. Asynchronous PEAs (APEAs) continuously generates a new solution without waiting for evaluations of other solutions, unlike conventional synchronous PEAs (SPEAs) that need to wait for all solutions. Since APEAs continuously evolve solutions while evaluating solutions in parallel, it is possible to efficiently search solutions in a situation where the evaluation of solutions takes much computational time and differs from each other [8,18,19].

On the other hand, our previous works have proposed a semi-asynchronous PEA (SAPEA) [9,10] that introduces a new parameter into PEA, named the asynchrony parameter. The asynchrony is used to decide the number of solution evaluations to be waited to generate new solutions. The previous work applied the semi-asynchronous approach to a multi-objective EA (MOEA) and revealed that an appropriate asynchrony improves the performance of PEAs especially if the variance of the evaluation time is enormous.

This paper attempts another approach to take a balance between the search capability and the computational efficiency by limiting the waiting time for other solutions after the first solution evaluation completes. In concrete, instead of controlling the number of solution evaluations to waited as SAPEA, the proposed method controls the maximum waiting time decided from the average evaluation time. This paper introduces a novel asynchrony parameter to accomplish such control. This paper denotes the proposed approach as the time-limitation based APEA (TLAPEA).

This paper conducts an experiment to investigate the effectiveness of the proposed TLAPEA on multi-objective optimization benchmarks. This paper applies TLAPEA to a state-of-the-art indicator-based MOEA method, $I_{SDE}+$ [17], and TLAPEAs with different parameters are compared with SPEA, APEA. This experiment is conducted on a pseudo parallel computing environment based on the work of [22].

2   Semi-asynchronous Parallel Evolutionary Algorithm

The previous works have proposed a *semi-asynchronous* PEA (SAPEA) that waits the pre-defined number of solution evaluations to generate new solutions [9, 10]. Concretely, an asynchrony parameter α was introduced, and SAPEA waits for $n = \lceil \alpha \times \lambda \rceil (1/\lambda \le \alpha \le 1)$ solution evaluations of slave nodes, unlike a (full) APEA waits for only one evaluation. In other words, an SAPEA is $(\mu + \lceil \alpha\lambda \rceil)$ EA that selects μ better solutions from original μ solutions and newly evaluated $\lceil \alpha\lambda \rceil$ solutions. Note that $\lceil x \rceil$ indicates the ceiling function that maps a real number x to the smallest next integer.

Algorithm 1. A pseudo-code of an SAPEA

1: $P_0 \leftarrow$ Initialize()
2: $R_0 \leftarrow$ Variation($P_0, |P_0|$)
3: Send R_0 to slave nodes to start evaluation
4: $g \leftarrow 0$
5: **while** Termination condition **do**
6:     $Q_g \leftarrow$ wait $\alpha \times |P_g|$ solution evaluations
7:     $P_{g+1} \leftarrow$ Replacement($P_g, Q_g, |P_g|$)
8:     $R_{g+1} \leftarrow$ Variation($P_{g+1}, |Q_g|$)
9:     Send R_{g+1} to slave nodes to start evaluation
10:     $g \leftarrow g + 1$
11: **end while**

High asynchrony value means that an SAPEA gets close to a synchronous-like EA, e.g., waits for λ solutions when $\alpha = 1$, which is the same as a full SPEA.

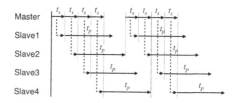

Fig. 1. $(\mu + \alpha\lambda)$ SAPEA where $\lambda = 4$ slave nodes and the asynchrony parameter $\alpha = 0.5$, i.e., $n = \alpha\lambda = 2$ evaluations out of four slave nodes are waited to execute the master process

While low asynchrony value means that it gets close to an asynchronous-like EA, e.g., waits for only one solution when $\alpha = 1/\lambda$, which is the same as a full APEA. From this fact, an SAPEA is a general representation of a master-slave PEA, including full synchronous and full asynchronous approaches.

Algorithm 1 shows a pseudo-code of an SAPEA. In Algorithm 1, the procedure of Initialization() generates the initial population. The procedure of Replacement(P, Q, n) selects n solutions from two solution sets of P and Q. The procedure of Variation(P, n) generates new n solutions from a solution set P by using genetic operators such as crossover and mutation. After generating and evaluating the initial population, the main procedure starts. For each step, SAPEA waits for $\alpha \times |P_g|$ solution evaluations and updates the population from the current population P_g and newly evaluated $\alpha \times |P_g|$ solutions. The new $\alpha \times |P_g|$ solutions are generated from the population, and they are sent to the slave nodes for the fitness evaluation. Figure 1 depicts an illustration of an SAPEA with the asynchrony parameter $\alpha = 2/\lambda$, i.e., $n = \lambda/2 = 2$. In this situation, an SAPEA waits for $\alpha\lambda$ evaluations (two evaluations in Fig. 1) and generates new $\alpha\lambda$ solutions.

An SAPEA cannot use arbitrary values of α within the range of $1/\alpha$ to 1 because the incorrect setting of α causes the ineffectual synchronization of

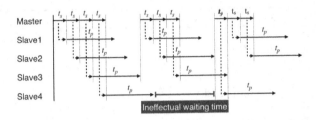

Fig. 2. An example of an ineffectual asynchrony of $(\mu + \alpha\lambda)$ SAPEA where $\lambda = 4$ slave nodes and the asynchrony parameter $\alpha = 3/4$, i.e., $n = \alpha\lambda = 3$ evaluations out of four slave nodes are waited to execute the master process

slave nodes. Concretely, an effectual α should satisfy the restriction of $\lambda \equiv 0$ (mod $\lceil \alpha\lambda \rceil$), where $a \equiv b$ (mod n) expresses congruent modulo. This is because if α does not satisfy this restriction and there exists some k that satisfies $\lambda \equiv k$ (mod $\lceil \alpha\lambda \rceil$), k slave nodes cannot be synchronized with other slave nodes conjunctively and ineffectual waiting time occurs.

Figure 2 shows an example of an ineffectual asynchrony setting, where $\lambda = 4$, $\alpha = 3/4$, and $\lambda \equiv 1$ (mod $\lceil \alpha\lambda \rceil$). In that case, as shown in Fig. 2, the first three evaluations by Slaves 1 to 3 are synchronized, and the next three solutions are generated, and three slave nodes start their evaluations. Then the next evaluation by Slave 4 completes soon after evaluation of Slave 3 completes. However, since other slaves just start their evaluations, Slave 4 must wait for evaluations of the other two slaves out of three, which causes the ineffectual idling time. Such an ineffectual situation may be avoided if evaluation times of solutions differ from each other. However, this paper supposes that the restriction of $\lambda \equiv k$ (mod $\lceil \alpha\lambda \rceil$) should be preserved in the proposed SAPEA.

3   Proposed Method

This paper proposes a novel scheme of PEAs that takes a balance between the search capability and the computational efficiency, named as time-limitation based PEA (TLAPEA). The previous SAPEA takes such a balance by deciding the number of solutions to be waited for before generating new solutions. However, although an SAPEA has to choose the asynchrony parameter from the effectual settings, it only takes discrete (effectual) values and is less flexible.

Instead of controlling the number of solutions to be waited for before generating new solutions as SAPEA, the proposed method controls the asynchrony based on the limitation of the maximum waiting time for other solutions before generating new solutions. Here let a new asynchrony parameter α_t define a parameter to decide the maximum waiting time before generating new solutions. By using α_t, the maximum waiting time is calculated as $\alpha_t \times \overline{T}$, where $\overline{T}$ is the average evaluation time of solutions so far.

Algorithm 2 shows a pseudo-code of the proposed TLAPEA. The difference from SAPEA shown in Algorithm 1 is that TLAPEA calculates the average evaluation time of evaluated solutions $\overline{T}$ and decides the waiting time for each step.

Algorithm 2. A pseudo-code of the time-limitation based PEA (TLAPEA)

1: $P_0 \leftarrow$ Initialize()
2: Evaluate all solution in P_0
3: Calculate the average evaluation time $\overline{T}$
4: $R_0 \leftarrow$ Variation($P_0, |P_0|$)
5: Send R_0 to slave nodes to start evaluation
6: $g \leftarrow 0$
7: **while** Termination condition **do**
8:     $s \leftarrow$ wait one solution evaluation
9:     $Q_g \leftarrow \{s\}$
10:    $t_{start} \leftarrow$ currenttime
11:    **while** $t_{now} - t_{start} < \alpha_t \times \overline{T} \vee |Q_g| = |P_g|$ **do**
12:        $s \leftarrow$ wait one solution evaluation
13:        $Q_g \leftarrow Q_g \cup \{s\}$
14:    **end while**
15:    Update the average evaluation time $\overline{T}$ from the evaluation times of solutions in Q_g
16:    $P_{g+1} \leftarrow$ Replacement($P_g, Q_g, |P_g|$)
17:    $R_{g+1} \leftarrow$ Variation($P_{g+1}, |Q_g|$)
18:    Send R_{g+1} to slave nodes to start evaluation
19:    $g \leftarrow g + 1$
20: **end while**

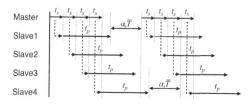

Fig. 3. The proposed time-limitation based APEA.

In Step 8 in Algorithm 2, when a slave node returns the first solution, the current time is recorded to t_{start}. Then, other evaluations are waited until the elapsed time $t_{now} - t_{start}$ reaches the decided maximum waiting time $\alpha_t \times \overline{T}$. After the time limitation, TLAPEA generates new solutions from the current population P_g and the evaluated solutions Q_g. On the other hand, if the evaluations of all solutions are completed during the time limitation, TLAPEA terminates the wait and generates new solutions.

Figure 3 depicts an illustration of the proposed TLAPEA. In this figure, when the first solution evaluation completes on Slave 1, the master node waits for other evaluations for $\alpha_t \overline{T}$ elapsed time. In this example, the evaluations by Slaves 2 and 3 complete within this time limitation, new solutions are generated by using solutions given by Slaves 1, 2, and 3. After that, the evaluation of Slave 4 completes, and the master node waits for other evaluations again. However, since no solution evaluation is completed within the time limitation, a new solution is generated using a solution given by Slave 4.

According to this setting, when $\alpha_t = 0$, TLAPEA only waits for one solution evaluation, which is the same as the full APEA. On the other hand, when $\alpha = \infty$, the maximum waiting time is infinity, and TLAPEA waits for all solution evaluations. This is same as the full SPEA. For this, TLAPEA is a general method that contains both of the full synchronous and asynchronous PEAs, which is a similar characteristic to the previous SAPEA. TLAPEA, on the other hand, can decide the setting of the asynchrony parameter more flexibly than SAPEA. Concretely, TLAPEA does not elapse much waiting time even if the variance of the evaluation times is enormous and the finishing times of the evaluations differ from each other. This is an advantage of TLAPEA, unlike SAPEA that suffers from waiting a much longer time if the asynchrony parameter is ineffectual.

4   Experiment

This paper conducts an experiment to investigate the effectiveness of the proposed TLAPEA. In particular, this paper compares TLAPEA with the full synchronous and asynchronous PEAs. The experiment applies the proposed method to multi-objective optimization problems (MOOPs).

4.1   Used Algorithm: $I_{\text{SDE}}+$

This paper uses $I_{\text{SDE}}+$ [17] as a state-of-the-art multi-objective EA (MOEA) method, $I_{\text{SDE}}+$ is an indicator-based MOEA and has a high search capability for multi- and many-objective optimization problems. $I_{\text{SDE}}+$ calculates the fitness of solutions as:

$$I_{\text{SDE}} + (p) = \min_{q \in P_{SB(p)}, p \neq q} \{dist(p, q')\} \tag{1}$$

where p is a solution to be evaluated, while $dist()$ returns the Euclidian distance on the objective space. $P_{SB(p)}$ is a subset of the population P of which solutions have a smaller sum of objectives (SB) value than p. SB is calculated as:

$$SB(x) = \sum_{i=1}^{m} f_i(x) \tag{2}$$

where $f_i(x)$ is a normalized ith objective function value, while m is the number of objectives. In Eq. 1, q' is a shifted position of a solution q. If the objectives are all minimization, q' is calculated as:

$$q(j)' = \begin{cases} p(j) & \text{if } q(j) < p(j) \\ q(j) & \text{otherwise} \end{cases} \quad j \in (1, 2, \ldots, m) \tag{3}$$

where $p(j)$ and $q(j)$ are the jth objective value of p and q, respectively. This shift adjusts the position (objective value) of q to the maximum point of p and q.

MOEA using $I_{SDE}+$ evolves solutions using this indicator for the mating selection and the environmental selection. Afterward, this paper denotes the $I_{SDE}+$ with the proposed TLAPEA as TL-$I_{SDE}+$, while the competitive synchronous and asynchronous PEAs as SP-$I_{SDE}+$ and AP-$I_{SDE}+$, respectively.

4.2 Settings

This paper uses a well-known MOOP benchmark set, WFG [11]. The WFG series consists of nine scalable, multi-objective test problems. This paper adopts two objectives and six decision variables ($k = 4, l = 2$) of WFG2, 3, 4, 5, 7, and 9.

This experiment is conducted on the pseudo (simulated) parallel computational environment based on the computational time model proposed in [22]. This model consists of a single master node and $\lambda = 100$ slave nodes work. The master node computes the primary process of the EA algorithm, i.e., initialization, selection, solution generation, and population maintenance in $t_s = 1$ simulation time. In contrast, the slave nodes evaluate one solution in the simulation time determined from the normal distribution with the mean t_p and the standard deviation $c_v \times t_p$. c_v is a parameter to determine the degree of the variance of the evaluation time. t_p is set as 1000 simulation time, which is 1000 times larger than the execution time of the master process. This paper tests several variances of $c_v = \{0.0, 0.02, 0.05, 0.10, 0.20\}$ are tested.

For TL-$I_{SDE}+$, this paper uses the asynchrony parameters $\alpha_t = \{0.01, 0.05, 0.1, 0.2, 0.3, 0.4, 0.5, 0.6, 0.7, 0.8, 0.9, 1.0\}$. When $\alpha_t = 0.01$, TL-$I_{SDE}+$ waits for 1% of the average evaluation time. On the other hand, when $\alpha_t = 1.0$, TL-$I_{SDE}+$ wait for the same computing time of the average evaluation time. For all asynchrony parameters, TL-$I_{SDE}+$ terminates the wait and proceeds to the next step when all solution evaluations, i.e., 100 evaluations, complete until the time limitation.

This experiment commonly employs the following genetic operations and the parameter settings:

- Population size $= 100\ (= \lambda)$
- The maximum evaluations $= 5.0 \times 10^4$ (500 generations of SPEA)
- Simulated Binary Crossover (SBX) [4] with $P_c = 0.9$ and $\eta_c = 20.0$
- Polynomial Mutation (PM) [5] with $P_m = 1/D$ and $\eta_m = 20.0$ (D is the dimension of the decision variable)

Our experiment is implemented using jMetal 5.0 framework [16]. 25 independent trials are conducted for all combinations of the benchmark problems, the asynchrony parameters α, and the variations of c_v.

4.3 Evaluation Criteria

This paper compares the computational time to obtain a certain quality of solutions for each problem to assess each method. In particular, this paper uses the Hypervolume (HV) indicator [21] for a quality assessment. HV computes the area dominated by the obtained non-dominated solutions on the objective space. This paper calculates the percentage of HV by comparing obtained HV at each elapsed time with HV of the true Pareto front (PF). Let $HV(t)$ be the HV value at the computing time t, and HV_{true} be the HV value of the true PF. This paper defines $T(x\%)$ as the computational time to reach $x\%$ of the true HV as: $T(x\%) = \min_{t \geq 0} \{t \mid 100 \times HV(t)/HV_{true} \geq x\}$. By using $T(x\%)$, the reduction ratio of computational time of each asynchrony parameter of TL-$I_{\text{SDE}}+$ is calculated as: $\Delta T(x\%; \alpha_t) = (T_{sync}(x\%) - T_{\alpha_t}(x\%))/T_{sync}(x\%)$, where $T_{sync}(x\%)$ is the median $T(x\%)$ of S-$I_{\text{SDE}}+$, while $T_{\alpha_t}(x\%)$ is $T(x\%)$ of TL-$I_{\text{SDE}}+$ with a certain α_t. This paper decides the percentage for each benchmark from the prior experiment as: 99% for WFG2, WFG4, and WFG7; 85% for WFG3 and WFG5; 95% for WFG9.

5   Result

Table 1 shows the median value of $\Delta T(x\%; \alpha_t)$ and the results of the statistical test with the Mann-Whitney U test [15] with 5% of the significance level. In this table, the "Prob." column indicates the benchmark problem. The "c_v" column indicates the variance parameter of the evaluation time of solutions. The "Async." column shows the result of the full asynchronous $I_{\text{SDE}}+$. The columns from "0.01" to "1.0" indicate the result of TL-$I_{\text{SDE}}+$ with the corresponding α_t value. The "p-value" column indicates the p-value of the Kruskal-Wallis test [14] where the cells with the value less than 0.05 are denoted in the bold style.

Table 1 shows that when the variance of the evaluation time is nothing ($c_v = 0.0$), the significant difference in the methods is found in WFG4 and WFG5 from the Kruskal-Wallis test. In WFG4, the full asynchronous $I_{\text{SDE}}+$ is significantly worse than the full synchronous one and some of the results of TL-$I_{\text{SDE}}+$. Similar to this, in WFG5, TL-$I_{\text{SDE}}+$ with $\alpha_t \geq 0.1$ outperform the full asynchronous $I_{\text{SDE}}+$. This is because TL-$I_{\text{SDE}}+$ with $\alpha_t \geq 0.1$ works the same as the full synchronous one, which can efficiently evolve solutions when the variance of the evaluation times small.

When the variance of the evaluation time is small ($c_v = 0.02$), the significant difference in the methods is found in WFG3 and WFG5. In WFG3, TL-$I_{\text{SDE}}+$ variants with the smaller $\alpha \leq 0.05$ are significantly worse than the full synchronous one. This is a similar tendency to the full asynchronous one. On the other hand, in WFG5, TL-$I_{\text{SDE}}+$ with the higher asynchrony parameters ($\alpha = \{0.2, 0.3, 0.4, 1.0\}$) significantly outperform both the full synchronous and full asynchronous $I_{\text{SDE}}+$.

When the variance of the evaluation time is middle ($c_v = 0.05$), the significant difference in the methods is found in WFG4, WFG5, and WFG7. In particular, TL-$I_{\text{SDE}}+$ variants with $\alpha = \{0.2, 0.3\}$ are significantly worse than both the full synchronous and full asynchronous $I_{\text{SDE}}+$. Moreover, TL-$I_{\text{SDE}}+$ variants with a higher asynchrony parameter shows the tendency to get worse.

When the variance of the evaluation time is large, i.e., $c_v = \{0.1, 0.2\}$, the significant difference in the methods is found in all benchmarks, and a clear

Table 1. Median $\Delta T(x\%; \alpha)$ and the statistical test results with the Mann-Whitney U test. $s+$ and $a+$ indicate the corresponding TL-$I_{\mathrm{SDE}}+$ is significantly better (i.e., shorter computational time) than the full synchronous and full asynchronous $I_{\mathrm{SDE}}+$, respectively. Meanwhile, $s-$ and $a-$ indicate that TL-$I_{\mathrm{SDE}}+$ is significantly worse than the full synchronous and full asynchronous $I_{\mathrm{SDE}}+$, respectively. $\approx$ symbol indicates that there is no significant difference. The p-value indicates the result of the Kruskal-Wallis test.

Prob	c_v	Async	0.01	0.05	0.1	0.2	0.3	0.4	0.5	0.6	0.7	0.8	0.9	1.0	p-value
WFG2	0.0	$-2.1\%^{s\approx}$	$6.3\%^{s\approx}_{a\approx}$	$4.4\%^{s\approx}_{a\approx}$	$-1.7\%^{s\approx}_{a\approx}$	$-1.7\%^{s\approx}_{a\approx}$	$-3.4\%^{s\approx}_{a\approx}$	$3.4\%^{s\approx}_{a\approx}$	$5.1\%^{s\approx}_{a\approx}$	$-5.1\%^{s\approx}_{a\approx}$	$-6.8\%^{s\approx}_{a\approx}$	$3.4\%^{s\approx}_{a\approx}$	$6.8\%^{s\approx}_{a\approx}$	$-11.9\%^{s\approx}_{a\approx}$	0.62
	0.02	$0.8\%^{s\approx}$	$-11.2\%^{s\approx}_{a-}$	$-6.1\%^{s\approx}_{a\approx}$	$-6.0\%^{s\approx}_{a\approx}$	$-16.4\%^{s-}_{a-}$	$-3.5\%^{s\approx}_{a\approx}$	$-9.0\%^{s-}_{a-}$	$-16.7\%^{s-}_{a-}$	$-5.4\%^{s\approx}_{a\approx}$	$-9.2\%^{s\approx}_{a\approx}$	$-10.9\%^{s\approx}_{a\approx}$	$-7.1\%^{s\approx}_{a\approx}$	$-12.6\%^{s\approx}_{a\approx}$	0.12
	0.05	$6.9\%^{s+}$	$13.7\%^{s+}_{a\approx}$	$2.6\%^{s\approx}_{a\approx}$	$-1.3\%^{s\approx}_{a-}$	$4.4\%^{s\approx}_{a\approx}$	$-1.5\%^{s\approx}_{a-}$	$5.0\%^{s+}_{a\approx}$	$3.7\%^{s\approx}_{a\approx}$	$-3.2\%^{s\approx}_{a-}$	$0.4\%^{s\approx}_{a-}$	$-2.7\%^{s\approx}_{a\approx}$	$-0.8\%^{s\approx}_{a\approx}$	$2.0\%^{s\approx}_{a\approx}$	0.32
	0.1	$12.0\%^{s+}$	$21.4\%^{s+}_{a\approx}$	$15.0\%^{s+}_{a\approx}$	$1.5\%^{s\approx}_{a\approx}$	$9.7\%^{s\approx}_{a\approx}$	$0.3\%^{s\approx}_{a-}$	$-0.2\%^{s\approx}_{a-}$	$-9.9\%^{s\approx}_{a-}$	$-11.4\%^{s\approx}_{a-}$	$-8.7\%^{s\approx}_{a-}$	$-7.0\%^{s-}_{a-}$	$-1.6\%^{s\approx}_{a-}$	$-9.9\%^{s\approx}_{a-}$	**< 0.01**
	0.2	$29.1\%^{s+}$	$25.1\%^{s+}_{a\approx}$	$29.1\%^{s+}_{a\approx}$	$26.1\%^{s+}_{a\approx}$	$20.4\%^{s+}_{a-}$	$18.3\%^{s+}_{a-}$	$20.5\%^{s+}_{a-}$	$14.5\%^{s+}_{a-}$	$5.2\%^{s\approx}_{a-}$	$10.1\%^{s\approx}_{a-}$	$-0.0\%^{s\approx}_{a-}$	$6.6\%^{s\approx}_{a-}$	$-1.8\%^{s\approx}_{a-}$	**< 0.01**
WFG3	0.0	$-1.0\%^{s\approx}$	$-1.9\%^{s\approx}_{a\approx}$	$-0.5\%^{s\approx}_{a\approx}$	$5.0\%^{s\approx}_{a+}$	$5.0\%^{s\approx}_{a\approx}$	$5.0\%^{s\approx}_{a+}$	$5.0\%^{s\approx}_{a+}$	$0.0\%^{s\approx}_{a\approx}$	$0.0\%^{s\approx}_{a\approx}$	$-5.0\%^{s\approx}_{a\approx}$	$5.0\%^{s\approx}_{a+}$	$0.0\%^{s\approx}_{a\approx}$	$0.0\%^{s\approx}_{a\approx}$	0.37
	0.02	$-13.9\%^{s-}$	$-14.6\%^{s-}_{a\approx}$	$-11.7\%^{s-}_{a\approx}$	$-6.3\%^{s\approx}_{a\approx}$	$-8.5\%^{s\approx}_{a\approx}$	$0.2\%^{s\approx}_{a+}$	$-0.2\%^{s\approx}_{a+}$	$-5.2\%^{s\approx}_{a\approx}$	$-5.1\%^{s\approx}_{a\approx}$	$10.4\%^{s\approx}_{a+}$	$-5.5\%^{s\approx}_{a+}$	$-0.1\%^{s\approx}_{a+}$	$-5.1\%^{s\approx}_{a\approx}$	**< 0.01**
	0.05	$5.2\%^{s+}$	$4.6\%^{s\approx}_{a\approx}$	$6.8\%^{s+}_{a\approx}$	$-0.0\%^{s\approx}_{a-}$	$0.6\%^{s\approx}_{a-}$	$2.0\%^{s\approx}_{a-}$	$0.5\%^{s\approx}_{a\approx}$	$0.9\%^{s\approx}_{a\approx}$	$0.2\%^{s\approx}_{a-}$	$4.7\%^{s\approx}_{a\approx}$	$0.2\%^{s\approx}_{a-}$	$0.2\%^{s\approx}_{a-}$	$0.3\%^{s\approx}_{a-}$	0.40
	0.1	$12.2\%^{s+}$	$11.7\%^{s+}_{a\approx}$	$11.8\%^{s+}_{a\approx}$	$11.9\%^{s+}_{a\approx}$	$8.3\%^{s\approx}_{a\approx}$	$1.0\%^{s\approx}_{a-}$	$-1.7\%^{s\approx}_{a-}$	$-6.5\%^{s-}_{a-}$	$2.4\%^{s\approx}_{a-}$	$8.7\%^{s\approx}_{a\approx}$	$10.1\%^{s+}_{a\approx}$	$3.9\%^{s\approx}_{a-}$	$5.1\%^{s\approx}_{a\approx}$	**< 0.01**
	0.2	$13.5\%^{s+}$	$17.1\%^{s+}_{a\approx}$	$11.0\%^{s+}_{a\approx}$	$12.5\%^{s+}_{a\approx}$	$13.8\%^{s+}_{a\approx}$	$4.2\%^{s\approx}_{a-}$	$1.1\%^{s\approx}_{a-}$	$-7.5\%^{s\approx}_{a-}$	$-4.2\%^{s\approx}_{a-}$	$-6.3\%^{s\approx}_{a-}$	$-10.0\%^{s\approx}_{a-}$	$-9.4\%^{s-}_{a-}$	$-30.5\%^{s-}_{a-}$	**< 0.01**
WFG4	0.0	$-13.6\%^{s-}$	$-8.0\%^{s\approx}_{a\approx}$	$-16.6\%^{s-}_{a\approx}$	$-9.8\%^{s\approx}_{a+}$	$-7.3\%^{s\approx}_{a+}$	$-7.3\%^{s\approx}_{a+}$	$-17.1\%^{s-}_{a\approx}$	$-2.4\%^{s\approx}_{a+}$	$-14.6\%^{s-}_{a\approx}$	$-12.2\%^{s\approx}_{a+}$	$-12.2\%^{s\approx}_{a+}$	$-7.3\%^{s\approx}_{a+}$	$-9.8\%^{s\approx}_{a+}$	**0.02**
	0.02	$-1.0\%^{s\approx}$	$0.1\%^{s\approx}_{a\approx}$	$-1.9\%^{s\approx}_{a\approx}$	$-3.6\%^{s\approx}_{a\approx}$	$0.6\%^{s\approx}_{a\approx}$	$0.3\%^{s\approx}_{a\approx}$	$-3.9\%^{s\approx}_{a\approx}$	$0.3\%^{s\approx}_{a\approx}$	$-6.2\%^{s\approx}_{a\approx}$	$2.7\%^{s+}_{a\approx}$	$-1.8\%^{s\approx}_{a\approx}$	$0.4\%^{s+}_{a\approx}$	$2.7\%^{s+}_{a\approx}$	0.65
	0.05	$-4.3\%^{s\approx}$	$-4.7\%^{s\approx}_{a\approx}$	$1.1\%^{s\approx}_{a\approx}$	$-4.6\%^{s\approx}_{a\approx}$	$-12.2\%^{s-}_{a-}$	$-16.1\%^{s-}_{a-}$	$-2.2\%^{s\approx}_{a\approx}$	$-8.5\%^{s\approx}_{a\approx}$	$0.4\%^{s\approx}_{a\approx}$	$-4.0\%^{s\approx}_{a\approx}$	$-4.3\%^{s\approx}_{a\approx}$	$-4.0\%^{s\approx}_{a\approx}$	$-2.1\%^{s\approx}_{a\approx}$	**0.02**
	0.1	$18.4\%^{s+}$	$16.4\%^{s+}_{a\approx}$	$17.8\%^{s+}_{a\approx}$	$10.4\%^{s+}_{a-}$	$8.0\%^{s+}_{a-}$	$7.2\%^{s+}_{a-}$	$2.3\%^{s\approx}_{a-}$	$4.9\%^{s\approx}_{a-}$	$-10.4\%^{s-}_{a-}$	$-0.5\%^{s\approx}_{a-}$	$1.8\%^{s\approx}_{a-}$	$6.2\%^{s+}_{a-}$	$1.8\%^{s\approx}_{a-}$	**< 0.01**
	0.2	$25.6\%^{s+}$	$26.6\%^{s+}_{a\approx}$	$22.7\%^{s+}_{a\approx}$	$22.7\%^{s+}_{a-}$	$17.3\%^{s+}_{a-}$	$18.7\%^{s+}_{a-}$	$12.5\%^{s+}_{a-}$	$9.5\%^{s+}_{a-}$	$9.6\%^{s+}_{a-}$	$3.2\%^{s\approx}_{a-}$	$-3.2\%^{s\approx}_{a-}$	$-9.1\%^{s-}_{a-}$	$-9.6\%^{s\approx}_{a-}$	**< 0.01**
WFG5	0.0	$-1.6\%^{s\approx}$	$-6.1\%^{s-}_{a\approx}$	$0.8\%^{s\approx}_{a\approx}$	$5.7\%^{s\approx}_{a+}$	$5.7\%^{s\approx}_{a+}$	$5.7\%^{s+}_{a+}$	$5.7\%^{s\approx}_{a+}$	$1.9\%^{s\approx}_{a\approx}$	$1.9\%^{s\approx}_{a\approx}$	$5.7\%^{s\approx}_{a+}$	$1.9\%^{s\approx}_{a\approx}$	$1.9\%^{s\approx}_{a\approx}$	$3.8\%^{s\approx}_{a\approx}$	**0.02**
	0.02	$4.3\%^{s\approx}$	$2.0\%^{s\approx}_{a\approx}$	$2.0\%^{s\approx}_{a\approx}$	$-4.1\%^{s\approx}_{a\approx}$	$9.2\%^{s+}_{a+}$	$6.1\%^{s+}_{a+}$	$9.4\%^{s+}_{a+}$	$4.2\%^{s\approx}_{a\approx}$	$5.8\%^{s\approx}_{a\approx}$	$4.0\%^{s\approx}_{a\approx}$	$7.7\%^{s\approx}_{a+}$	$4.1\%^{s\approx}_{a\approx}$	$7.7\%^{s+}_{a+}$	**< 0.01**
	0.05	$-6.0\%^{s\approx}$	$-4.6\%^{s\approx}_{a\approx}$	$-5.7\%^{s\approx}_{a\approx}$	$-6.3\%^{s-}_{a\approx}$	$-9.7\%^{s-}_{a-}$	$-10.4\%^{s-}_{a\approx}$	$-5.5\%^{s\approx}_{a\approx}$	$-4.2\%^{s-}_{a\approx}$	$-6.6\%^{s-}_{a\approx}$	$-6.3\%^{s-}_{a\approx}$	$-7.6\%^{s-}_{a\approx}$	$-3.8\%^{s\approx}_{a\approx}$	$-4.0\%^{s\approx}_{a\approx}$	**0.02**
	0.1	$12.4\%^{s+}$	$12.4\%^{s+}_{a\approx}$	$10.9\%^{s+}_{a\approx}$	$9.1\%^{s+}_{a-}$	$5.3\%^{s+}_{a-}$	$3.0\%^{s\approx}_{a-}$	$-0.4\%^{s\approx}_{a-}$	$1.0\%^{s\approx}_{a-}$	$-9.2\%^{s-}_{a-}$	$-3.1\%^{s\approx}_{a-}$	$-3.2\%^{s\approx}_{a-}$	$0.5\%^{s\approx}_{a-}$	$0.3\%^{s\approx}_{a-}$	**< 0.01**
	0.2	$24.2\%^{s+}$	$22.1\%^{s+}_{a-}$	$19.0\%^{s+}_{a-}$	$16.8\%^{s+}_{a-}$	$16.7\%^{s+}_{a-}$	$10.1\%^{s+}_{a-}$	$13.1\%^{s+}_{a-}$	$10.6\%^{s+}_{a-}$	$9.1\%^{s+}_{a-}$	$-2.0\%^{s\approx}_{a-}$	$-8.9\%^{s-}_{a-}$	$-4.4\%^{s-}_{a-}$	$-5.4\%^{s\approx}_{a-}$	**< 0.01**
WFG7	0.0	$-2.5\%^{s\approx}$	$-1.6\%^{s\approx}_{a\approx}$	$0.4\%^{s\approx}_{a\approx}$	$0.0\%^{s\approx}_{a\approx}$	$2.0\%^{s\approx}_{a+}$	$-8.2\%^{s-}_{a\approx}$	$0.0\%^{s\approx}_{a\approx}$	$0.0\%^{s\approx}_{a\approx}$	$2.0\%^{s\approx}_{a+}$	$0.0\%^{s\approx}_{a\approx}$	$-2.0\%^{s\approx}_{a\approx}$	$-2.0\%^{s\approx}_{a\approx}$	$0.0\%^{s\approx}_{a\approx}$	0.47
	0.02	$-2.3\%^{s\approx}$	$-2.9\%^{s\approx}_{a\approx}$	$2.6\%^{s\approx}_{a\approx}$	$2.8\%^{s\approx}_{a\approx}$	$4.0\%^{s\approx}_{a\approx}$	$0.1\%^{s\approx}_{a\approx}$	$-1.9\%^{s\approx}_{a\approx}$	$2.1\%^{s\approx}_{a\approx}$	$-6.0\%^{s\approx}_{a\approx}$	$-1.9\%^{s\approx}_{a\approx}$	$2.0\%^{s\approx}_{a\approx}$	$-0.0\%^{s\approx}_{a\approx}$	$1.8\%^{s\approx}_{a\approx}$	0.92
	0.05	$6.4\%^{s+}$	$4.3\%^{s+}_{a\approx}$	$4.3\%^{s\approx}_{a\approx}$	$1.2\%^{s\approx}_{a\approx}$	$-4.0\%^{s\approx}_{a-}$	$-4.0\%^{s\approx}_{a-}$	$-3.8\%^{s\approx}_{a-}$	$-2.2\%^{s\approx}_{a-}$	$-0.2\%^{s\approx}_{a-}$	$0.2\%^{s\approx}_{a-}$	$2.4\%^{s\approx}_{a\approx}$	$-7.8\%^{s\approx}_{a-}$	$-0.1\%^{s\approx}_{a-}$	**0.02**
	0.1	$13.8\%^{s+}$	$13.2\%^{s+}_{a\approx}$	$6.4\%^{s+}_{a-}$	$9.1\%^{s+}_{a-}$	$7.6\%^{s+}_{a-}$	$4.8\%^{s\approx}_{a-}$	$0.1\%^{s\approx}_{a-}$	$-7.6\%^{s-}_{a-}$	$-10.4\%^{s-}_{a-}$	$-0.6\%^{s\approx}_{a-}$	$-1.4\%^{s\approx}_{a-}$	$-1.1\%^{s\approx}_{a-}$	$3.5\%^{s\approx}_{a-}$	**< 0.01**
	0.2	$23.7\%^{s+}$	$19.9\%^{s+}_{a\approx}$	$22.5\%^{s+}_{a\approx}$	$20.9\%^{s+}_{a\approx}$	$20.0\%^{s+}_{a-}$	$11.5\%^{s+}_{a-}$	$7.3\%^{s+}_{a-}$	$9.9\%^{s+}_{a-}$	$8.6\%^{s+}_{a-}$	$-3.8\%^{s\approx}_{a-}$	$-2.3\%^{s\approx}_{a-}$	$-12.3\%^{s-}_{a-}$	$-13.1\%^{s-}_{a-}$	**< 0.01**
WFG9	0.0	$-9.2\%^{s\approx}$	$-18.9\%^{s\approx}_{a\approx}$	$-9.6\%^{s\approx}_{a\approx}$	$-4.8\%^{s\approx}_{a+}$	$-9.5\%^{s\approx}_{a\approx}$	$-4.8\%^{s\approx}_{a\approx}$	$-4.8\%^{s\approx}_{a\approx}$	$-4.8\%^{s\approx}_{a\approx}$	$-4.8\%^{s\approx}_{a\approx}$	$-14.3\%^{s\approx}_{a\approx}$	$0.0\%^{s\approx}_{a+}$	$-4.8\%^{s\approx}_{a\approx}$	$0.0\%^{s\approx}_{a\approx}$	0.08
	0.02	$-2.6\%^{s\approx}$	$-3.5\%^{s\approx}_{a\approx}$	$-1.9\%^{s\approx}_{a\approx}$	$-4.9\%^{s-}_{a\approx}$	$-9.4\%^{s-}_{a\approx}$	$-0.6\%^{s\approx}_{a\approx}$	$-5.3\%^{s\approx}_{a\approx}$	$-0.1\%^{s\approx}_{a\approx}$	$-0.4\%^{s\approx}_{a\approx}$	$-0.1\%^{s\approx}_{a\approx}$	$-9.4\%^{s\approx}_{a\approx}$	$-5.0\%^{s-}_{a\approx}$	$-5.0\%^{s\approx}_{a\approx}$	0.79
	0.05	$-6.5\%^{s\approx}$	$-3.4\%^{s\approx}_{a\approx}$	$2.2\%^{s\approx}_{a\approx}$	$-11.6\%^{s\approx}_{a\approx}$	$-5.2\%^{s\approx}_{a\approx}$	$-6.1\%^{s\approx}_{a\approx}$	$-9.4\%^{s\approx}_{a\approx}$	$-9.4\%^{s\approx}_{a\approx}$	$4.2\%^{s\approx}_{a\approx}$	$8.9\%^{s+}_{a+}$	$-5.2\%^{s\approx}_{a\approx}$	$-0.8\%^{s\approx}_{a\approx}$	$-4.5\%^{s\approx}_{a\approx}$	0.45
	0.1	$7.7\%^{s+}$	$-0.2\%^{s\approx}_{a\approx}$	$-2.3\%^{s\approx}_{a\approx}$	$-5.6\%^{s\approx}_{a-}$	$0.3\%^{s\approx}_{a-}$	$-22.8\%^{s-}_{a-}$	$-21.1\%^{s-}_{a-}$	$-14.7\%^{s-}_{a-}$	$-25.1\%^{s-}_{a-}$	$-16.5\%^{s-}_{a-}$	$-21.3\%^{s-}_{a-}$	$-1.2\%^{s\approx}_{a-}$	$-5.3\%^{s\approx}_{a-}$	**< 0.01**
	0.2	$25.8\%^{s+}$	$22.9\%^{s+}_{a\approx}$	$20.8\%^{s+}_{a\approx}$	$22.9\%^{s+}_{a\approx}$	$20.2\%^{s+}_{a\approx}$	$11.5\%^{s+}_{a-}$	$12.2\%^{s+}_{a-}$	$4.8\%^{s\approx}_{a-}$	$3.1\%^{s\approx}_{a-}$	$4.4\%^{s\approx}_{a-}$	$-5.0\%^{s\approx}_{a-}$	$-11.0\%^{s-}_{a-}$	$-4.9\%^{s\approx}_{a-}$	**< 0.01**

tendency can be found. For small asynchrony parameters, $\alpha_t = \{0.01, 0.05, 0.1\}$, TL-$I_{SDE}+$ significantly outperforms the full synchronous $I_{SDE}+$, while it performs the equivalent reduction time to the full asynchronous one. On the other hand, TL-$I_{SDE}+$ with high asynchrony parameters, i.e., $\alpha_t \geq 0.3$, is significantly worse than the full asynchronous $I_{SDE}+$. Furthermore, when $\alpha_t \geq 0.8$, TL-$I_{SDE}+$ is also significantly worse than the full synchronous one.

From the overall results of the statistical tests, it can be confirmed that TL-$I_{SDE}+$ with smaller asynchrony parameters ($\alpha_t \leq 0.3$) is mostly better than or equal to the full synchronous $I_{SDE}+$ for any variance of the evaluation time. A similar tendency can be found against the full asynchronous $I_{SDE}+$. Concretely, TL-$I_{SDE}+$ variants with smaller asynchrony parameters ($\alpha_t \leq 0.2$) are mostly better than or equal to the full asynchronous $I_{SDE}+$ for any variance of the evaluation time. However, TL-$I_{SDE}+$ variants with larger asynchrony parameters ($\alpha_t \geq 0.3$) are significantly worse than the asynchronous one, especially when the variance is enormous.

These results reveal that TL-$I_{SDE}+$ variants with smaller asynchrony parameters ($\alpha_t \leq 0.2$) perform better search capability than the full synchronous and full asynchronous $I_{SDE}+$ regardless of the variance of the evaluation time. Meanwhile, larger asynchrony parameters ($\alpha_t \geq 0.3$) are not suitable, especially TL-$I_{SDE}+$ with such parameters are worse than the full asynchronous one if the variance of the evaluation time is enormous.

6   Conclusion

This paper proposed a novel PEA approach called time-limitation asynchronous PEA (TLAPEA). TLAPEA limits the maximum waiting time for other solution evaluations before generating new solutions. In particular, an asynchrony parameter α_t is introduced, which decides the maximum waiting time by multiplying the average evaluation time of solutions obtained so far by α_t. This approach enables waiting solution evaluations to utilize them to new solution generation while reducing the waste time for waiting for slower solution evaluation.

This paper conducted an experiment on multi-objective optimization benchmarks, the WFG series. This paper adopted $I_{SDE}+$ as a state-of-the-art MOEA method to be applied to PEA schemes. In the experiment, the pseudo parallel computational environment was used. The evaluation time of solutions is determined from the normal distribution with several variances.

The experimental results revealed that TLAPEA with smaller asynchrony parameters ($\alpha_t \leq 0.2$) performs better search capability than the full synchronous and full asynchronous ones for any variances of the evaluation time. Meanwhile, larger asynchrony parameters ($\alpha_t \geq 0.3$) are not suitable, in particular, TLAPEA with such parameters are worse than the full asynchronous one if the variance of the evaluation time is enormous.

Future works will analyze further detailed behavior of TLAPEA by applying it to other single- and multi-objective optimizations and other EA methods. Additionally, it should be explored how to find appropriate asynchronous parameter according to the behavior of the evolution or the characteristics of the evaluation time of solutions. Moreover, other approaches to reduce the computing time have been proposed, for example, surrogate-assisted EAs [12] or model-based approaches [2]. Future research will focus on the integration of such approaches with TLAPEA.

References

1. Chang, J.F., Chu, S.C., Roddick, J.F., Pan, J.S.: A parallel particle swarm optimization algorithm with communication strategies. J. Inf. Sci. Eng. **21**(4), 809–818 (2005)
2. Cheng, R., He, C., Jin, Y., Yao, X.: Model-based evolutionary algorithms: a short survey. Complex Intell. Syst. **4**(4), 283–292 (2018). https://doi.org/10.1007/s40747-018-0080-1
3. Chipperfield, A., Fleming, P.: Parallel Genetic Algorithms, pp. 1118–1143. McGraw-Hill, New York (1996)
4. Deb, K., Agrawal, R.B.: Simulated binary crossover for continuous search space. Complex Syst. **9**, 115–148 (1995). citeseer.ist.psu.edu/deb95simulated.html
5. Deb, K., Goyal, M.: A combined genetic adaptive search (GeneAS) for engineering design. Comput. Sci. Inf. **26**, 30–45 (1996)
6. Durillo, J.J., Zhang, Q., Nebro, A.J., Alba, E.: Distribution of computational effort in parallel MOEA/D. In: Coello, C.A.C. (ed.) LION 2011. LNCS, vol. 6683, pp. 488–502. Springer, Heidelberg (2011). https://doi.org/10.1007/978-3-642-25566-3_38
7. Goldberg, D.E.: Genetic Algorithms in Search, Optimization and Machine Learning, 1st edn. Addison-Wesley Longman Publishing Co., Inc., Boston (1989)
8. Harada, T., Takadama, K.: Asynchronous evaluation based genetic programming: comparison of asynchronous and synchronous evaluation and its analysis. In: Krawiec, K., Moraglio, A., Hu, T., Etaner-Uyar, A.Ş., Hu, B. (eds.) EuroGP 2013. LNCS, vol. 7831, pp. 241–252. Springer, Heidelberg (2013). https://doi.org/10.1007/978-3-642-37207-0_21
9. Harada, T., Takadama, K.: Performance comparison of parallel asynchronous multi-objective evolutionary algorithm with different asynchrony. In: 2017 IEEE Congress on Evolutionary Computation (CEC), pp. 1215–1222, June 2017. https://doi.org/10.1109/CEC.2017.7969444
10. Harada, T., Takadama, K.: Analysis of semi-asynchronous multi-objective evolutionary algorithm with different asynchronies. Soft Comput. **24**(4), 2917–2939 (2020). https://doi.org/10.1007/s00500-019-04071-7
11. Huband, S., Barone, L., While, L., Hingston, P.: A scalable multi-objective test problem toolkit. In: Coello Coello, C.A., Hernández Aguirre, A., Zitzler, E. (eds.) EMO 2005. LNCS, vol. 3410, pp. 280–295. Springer, Heidelberg (2005). https://doi.org/10.1007/978-3-540-31880-4_20
12. Jin, Y.: Surrogate-assisted evolutionary computation: recent advances and future challenges. Swarm Evol. Comput. **1**(2), 61–70 (2011). https://doi.org/10.1016/j.swevo.2011.05.001, http://www.sciencedirect.com/science/article/pii/S2210650211000198
13. Koza, J.: Genetic Programming On the Programming of Computers by Means of Natural Selection. MIT Press, Cambridge (1992)

14. Kruskal, W.H., Wallis, W.A.: Use of ranks in one-criterion variance analysis. J. Am. Stat. Assoc. **47**(260), 583–621 (1952). https://doi.org/10.2307/2280779

15. Mann, H.B., Whitney, D.R.: On a test of whether one of two random variables is stochastically larger than the other. Ann. Math. Stat. **18**(1), 50–60 (1947). https://doi.org/10.1214/aoms/1177730491

16. Nebro, A.J., Durillo, J.J., Vergne, M.: Redesigning the jMetal multi-objective optimization framework. In: Proceedings of the Companion Publication of the 2015 Annual Conference on Genetic and Evolutionary Computation, pp. 1093–1100. GECCO Companion 2015. ACM, New York (2015). https://doi.org/10.1145/2739482.2768462, https://doi.acm.org/10.1145/2739482.2768462

17. Pamulapati, T., Mallipeddi, R., Suganthan, P.N.: I_{SDE} +—an indicator for multi and many-objective optimization. IEEE Trans. Evol. Comput. **23**(2), 346–352 (2019). https://doi.org/10.1109/TEVC.2018.2848921

18. Scott, E.O., De Jong, K.A.: Evaluation-time bias in asynchronous evolutionary algorithms. In: Proceedings of the Companion Publication of the 2015 Annual Conference on Genetic and Evolutionary Computation, pp. 1209–1212. GECCO Companion 2015. ACM, New York (2015). https://doi.org/10.1145/2739482.2768482, https://doi.acm.org/10.1145/2739482.2768482

19. Scott, E.O., De Jong, K.A.: Understanding simple asynchronous evolutionary algorithms. In: Proceedings of the 2015 ACM Conference on Foundations of Genetic Algorithms XIII, pp. 85–98. FOGA 2015. ACM, New York (2015). https://doi.org/10.1145/2725494.2725509, https://doi.acm.org/10.1145/2725494.2725509

20. Tasoulis, D.K., Pavlidis, N.G., Plagianakos, V.P., Vrahatis, M.N.: Parallel differential evolution. In: Proceedings of the 2004 Congress on Evolutionary Computation (IEEE Cat. No. 04TH8753), vol. 2, pp. 2023–2029, June 2004. https://doi.org/10.1109/CEC.2004.1331145

21. Zitzler, E., Thiele, L.: Multiobjective optimization using evolutionary algorithms—a comparative case study. In: Eiben, A.E., Bäck, T., Schoenauer, M., Schwefel, H.-P. (eds.) PPSN 1998. LNCS, vol. 1498, pp. 292–301. Springer, Heidelberg (1998). https://doi.org/10.1007/BFb0056872

22. Zăvoianu, A.C., Lughofer, E., Koppelstätter, W., Weidenholzer, G., Amrhein, W., Klement, E.P.: Performance comparison of generational and steady-state asynchronous multi-objective evolutionary algorithms for computationally-intensive problems. Knowl. Based Syst. **87**(C), 47–60 (2015). https://doi.org/10.1016/j.knosys.2015.05.029

Nonlinear Regression in Dynamic Environments Using Particle Swarm Optimization

Cry Kuranga⬤ and Nelishia Pillay$^{(\boxtimes)}$ ⬤

Department of Computer Science, University of Pretoria,
Lynnwood Road, Hillcrest, Pretoria 0002, South Africa
kurangacry@gmail.com, npillay@cs.up.ac.za

Abstract. This paper extends a PSO-based nonlinear regression technique to dynamic environments whereby the induced model dynamically adjusts when an environmental change is detected. As such, this work hybridizes a PSO designed for dynamic environments with a least-squares approximation technique to induce structurally optimal nonlinear regression models. The proposed model was evaluated experimentally and compared with the dynamic PSOs, namely multi-swarm, reinitialized, and charged PSOs, to optimize the model structure and the regression parameters in the dynamic environment. The obtained results show that the proposed model was adaptive to the changing environment to yield structurally optimal models which consequently, outperformed the dynamic PSOs for the given datasets.

Keywords: Dynamic PSO · Least-squares · Nonlinear regression · Dynamic environments

1 Introduction

Regression models can be classified as either linear or nonlinear. Nonlinear models can be induced by either classical techniques such as Gauss-Newton [1] and Levenberg-Marquardt methods [2] or machine learning techniques such as evolutionary computation [3–5] and artificial neural networks [6, 7].

Nonlinear regression-based prediction, in static environments, has been successfully applied in the literature where a static prediction model is constructed once and then used to predict for instances not used during training. The main objective is to minimize the nonlinear least-squares error. Therefore, nonlinear regression-based prediction can be considered as an optimization problem where the optimal parameters can be estimated by either classical or heuristic optimization techniques. However, classical techniques are usually trapped in local minima [8]. As such, metaheuristics have been considered as an alternative [3–5].

Particle swarm optimization (PSO) has been successfully applied to nonlinear regression problems, in static environments, w.r.t accuracy [9, 10]. However, the structure of the approximator needs to be optimized as well. Usually, real-world nonlinear regression problems are dynamic. As such, the objective function in a dynamic environment tends

© Springer Nature Switzerland AG 2020
C. Martín-Vide et al. (Eds.): TPNC 2020, LNCS 12494, pp. 133–144, 2020.
https://doi.org/10.1007/978-3-030-63000-3_11

to change, which results in changes in the search space structure and the position of optima. Therefore, the performance of the prediction model constructed using the past environment is bound to deteriorate. Thus, making a continuous adaptation of the prediction model becomes a necessity. However, a standard PSO in a changing environment is prune to outdated memory problem and diversity loss [11].

This work aims to extend a PSO-based nonlinear regression technique to dynamic environments whereby the induced model dynamically adjusts when an environmental change is detected. As such, this work hybridizes a PSO designed for dynamic environments with a least-squares approximation technique to induce structurally optimal nonlinear regression models in dynamic environments. This hybridization decreases the performance deterioration that usually results from the environmental changes and consequently, improves the algorithm's performance. Also, this work evaluates experimentally and compared with dynamic PSO algorithms, namely multi-swarm, reinitialized, and charged PSOs, to optimize the model structure and the regression parameters in the dynamic environment. Dynamic PSO algorithms are PSO variants that can adapt in dynamic environments.

This paper is structured as follows: Sect. 2 discusses related work. Section 3 discusses the proposed model whereas Sect. 4 discusses the experimental setup and present the results. Section 5 provides a conclusion to the paper.

2 Related Work

Regression analysis is a statistical-based model induction technique that models a relationship between variables (quantitative), ideal to predict a selected variable from one or more other variables [12]. Regression analysis uses equations to describe the given dataset whereby a regression model consists of the following components [13]: a response variable(s), i.e., a real-world output, y; a vector of predictor variables, i.e., an input vector $x = x_1; x_2; \ldots; x_n$; and an unknown parameter, θ, which can be a vector or scalar.

Given that x is an input vector and y is a real-world output, a nonlinear model between x and y is of the form:

$$y = f(x; \theta) + \varepsilon \tag{1}$$

where ε is a random error. A process of fitting the best approximation to a dataset of $n = |N|$ data points $\{(x_1, y_1), \ldots, (x_n, y_n)\}$ is commonly referred to as least-squares approximation [14, 15]. Least-squares approximation minimizes the least-squares error, E_{ss}, to an arbitrary set of m data points:

$$E_{ss} = \sum_{i=1}^{m} \left[y_i - \dot{y}_i \right]^2$$

where $\dot{y}_i$ is the predicted output and y_i is the target value, e.g.

$$\dot{y}_i = \tau_0 + \tau_1 x_i + \ldots + \tau_{p-1} x_i^{p-1} + \tau_p x_i^p$$

$$= \sum_{j=0}^{p} \tau_j x_i^j \tag{2}$$

where p is the maximum number of terms. The determination of coefficients $(\tau_0, \ldots, \tau_n)$ is realized through solving the linear system:

$$y \approx X\tau$$

where $\tau^T = [\tau_0, \tau_1, \ldots \tau_{p-1}, \tau_p]$ and $y^T = [y_0, y_1, \ldots y_{p-1}, y_p]$. Therefore, the solution to the least-squares problem can be obtained by solving the overdetermined system:

$$(X^T X)\tau = X^T y$$

Least-squares problems are usually solved using numerous techniques such as normal equation, singular value decomposition and QR decomposition technique. The normal equation technique is very fast though the least precise whereas singular value decomposition is the most precise though the slowest. The QR decomposition technique strikes the balance between precision and computational load [15]. QR decomposition can be computed using several methods such as Givens rotations, Householder transform, and Gram-Schmidt.

The implementation of PSO, in a static environment, for regression problems has yielded favorable results [9, 10]. However, since PSO in a changing environment is prune to outdated memory problem and diversity loss [11], few PSO variants that can adapt in dynamic environments were selected based on the classification given in [16]: a memory scheme - reinitialized PSO; a multi-population scheme - multiPSO; and a diversity maintenance scheme - charged PSO. A brief description of the selected algorithms is provided below.

A charged PSO proposed by Blackwell and Branke, referred to as quantum PSO (QPSO), is based on the model of an atom [17–19]. A swarm consists of both quantum particles and non-quantum particles. For quantum particles, instead of using the position equation as in the standard PSO, the position of each quantum particle is determined by a probability distribution. To preserve the swarm diversity, the quantum particles are randomized at each iteration. The non-quantum particles behave like standard PSO particles which use velocity and position equations to improve the current solution. As such, quantum particles search for new solutions [17].

Multi-swarm PSO implements multiple populations, each optimizing a single solution from the set of solutions [17]. The algorithm keeps the swarm diverse by using anti-convergence methods and repulsion. The convergence of all sub-swarms is determined by a convergence radius whereby if all sub-swarm are within r_{excl} then one sub-swarms, usually the one with the worst fitness, is reinitialized.

In reinitialized PSO, the swarm or part of it is randomly re-initialized within the search space when a change in the environment occurs to enhance diversity [20]. Usually, the best particles are maintained within their neighborhood to monitor the best-known positions. If a change is detected, the particle velocity is reset and the particle's current position becomes the particle's best position. As such, particles are discouraged to be attracted to their former position. In this work, a nonlinear regression model designed for dynamic environments is proposed that hybridize a QR decomposition, computed using Gram-Schmidt technique and a dynamic PSO algorithm.

3 Particle Swarm Optimization in Regression Analysis

The proposed dynamic PSO-based nonlinear regression model consists of a QR decomposition technique to determine the coefficients of the model and a dynamic PSO to induce an optimal model structure that can adapt whenever a change in the environment occurs.

Considering a QR decomposition technique, the predicted output, $\dot{y}_i$, in Eq. (2), when the dimensionality of the input space, d, is taken into consideration, can be rewritten as [5]:

$$\dot{y}_i = \sum_{j=1}^{p} \sum_{\beta_j=0}^{d} \left(\tau(\beta_1, \beta_2, \ldots, \beta_d) \prod_{q=1}^{d} x_{i,q}^{\beta_d} \right) \tag{3}$$

where $\tau(\beta_1, \beta_2, \ldots, \beta_d)$ is a real-valued coefficient and β_d is the order of attribute $x_{i,q}$. Considering $d = 2$ and $p = 2$, Eq. (3) lets the representation of function such as:

$$\dot{y}_i = \tau_{(0,0)} + \tau_{(1,0)} x_{i,1} + \tau_{(0,1)} x_{i,2} + \tau_{(1,1)} x_{i,1} x_{i,2} + \tau_{(2,0)} x_{i,1}^2 + \tau_{(0,2)} x_{i,2}^2$$

As such, QR decomposition determines the value of the coefficients, $\tau(\beta_1, \beta_2, \ldots, \beta_d)$. Therefore, the dynamic PSO is tasked to determine only the optimal model structure.

Each particle in dynamic PSO is a representation of Eq. (3) and consists of unique, term-coefficient mappings from a set, S: [5]

$$S = \left\{ (t_0 \rightarrow \tau_o), \ldots, \left(t_{n_p} \rightarrow \tau_{n_p} \right) \right\} \tag{4}$$

where $\tau_j, j \in \{0, \ldots, n_p\}$ is a real-valued coefficient and n_p is the maximum number of terms. Each term, t_j, consists of a set, T, of unique, variable-order mappings e.g.

$$T = \left\{ (x_{i,1} \rightarrow \beta_1), \ldots, (x_{i,d} \rightarrow \beta_d) \right\}$$

where $x_{i,j}, j \in \{1, \ldots, n\}$ is an input variable-integer representation, n is the number of input variables and β_j is a natural-valued order. The coefficients of term-coefficient mappings are determined by reducing $y \approx X\tau$. Algorithm 1 summarizes a dynamic PSO-based nonlinear regression technique.

Algorithm 1 Dynamic PSO-based Nonlinear Regression
    BEGIN
        Initialize particles using Eqn (3)
        DO
            Run n iterations of the dynamic PSO algorithm
            IF an environment_change is detected
                Update the coefficients of term-coefficient mappings in each particle
                by reducing $y \approx Xr$.
            END
        UNTIL termination condition satisfied;
    END

3.1 Fitness Function

The adjusted coefficient of determination, R_a^2, is used to measure the fitness of each particle and is defined as:

$$R_a^2 = 1 - \frac{\sum_{i=1}^{n}(y_i - y_{I,i})^2}{\sum_{i=1}^{n}(y_i - \bar{y})^2} \times \frac{n - 1}{n - k}$$

where the predicted output of particle I for the pattern i is $y_{I,i}$, the target output is y_i, n is a size of data patterns and k is the number of coefficients. The R_a^2 penalizes a model that has a larger number of coefficients, k. Thus, the objective of R_a^2 is to minimize the model's architecture, whereas maximizing the correlation between the dataset and the induced model.

3.2 Detecting Environmental Changes

For an algorithm to efficiently optimize in a dynamic environment, there is a need for the algorithm to detect an environmental change [21]. Various indicators can be used to detect an environmental change in a dynamic environment such as the time-averaged best performance or the deterioration of the population performance [22]. In this work, a simple and efficient method to detect environment change used in [23] was adopted that uses the *personal Best* position of each particle which is re-evaluated before being updated. As such, fitness deterioration implies that an environmental change had occurred.

4 Experimental Setup and Results

In this section, the multi-swarm, reinitialized and charged PSOs and the proposed model were experimentally evaluated. All experiments were implemented in MATLAB programming environment [24] on an Intel Core i7 processor (3.1 GHz) desktop with 16 GB of memory running on a Linux Centos 7 system. For reinitialized PSO, 50% of the swarm was reinitialized when an environmental change was detected. The following PSO parameters in the literature were used $c_1 = c_2 = 1.496180$, $\omega = 0.729844$, $r_{excl} = quantum\_radius = 2$, $swarm\_size = 50$ and QR decomposition: $n_p = \beta_j = 10$. For each experiment, 1000 iterations were executed for each algorithm.

The training algorithms were categorized into QR_PSOs and nonQR_PSOs. The QR_PSOs consist of dynamic PSOs namely, charged PSO (QPSO), multi-swarm PSO (mPSO) and re-initialized PSO (rePSO) that implemented the proposed Algorithm 1 and therefore, referred to as QR_QPSO, QR_mPSO and QR_rePSO respectively. To benchmark, the performance of the proposed model, nonQR_PSOs (QPSO, mPSO and rePSO) were implemented in all experiments. The initial swarm for each algorithm was initialized using Eq. (3).

To simulate dynamic environments, a windowing technique was used. A sliding window of analysis was set to ws data patterns. A data pattern consists of the inputs and target output for the given dataset. Each sliding window was split to training and generalization datasets using the ratio 4:1 respectively.

4.1 Performance Measure

The off-line performance was used to evaluate the performance of the algorithm, computed at each time step as the best fitness found so far [22]. A total of 30 independent runs were executed on each experiment for each algorithm and then averaged. The Mann-Whitney U test was performed, at a significance level of 0.05, to determine if there was a statistically significant difference between the mean fitness values of the training algorithms for each experiment [25]. A test was performed for the algorithms' mean fitness values, μ_1 and μ_2, whereby $H_0 : \mu_1 = \mu_2$, and $H_1 : \mu_1 \neq \mu_2$. These tests were performed for every combination of algorithms and all problems. The number of wins and losses for each algorithm was determined using U-values. The overall performances were ranked based on the difference between wins and losses of each algorithm.

4.2 Dataset

Real-world nonlinear regression datasets in dynamic environments enable to evaluate the performance of the induced model in real-world conditions. However, the existence of a real drift in the data is unknown or if the drift exists, it may be unknown when exactly it occurs. As such, it becomes difficult to have an in-depth analysis of the behavior of the predictive models. Therefore, an artificially generated dataset with induced drifts becomes favorable.

a) Benchmark Dataset

Auto-generated datasets of 10000 patterns with 100 timesteps were used in the experiments conducted in this work on different types of change period. The datasets were generated using the benchmark nonlinear Bennett5 function computed as [26]:

$$f(x, \theta) = \theta_1 + (\theta_2 + x)^{-\frac{1}{\theta_3}}$$

The starting values for Bennett5 function were provided in the literature. An environmental change is simulated by adding drift to each parameter, $\theta_i = \theta_i + \delta\sigma$ where δ is the drift and σ is the probability of altering the direction of change. The following equation was used to simulate the drift:

$$f(\delta) = 0.6\delta^2 + 0.02\delta + 0.01$$

The impact of the drifts was smaller at the beginning and then improves along with an increase in the frequency (f).

A sliding window of size of 100 patterns slides from one timestep, which consists of 100 patterns, to the next. The change period occurs at severities and frequencies of 1 to 5. The severity of change determines the probability of altering the direction of change, σ, where a value of 5 implies that the reverse direction of change is certain at each change period. The timestep at which the change occurs is determined by the frequency of change and was computed as:

$$changePoint = \frac{f}{10} \times T$$

where T is the total number of iteration and f is the frequency. A high value of f implies that fewer changes were occurring to the dataset.

b) Electricity Pricing

A real-world dataset, Electricity pricing that consists of 27552 data patterns, was also implemented in this work [27]. The Electricity pricing dataset was built on the electricity market in the Australian state of New South Wales. This dataset exhibits both long-term regular changes happening as a result of seasonal changes and short-term irregular changes happening as a result of weather fluctuations.

To determine the electricity price, the current electricity demand is matched with the combination of all available power stations with the least expensive electricity. The task of the proposed model was to induce a predictive model that determines the electricity price from the given parameters.

The sliding window size (ws) was set to 100 data patterns. The training algorithm requires 275 slides to traverse the complete dataset. Given that 100 iterations were executed before the sliding window slides. Therefore, for the training algorithm to traverse the complete dataset, 27 600 iterations were executed.

4.3 Results

The results were analyzed using mean squared errors (E_{MS}) and adjusted coefficient of determination (R_a^2) on training and generalization for different severities and frequencies. The p-values corresponding to the comparison of the training algorithms on $E_{MS}T$ (training) and $E_{MS}G$ (generalization) for 30 independent runs were reported in Appendix 1 where $p \leq 0.0001$ was recorded as 0.0001 for convenience. Table 1 presents the average (avgs) and standard deviation (SD at the 95% confidence interval) of Bennett5 dataset for R_a^2 and E_{MS} on training and generalization for each algorithm.

Table 1. Avgs and SD for R_a^2 and E_{MS} for each algorithm

Algorithm	Training		Generalization	
	R^2	E_{MS}	R^2	E_{MS}
QR_QPSO	0.7075 ± 0.0731	0.3106 ± 0.0142	0.8236 ± 0.0598	0.2183 ± 0.0621
QPSO	0.4227 ± 0.1782	0.3103 ± 0.0097	0.7598 ± 0.0699	0.4504 ± 0.0954
QR_rePSO	0.6169 ± 0.0901	0.3123 ± 0.0099	0.8059 ± 0.0762	0.4043 ± 0.1150
rePSO	0.0769 ± 0.0110	0.3507 ± 0.0223	0.4237 ± 0.0452	0.4992 ± 0.0774
QR_mPSO	0.6407 ± 0.0583	0.3141 ± 0.0132	0.8121 ± 0.0649	0.4807 ± 0.0849
mPSO	0.0912 ± 0.0973	0.3228 ± 0.0192	0.4068 ± 0.0527	0.4271 ± 0.0326

The results presented in Table 1 show that QR_QPSO obtained the best R_a^2 on both training and generalization whereas mPSO obtained the worst performance on generalization and rePSO on training. As presented in Table 1, QR_PSOs yielded improved performances compared to nonQR_PSOs on both R_a^2 and E_{MS}, except for QPSO on R_a^2.

This performance improvement could have been attributed by the capability of the proposed technique to track and adapt the nonlinear regression model as the environment changes. Also, the value of R_a^2 above 0.7 suggests structurally optimal models generated by QR_PSOs. Considering QR_PSOs only, QR_QPSO exhibit superior performance whereas QR_rePSO exhibit the worst performance.

The averages for R_a^2 and EMS on generalization per frequency and severity are graphically illustrated in Fig. 1. As illustrated in Fig. 1, the performance of all training algorithms improved as the frequency increased on both R_a^2 and E_{MS}. However, QR_PSOs exhibit superior performance evident with high R_a^2 and low E_{MS}. Also, QR_QPSO outperformed all other algorithms on both R_a^2 and E_{MS} for all frequencies and severities.

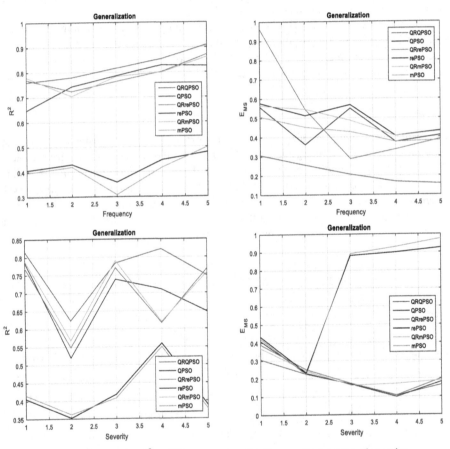

Fig. 1. Averages for R_a^2 and E_{MS} on generalization per frequency and severity

The average ranks obtained on training algorithms for R_a^2 and E_{MS} on both training and generalization for the given frequencies and severities were illustrated in Fig. 2 and Fig. 3. As illustrated in Fig. 2, rePSO and mPSO exhibit the worst performance on both R_a^2 and E_{MS}. On training, QR_rePSO and QR_mPSO exhibit improved performance on

E_{MS}. On generalization, QR_QPSO outperformed all other training algorithms on both R_a^2 and E_{MS}. Generally, as the frequency increased, the performance of nonQR_PSOs deteriorated on both R_a^2 and E_{MS} especially for QPSO.

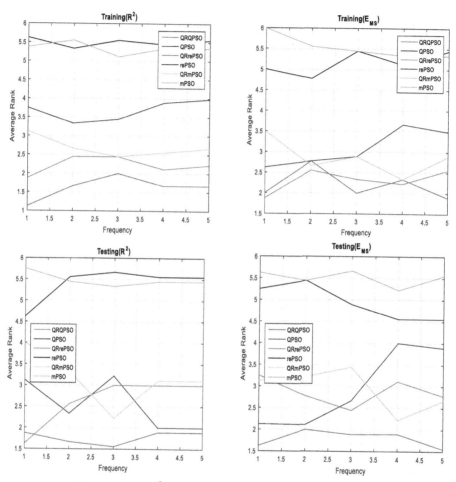

Fig. 2. Ranks of R_a^2 and E_{MS} per frequency on training and testing

As illustrated in Fig. 3, QR_QPSO also outperformed all other algorithms on both R_a^2 and E_{MS} whereas rePSO and mPSO exhibit the worst performance on both R_a^2 and E_{MS}. The performance of QR_mPSO improved as the severity increased to outperform QR_rePSO on generalization on both R_a^2 and E_{MS}. This performance improvement for QR_mPSO suggests the improved adaptive traits of QR_mPSO under severe changing environment.

Generally, the performance of nonQR_PSO on both R_a^2 and E_{MS} deteriorated as the severity increased whereas QR_PSOs exhibit an improved performance as the severity increased which suggests improved adaptive traits to a changing environment.

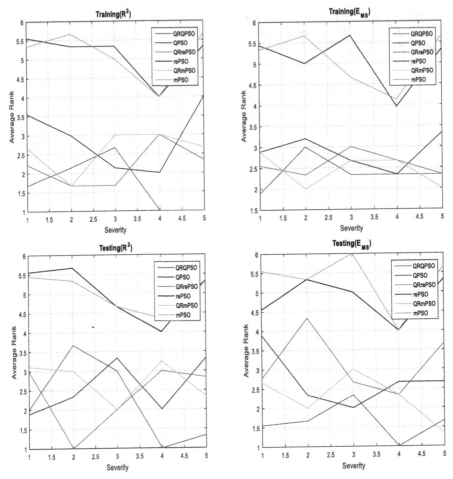

Fig. 3. Ranks of R_a^2 and E_{MS} per severity on training and testing

Table 2 presents the average (avgs) and standard deviation (SD at the 95% confidence interval) for R_a^2 and E_{MS} on training and generalization for each algorithm on Electricity pricing dataset.

As observed in Table 1, the results presented in Table 2 show that QR_QPSO obtained the best R_a^2 on both training and generalization whereas rePSO obtained the worst performance on generalization and training. Also, QR_PSOs yielded improved performances compared to nonQR_PSOs on both R_a^2 and E_{MS}. As already explained, the performance improvement could have been attributed by the capability of the proposed technique to track and adapt the nonlinear regression model as the environment changes.

Table 2. Avgs and SD for R_a^2 and E_{MS} for Electricity Pricing Dataset

Algorithm	Training		Generalization	
	R^2	E_{MS}	R^2	E_{MS}
QR_QPSO	0.8874 ± 0.1794	0.0001 ± 0.0004	0.8097 ± 0.2979	0.0011 ± 0.0005
QPSO	0.8646 ± 0.1630	0.0001 ± 0.0004	0.7316 ± 0.3697	0.0041 ± 0.0010
QR_rePSO	0.8671 ± 0.1496	0.0001 ± 0.0004	0.7744 ± 0.3384	0.0032 ± 0.0011
rePSO	0.6670 ± 0.1931	0.0003 ± 0.0012	0.7259 ± 0.3234	0.0043 ± 0.0007
QR_mPSO	0.8694 ± 0.1712	0.0001 ± 0.0003	0.7837 ± 0.2649	0.0028 ± 0.0008
mPSO	0.7108 ± 0.1253	0.0002 ± 0.0009	0.7305 ± 0.3234	0.0042 ± 0.0009

5 Conclusion

The obtained results suggest the capability of the proposed dynamic PSO-based nonlinear regression technique to track and adapt the induced model as the environment changes. Therefore, yield improved performance and consequently, outperformed the dynamic PSOs on the given datasets. The hybridization of the dynamic PSOs with QR decomposition technique indeed decreased the performance deterioration of the induced model that resulted from the environmental changes. The obtained values of R_a^2 suggests that the dynamic PSO-based nonlinear regression technique induced structurally optimal nonlinear regression models.

Future work could extend the dynamic PSO-based nonlinear regression technique to induce the nonlinear regression models using the most recent and relevant data points from the presented dataset by excluding the irrelevant data points provided in the data window. Also, to perform a comparative study of dynamic PSO-based nonlinear regression technique with non-PSO machine learning approaches and neural networks.

References

1. Gray, R.A., Docherty, P.D., Fisk, L.M., Murray, R.: A modified approach to objective surface generation within the Gauss-Newton parameter identification to ignore outlier data points. Biomed. Signal Process. Control **30**, 162–169 (2016)
2. Basics on Continuous Optimization, November 2019. http://www.brnt.eu/phd/node10.html
3. Erdoğmuş, P., Ekiz, S.: Nonlinear regression using particle swarm optimization and genetic algorithm. Int. J. Comput. Appl. **153**(6), 28–36 (2016)
4. Potgieter, G., Engelbrecht, A.P.: Genetic algorithm for structurally optimisation of learned polynomial expressions. Appl. Math. Comput. **186**, 1441–1466 (2007)
5. Özel, T., Karpat, Y.: Identification of constitutive material model parameters for high-strain rate metal cutting conditions using evolutionary computational algorithms. Mater. Manuf. Processes **22**(5), 659–667 (2007)
6. Hornik, K.: Multilayer feedforward networks are universal approximators. Neural Netw. **2**, 359–366 (1989)

7. Atici, U.: Prediction of the strength of mineral admixture concrete using multivariable regression analysis and an artificial neural network. Expert Syst. Appl. **38**(8), 9609–9618 (2011)
8. Lu, Z., Yang, C., Qin, D., Luo, Y., Momayez, M.: Estimating ultrasonic time-of-flight through echo signal envelope and modified Gauss-Newton method. Measurement **94**, 355–363 (2016)
9. Cheng, S., Zhao, C., Wu, J., Shi, Y.: Particle swarm optimization in regression analysis: a case study. In: Tan, Y., Shi, Y., Mo, H. (eds.) ICSI 2013. LNCS, vol. 7928, pp. 55–63. Springer, Heidelberg (2013). https://doi.org/10.1007/978-3-642-38703-6_6
10. Abdullah, S.M., Yassin, A.I.M., Tahir, N.M.: Particle swarm optimization and least squares estimation of NARMAX. ARPN J. Eng. Appl. Sci. **10**(22), 10722–10726 (2015)
11. Blackwell, T.M.: Particle swarm optimization in dynamic environments. Evol. Comput. Dyn. Uncertain Environ. **51**, 29–49 (2007)
12. Draper, N.R., Smith, H.: Applied Regression Analysis, vol. 326. Wiley, Hoboken (1998)
13. Hastie, T., Tibshirani, R., Friedman, J.: The Elements of Statistical Learning. SSS. Springer, New York (2009). https://doi.org/10.1007/978-0-387-84858-7
14. Fraleigh, J.B., Beauregard, R.A.: Linear Algebra, 3rd edn. Addison-Wesley Publishing Company, Upper Saddle River (1995)
15. Stigler, S.M.: Gauss and the invention of least squares. Ann. Stat. **9**(3), 465–474 (1981)
16. Yang, S., Yao, X.: A comparative study on particle swarm optimization in dynamic environments. In: Yang, S., Yao, X. (eds.) Evolutionary Computation for DOPs, pp. 109–136. Springer, Heidelberg (2013)
17. Blackwell, T., Branke, J.: Multi-swarm optimisation in dynamic environments. Appl. Evol. Comput. **3005**, 489–500 (2004)
18. Blackwell, T.M., Bentley, P.J.: Don't push me! Collision-avoidance swarms. In: Proceedings of the IEE Congress on Evolutionary Computation, vol. 2, pp. 1691–1696 (2002)
19. Blackwell, T.M., Bentley, P.J.: Dynamic search with charged swarms. In: Proceedings of the Genetic and Evolutionary Computation Conference, vol. 2, pp. 19–26 (2002)
20. Blackwell, T.M., Branke, J.: Multiswarms, exclusion, and anti-convergence in dynamic environments. IEEE Trans. Evol. Comput. **10**(4), 459–472 (2006)
21. Richter, H.: Detecting change in dynamic fitness landscapes. In: Proceedings of Congress on Evolutionary Computation, pp. 1613–1620 (2009)
22. Branke, J.: Evolutionary Optimization in Dynamic Environments. Kluwer, Norwell (2002)
23. Parrott, D., Li, X.: Locating and tracking multiple dynamic optima by a particle swarm model using speciation. IEEE Trans. Evol. Comput. **10**(4), 440–458 (2006)
24. Mathworks: MATLAB. www.mathworks.com
25. McKnight, P.E., Najab, J.: Issues with performance measures for dynamic multi-objective optimization. In: Proceedings of IEEE Symposium on Computational Intelligence in Dynamic and Uncertain Environments, pp. 17–24 (2013)
26. Bennett, L., Swartzendruber, L., Brown, H.: Superconductivity magnetization modeling. In: NIST (1994)
27. Harries, M.: Splice-2 comparative evaluation: electricity pricing. Technical Report UNSW-CSE-TR-9905. Artificial Intelligence Group, School of Computer Science and Engineering, The University of New South Wales, Sydney 2052, Australia (1999)

Theta Palindromes in Theta Conjugates

Kalpana Mahalingam⬤, Palak Pandoh$^{(\boxtimes)}$⬤, and Anuran Maity⬤

Department of Mathematics, Indian Institute of Technology Madras,
Chennai 600036, India
kmahalingam@iitm.ac.in, palakpandohiitmadras@gmail.com,
anuran.maity@gmail.com

Abstract. A DNA string is a Watson-Crick (WK) palindrome when the complement of its reverse is equal to itself. The Watson-Crick mapping θ is an involution that is also an antimorphism. θ-conjugates of a word is a generalization of conjugates of a word that incorporates the notion of WK-involution θ. In this paper, we study the distribution of palindromes and Watson-Crick palindromes, also known as θ-palindromes among both the set of conjugates and θ-conjugates of a word w. We also consider some general properties of the set $C_\theta(w)$, i.e., the set of θ-conjugates of a word w, and characterize words w such that $|C_\theta(w)| = |w| + 1$, i.e., with the maximum number of elements in $C_\theta(w)$. We also find the structure of words that have at least one (WK)-palindrome in $C_\theta(w)$.

Keywords: Theoretical DNA computing · Combinatorics of words · Palindromes · Watson-Crick palindromes · Conjugacy

1 Introduction

The study of sequences have applications in numerous fields such as biology, computer science, mathematics, and physics. DNA molecules, which carry the genetic information in almost all organisms, play an important role in molecular biology (see [4–6,16]). DNA computing experiments use information-encoding strings that possess Watson-Crick complementarity property between DNA single-strands which allows information-encoding strands to potentially interact. Formally, the Watson-Crick complementarity property on strings over Σ is an involution θ with the additional property that $\theta(uv) = \theta(v)\theta(u)$ for all strings $u, v \in \Sigma^*$ where θ is an involution, i.e., θ^2 equals the identity.

The notion of θ-palindrome was defined in [9] to study palindromes from the perspective of DNA computing. It was defined independently in [14], where closure operators for θ-palindromes were considered. The classical results on conjugacy and commutativity of words are present in [17]. In [3], the authors study the properties of θ-primitive words. They prove the existence of a unique θ-primitive root of a given word, and provided some constraints under which two distinct words share their θ-primitive root. The combinatorial properties of strings in connection to partial words were investigated in [2]. The notions

© Springer Nature Switzerland AG 2020
C. Martín-Vide et al. (Eds.): TPNC 2020, LNCS 12494, pp. 145–156, 2020.
https://doi.org/10.1007/978-3-030-63000-3_12

of conjugacy and commutativity was generalized to incorporate the notion of Watson-Crick complementarity of DNA single-strands in [9]. The authors define and study properties of Watson-Crick conjugate and commutative words, as well as Watson-Crick palindromes. They provide a complete characterization of the set of all words that are not Watson-Crick palindromes. Some properties that link the Watson-Crick palindromes to classical notions such as that of primitive words are established in [10]. The authors show that the set of Watson-Crick-palindromic words that cannot be written as the product of two non-empty Watson-Crick-palindromes equals the set of primitive Watson-Crick-palindromes.

In molecular biology, it is important to retrieve information from DNA sequences, align these sequences and to analyse the exact orders of DNA sequences. Researchers have considered several chromosomal operations on DNA sequences including inversions, pseudo-inversions, translocations, swaps and pseudoknots in the past. Swap is an important operation for bio-sequences such as DNA or RNA sequences, and is closely related to mutations. This operation is extensively studied in [1,11,12]. We consider a special kind of swap operation called θ-conjugate where θ is an antimorphic involution. In this paper, we extend the notion of palindromes in conjugacy class of a word to Watson-Crick palindromes and Watson-Crick conjugates of a word. The number of palindromes in the conjugacy class of a word is studied in [7]. We investigate the set of θ-conjugates of a word. We study the number of Watson-Crick palindromes in a conjugacy class. We then consider the number of palindromes and Watson-Crick palindromes in the Watson-Crick conjugacy set of a given word.

The paper is organised as follows. In Sect. 3, we study the properties of the set of θ-conjugates of a word. We first show that for a given word w, the maximum number of elements in the θ-conjugacy of a word is $|w| + 1$, and we also characterize the words that attain this maximum number. In Sect. 4, we study the distribution of θ-palindromes in the conjugacy class of a word. We show that the conjugacy class of a word can contain at most two distinct palindromes. In Sect. 5, we study the number of palindromes in the set of θ-conjugates of the word. We find the structure of the words which have at least one palindrome among its θ-conjugates. Lastly, in Sect. 5, we analyse the number of θ-palindromes in the set of θ-conjugates of a word. We find the structure of the words which have at least one θ-palindrome among its θ-conjugates. We end the paper with some concluding remarks.

2   Basic Definitions and Notations

An alphabet Σ is a finite non-empty set of symbols. A word over Σ is defined to be a finite sequence of symbols from Σ. Σ^* denotes the set of all words over Σ including the empty word λ and $\Sigma^+ = \Sigma^* \setminus \lambda$. The length of a word $w \in \Sigma^*$ is the number of symbols in a word and is denoted by $|w|$. The reversal of $w = a_1 a_2 \cdots a_n$ is defined to be a string $w^R = a_n \cdots a_2 a_1$ where $a_i \in \Sigma$. $Alph(w)$ denotes the set of all sub-words of w of length 1. A word w is said to be a palindrome if $w = w^R$.

A word $w \in \Sigma^+$ is called *primitive* if $w = u^i$ implies $w = u$ and $i = 1$. Let Q denote the set of all primitive words. For every word $w \in \Sigma^+$, there exists a unique word $\rho(w) \in \Sigma^+$, called the *primitive root* of w, such that $\rho(w) \in Q$ and $w = \rho(w)^n$ for some $n \geq 1$. A function $\theta : \Sigma^* \to \Sigma^*$ is said to be an *antimorphism* if $\theta(uv) = \theta(v)\theta(u)$. The function θ is called an *involution* if θ^2 is an identity on Σ^*.

A word $u \in \Sigma^*$ is said to be a factor of w if $w = xuy$ where $x, y \in \Sigma^*$. If $x = \lambda$, then u is a prefix of w and if $y = \lambda$, then u is a suffix of w. A word $u \in \Sigma^*$ is a conjugate of $w \in \Sigma^*$ if there exists $v \in \Sigma^*$ such that $uv = vw$. The set of all conjugates of w, denoted as $C(w)$, is the conjugacy class of w. A word u is a θ-conjugate of another word w if $uv = \theta(v)w$ for some $v \in \Sigma^*$. The set of all θ-conjugates of w is denoted by $C_\theta(w)$. For an antimorphic involution θ, a finite word w is called a θ-palindrome if $w = \theta(w)$. Consider $\Sigma = \{a, b\}$ and an antimorphic involution θ such that $\theta(a) = b$ and $\theta(b) = a$. Then, the word $abab$ is a θ-palindrome but not a palindrome. Throughout the paper, we take θ to be an antimorphic involution. For all other concepts in formal language theory and combinatorics on words, the reader is referred to [8, 13].

3   Conjugacy and Theta-Conjugacy of a Word

In this section, we study the conjugacy class and the θ-conjugacy set $C_\theta(w)$ for a word w. We show some general properties of the set $C_\theta(w)$. We also characterize words for which $|C_\theta(w)| = |w| + 1$ which is the maximum number of of θ-conjugates that a word of length $|w|$ can have.

We recall the following result from [9] for θ-conjugates of a word.

Proposition 1. *Let u be a θ-conjugate of w. Then, for an antimorphic involution θ, there exists $x, y \in \Sigma^*$ such that either $u = xy$ and $w = y\theta(x)$ or $w = \theta(u)$.*

Thus, we can deduce that for a word w,

$$C_\theta(w) = \{\theta(v)u \ : \ w = uv, \ u, v \in \Sigma^*\}$$

Also, Proposition 1 implies that the maximum number of elements in $C_\theta(w)$ is $|w| + 1$. It is also clear that if w is a θ-palindrome, then the maximum number of elements in $C_\theta(w)$ is $|w|$. We illustrate the concept of θ-conjugacy of a word with the help of some examples and show that the number of elements in the θ-conjugacy of a word w may or may not reach the maximum.

Example 2. Consider $\Sigma = \{a, b, c\}$ and θ such that $\theta(a) = b$, $\theta(b) = a$, $\theta(c) = c$.

1. If $w = aac$, then $C_\theta(w) = \{aac, caa, cba, cbb\}$ and $|C_\theta(w)| = 4 = |w| + 1$. Note that aac is a primitive word that is neither a palindrome nor a θ-palindrome.
2. If $w = abb$, then $C_\theta(w) = \{abb, aab, aaa\}$ and $|C_\theta(w)| = 3 < |w| + 1 = 4$. Note that abb is a primitive word that is neither a palindrome nor a θ-palindrome.
3. If $w = bccb$, then $C_\theta(w) = \{bccb, abcc, acbc, accb, acca\}$ and $|C_\theta(w)| = 5 = |w| + 1$. Note that $bccb$ is a palindrome.

4. If $w = aba$, then $C_\theta(w) = \{aba, bab, baa\}$ and $|C_\theta(w)| = 3 < |w| + 1$. Note that w is a palindrome.
5. If $w = ab$, then $C_\theta(ab) = \{ab, aa\}$ and $|C_\theta(w)| = 2 = |w|$. Note that w is a θ-palindrome.
6. If $w = abcab$, then $C_\theta(w) = \{abcab, aabca, ababc, abcaa\}$ and $|C_\theta(w)| = 4 < |w|$. Note that w is a θ-palindrome.
7. If $w = aaa$, then $C_\theta(w) = \{aaa, baa, bba, bbb\}$ and $|C_\theta(w)| = |w| + 1 = 4$. Note that w is not a primitive word but $|C_\theta(w)| = |w| + 1$.

It is well known that the maximum number of elements in a conjugacy class of a word w is $|w|$ and it is attained if w is primitive. This is not true in general for θ-conjugacy of w. It is clear from Example 2 that there are primitive words with the maximum number of elements in the set $C_\theta(w)$ to be less than $|w|$, equal to $|w|$ and equal to $|w| + 1$. It is also clear from Proposition 1 and Example 2 that the maximum number of elements in the set $C_\theta(w)$, i.e., $|w| + 1$, can be attained by both primitive as well as a non-primitive word.

We now characterize words w with exactly $|w| + 1$ elements in $C_\theta(w)$. We first recall some general results from [15].

Lemma 3. *Let $u, v, w \in \Sigma^+$.*

- *If $uv = vu$ then, u and v are powers of a common primitive word.*
- *If $uv = vw$ then, for $k \geq 0$, $x \in \Sigma^+$ and $y \in \Sigma^*$, $u = xy$, $v = (xy)^k x$, $w = yx$.*

We have the following result.

Proposition 4. *Let $w \in \Sigma^*$. Then, $|C_\theta(w)| = |w| + 1$ iff w is not of the form $(\alpha\beta)^{i+1}\alpha v$ where $\alpha, v \in \Sigma^*$, $\beta \in \Sigma^+$, $i \geq 0$ and α, β are θ-palindromes.*

Proof. Let $w \in \Sigma^*$. We prove that $|C_\theta(w)| < |w| + 1$ iff $w = (\alpha\beta)^{i+1}\alpha v$ where $\alpha, v \in \Sigma^*$, $\beta \in \Sigma^+$, $i \geq 0$ and α, β are θ-palindromes.

Let $|C_\theta(w)| < |w| + 1$, then at least two θ-conjugates of w are equal. Let $\theta(v)u$ and $\theta(y)x$ be the two θ-conjugates of w that are equal where $u, v, x, y \in \Sigma^*$ for $w = uv = xy$. Without loss of generality, let us assume that $|u| > |x|$. Then, $|v| < |y|$, $u = xy_1$ and $y = y_1v$ for some $y_1 \in \Sigma^+$. Now,

$$\theta(v)u = \theta(y)x \implies \theta(v)xy_1 = \theta(y_1v)x$$

$$\implies \theta(v)xy_1 = \theta(v)\theta(y_1)x \implies xy_1 = \theta(y_1)x.$$

Then by Lemma 3, $\theta(y_1) = \alpha\beta$, $x = (\alpha\beta)^i\alpha$ where $\beta \in \Sigma^+$, $\alpha \in \Sigma^*, i \geq 0$ such that α and β are θ-palindromes. Hence, $w = uv = xy = (\alpha\beta)^{i+1}\alpha v$ and α, β are θ-palindromes.

Conversely, let $w = (\alpha\beta)^{i+1}\alpha v$ where $\alpha, v \in \Sigma^*$, $\beta \in \Sigma^+$, $i \geq 0$ and α, β are θ-palindromes. Now, $w' = \theta(v)(\alpha\beta)^{i+1}\alpha \in C_\theta(w)$ and $w'' = \theta(\beta\alpha v)(\alpha\beta)^i\alpha \in C_\theta(w)$. Consider

$$w'' = \theta(v)\theta(\beta\alpha)(\alpha\beta)^i\alpha = \theta(v)\alpha\beta(\alpha\beta)^i\alpha = \theta(v)(\alpha\beta)^{i+1}\alpha = w'.$$

Therefore, $|C_\theta(w)| < |w| + 1$. □

We recall the following from [17].

Lemma 5. *Let $u = z^i$ for a primitive word z over Σ. Then the conjugacy class of u contains exactly $|z|$ words.*

We show that Lemma 5 do not hold for θ-conjugacy. Infact we show that for any word z, the number of θ-conjugates in z^i may not be equal to that of the number of θ-conjugates in the word z. We illustrate with the help of an example.

Example 6. Let $\Sigma = \{a, b, c\}$, and θ such that $\theta(a) = b, \theta(b) = a, \theta(c) = c$. Then,
1. $C_\theta(ac) = \{ac, ca, cb\}$;
2. $C_\theta((ac)^2) = \{acac, caca, cbac, cbca, cbcb\}$;
3. $C_\theta((ac)^3) = \{acacac, cacaca, cbacac, cbcaca, cbcbac, cbcbca, cbcbcb\}$.

We show that the number of θ-conjugates of a word z^i are greater than the number of θ-conjugates of a word z^j for $i > j$ and $z \in \Sigma^*$ and $|C_\theta(z)| \neq 1$. We have the following result.

Lemma 7. *Let $z \in \Sigma^*$. If $|C_\theta(z)| \neq 1$, then $|C_\theta(z)| < |C_\theta(z^2)|$.*

Proof. Let $z \in \Sigma^*$ such that $|C_\theta(z)| \neq 1$. Let $w = \theta(v)u \in C_\theta(z)$ such that $z = uv$. Now $z^2 = zz = uz'v$ where $z' = vu$. Then, $w_1 = \theta(v)uz' \in C_\theta(z^2)$. So for each element w in $C_\theta(z)$, there exist an element w_1 in $C_\theta(z^2)$ such that w is a prefix of w_1. Let $z = u_1v_1$. Then $w' = \theta(v_1)u_1 \in C_\theta(z)$. So there exist an element $w_1' = \theta(v_1)u_1z''$ in $C_\theta(z^2)$ where $z'' = v_1u_1$. Now if $w \neq w'$ then $w_1 \neq w_1'$. Hence, $|C_\theta(z)| \leq |C_\theta(z^2)|$.

Now $\theta(uv) \in C_\theta(z)$. Note that the words $\alpha_1 = \theta(vuv)u$ and $\alpha_2 = \theta(uv)uv \in C_\theta(z^2)$ have $\theta(uv)$ as their prefix. If $\alpha_1 = \alpha_2$, we get $\theta(v)u = uv$ such that $z = uv$ for all $u, v \in \Sigma^*$. Thus, we get $\theta(v)u = uv$ for all $u, v \in \Sigma^*$, so $C_\theta(z) = \{uv\}$, i.e., $|C_\theta(z)| = 1$ which is a contradiction. Therefore, there exist at least two distinct elements α_1 and α_2 in $C_\theta(z^2)$ whose prefix is $\theta(uv)$. Thus $|C_\theta(z)| < |C_\theta(z^2)|$. $\square$

We deduce an immediate result.

Corollary 8. *Let $z \in \Sigma^*$. If $|C_\theta(z)| \neq 1$, then $|C_\theta(z^i)| < |C_\theta(z^{i+1})|$ for $i \geq 1$.*

We recall the following from [10].

Proposition 9. *If $uv = \theta(v)u$ and θ is an antimorphic involution, then $u = x(yx)^i$, $v = yx$ where $i \geq 0$ and u, x, y are θ-palindromes, where $x \in \Sigma^*$, $y \in \Sigma^+$.*

Lemma 10. *Let $z \in \Sigma^*$ then $|C_\theta(z)| = 1$ iff $z = a^n$ such that $\theta(a) = a$ for $a \in \Sigma$.*

Proof. Let $|C_\theta(z)| = 1$, then z is a θ-palindrome. So, z is of the form $uv\theta(u)$ where v is a θ-palindrome. Let $u = au'$ where $a \in \Sigma$. As $|C_\theta(z)| = 1$, we have, $z = au'v\theta(u')\theta(a) = aau'v\theta(u')$. Then, $u'v\theta(u')\theta(a) = au'v\theta(u')$. Take $u'v\theta(u') = u_1$, then $u_1\theta(a) = au_1$. By Proposition 9, we have $\theta(u_1) = x(yx)^i$ and $\theta(a) = yx$ where $x \in \Sigma^*$, $y \in \Sigma^+$. Then, $x = \lambda$ and as y is a θ-palindrome, $u_1 = a^i$ and $\theta(a) = a$. Hence, $z = a^{i+1}$. Converse is straightforward. $\square$

Hence, we deduce the following by Corollary 8 and Lemma 10.

Theorem 11. *Let $z \in \Sigma^*$ such that $z \neq a^n$ for $a \in \Sigma$ such that $\theta(a) = a$, then $|C_\theta(z^i)| < |C_\theta(z^{i+1})|$ for $i \geq 1$.*

4   Theta Palindromes in the Conjugacy Class of a Word

The distribution of palindromes in the conjugacy class of a word was studied in [7]. The authors proved that there are at most two distinct palindromes in the conjugacy class of a given word. In this section, we show an analogous result pertaining to the distribution of θ-palindromes and prove that the conjugacy class of any given word also contains at most two θ-palindromes. We also provide the structure of such words. We begin by recalling the following from [7].

Lemma 12. *If the conjugacy class of a word contains two distinct palindromes, say uv and vu, then there exists a word x and a number i such that xx^R is primitive, $uv = (xx^R)^i$, and $vu = (x^R x)^i$.*

In this section, we study the distribution of θ-palindromes in the conjugacy class of a word.

We first observe the following.

Proposition 13. *If w^{n_1} is a θ-palindrome, then w^{n_2} is a θ-palindrome for $n_1, n_2 \geq 1$.*

We recall the following from [7].

Lemma 14. *If $u \neq u^R$ and $uu^R = z^i$ for a primitive word z then, i is odd and $z = xx^R$ for some x.*

We deduce the following.

Lemma 15. *Suppose $u \neq \theta(u)$ and $u\theta(u) = z^i$ for a primitive word z. Then, i is odd and $z = x\theta(x)$ for some x.*

Proof. If i is even, then $u\theta(u) = (z^{\frac{i}{2}})^2$. Hence, $u = \theta(u)$, contradicting the conditions of the lemma. So i is odd and then $|z|$ is even. Let $z = xx'$, where $|x| = |x'|$. We see that x is a prefix of u and x' is a suffix of $\theta(u)$. Hence, $x' = \theta(x)$, as required.   □

Lemma 16. *If the conjugacy class of a word contains two distinct θ-palindromes, say uv and vu, then there exists a word x and a number i such that $x\theta(x)$ is primitive, $uv = (x\theta(x))^i$, and $vu = (\theta(x)x)^i$.*

Proof. We use induction on $n = |uv|$. For $n = 2$, if there are two distinct θ-palindromes, then they must be of the form $x\theta(x)$ and $\theta(x)x$ where $x \in \Sigma$ and $x \neq \theta(x)$, i.e., $x\theta(x)$ is primitive. For the inductive step, assume $|u| \geq |v|$ without loss of generality. If $|u| = |v|$, then $v = \theta(u)$. By Lemma 15, we get $uv = (x\theta(x))^i$, $vu = (\theta(x)x)^i$ for a primitive word $x\theta(x)$ and $i \geq 1$.

Now let $|u| > |v|$. Then v is a prefix and suffix of $\theta(u)$. $\theta(u) = vw_1 = w_2v$ for $w_1, w_2 \in \Sigma^*$. This implies by Lemma 3, we obtain $v = (st)^i s$, and hence, $\theta(u) = (st)^{(i+1)}s$, for $s \neq \lambda$, and $i \geq 0$. Looking at the central factor of the palindromes

$$uv = (\theta(s)\theta(t))^{(i+1)}\theta(s)(st)^i s$$

$$vu = (st)^i s(\theta(s)\theta(t))^{(i+1)}\theta(s),$$

we see that st and ts are also θ-palindromes. If $t = \lambda$, then s is a θ-palindrome, implying $uv = vu$, which is a contradiction as uv and vu are distinct. If $st = ts$, then by Lemma 3, both s and t are powers of some primitive word z and by Proposition 13, s, t, and z are θ-palindromes, which again implie $uv = vu$ which is a contradiction. Thus, $st \neq ts$ with $|st| < n$ and by inductive hypothesis we get $st = (x\theta(x))^j$, $ts = (\theta(x)x)^j$ for some primitive word $x\theta(x)$. Then, we have

$$v = (x\theta(x))^{ji}s = s(\theta(x)x)^{ji} \tag{1}$$

Note that, if $s = (x\theta(x))^k x_1$ where $x = x_1 x_2$, then Eq. 1 becomes

$$(x_1 x_2 \theta(x_1 x_2))^{j(i+1)}(x\theta(x))^k x_1 = (x\theta(x))^k x_1 (\theta(x_1 x_2)x_1 x_2)^{j(i+1)}$$

Then by the comparing suffix, $x_2\theta(x)x_1 = \theta(x)x_1 x_2$ which is a contradiction, since all conjugates of $x\theta(x)$ are distinct by Lemma 5. The argument for the case when $s = (x\theta(x))^k x\theta(x_2)$ is similar. If $s = x(\theta(x)x)^k$, then Eq. 1 becomes

$$(x\theta(x))^{ji}(x\theta(x))^k = (x\theta(x))^k(\theta(x)x)^{ji}$$

and by comparing the suffix, we get $x\theta(x) = \theta(x)x$ which is a contradiction as $x\theta(x)$ is primitive. Thus, $s = (x\theta(x))^k x$ for some $k, 0 \leq k < j$. Then we can easily compute $t, \theta(s)$, and $\theta(t)$ by using s (we know the value of st) to get $uv = (x\theta(x))^{2j(i+1)}$, $vu = (\theta(x)x)^{2j(i+1)}$. Hence, the proof. $\qquad\square$

We give examples of words that have zero, one and two θ-palindromes each in their conjugacy class.

Example 17. Let $\Sigma = \{a, b, c\}$, and θ such that $\theta(a) = b$, $\theta(b) = a$ and $\theta(c) = c$. Then

1. The word aaa has zero θ-palindromes in its conjugacy class.
2. The word $cabab$ has exactly one θ-palindrome $abcab$ in its conjugacy class.
3. The word $abab$ has two exactly two θ-palindromes $abab$ and $baba$ in its conjugacy class.

We know from Example 17 that there exists words that contain exactly zero, one or two θ-palindromes in their conjugacy class. However, in the following result, we show that a conjugacy class of any word contains at most two distinct θ-palindromes and we also find the structure of words that contain exactly two θ-palindromes in their conjugacy class.

Theorem 18. *The conjugacy class of a word contains at most two θ-palindromes. It has exactly two θ-palindromes iff it contains a word of the form $(a\theta(a))^l$, where $a\theta(a)$ is primitive and $l \geq 1$. Note that such a word has even length.*

Proof. It is clear from Example 17 that a word can have upto 2 θ-palindromes. WLOG, we may assume that w is primitive. Suppose there are two θ-palindromic conjugates of a word w, then by Lemma 16, they are of the form $uv = x\theta(x)$ and $vu = \theta(x)x$ where $x\theta(x)$ is primitive. We show that the conjugacy class of w contains no other θ-palindromes.

Consider the conjugacy class of $w = x\theta(x)$. Let u_1 and u_2 be such that $u_1 u_2 = x\theta(x)$ and $u_2 u_1$ is a θ-palindrome. If $|u_1| \neq |u_2|$, say $|u_1| < |u_2|$, then we apply the same argument in Lemma 16 and obtain $u_1 u_2 = (y\theta(y))^{2k}$ for some y and k. But this is impossible, because $u_1 u_2 = x\theta(x)$ is primitive. Hence, $u_1 = u_2$, and $u_2 u_1 = \theta(x)x$. Thus, the conjugacy class contains exactly two θ-palindromes and the words are of the structure described in Lemma 16.   □

5   Palindromes in the Set of Theta-Conjugates of a Word

The concept of θ-conjugacy of a word was introduced in [9] to incorporate the notion of Watson-Crick involution map to the conjugacy relation. In this section, we count the number of distinct palindromes in $C_\theta(w)$, $w \in \Sigma^*$. We find the structure of words which have at least one palindrome in the set of their θ-conjugates. We also show that if a word is a palindrome, then there can be at most two palindromes among its θ-conjugates.

It is clear from Example 2, that the words acc, abb and aaa have zero, one and two palindromes, respectively, in their respective conjugacy classes. We now find the structure of words with at least one palindrome among their θ conjugates.

Theorem 19. *Given $w \in \Sigma^*$, $C_\theta(w)$ contains at least one palindrome iff $w = u\theta(x^R)x$ or $w = yv\theta(y^R)$ where $u, v, x, y \in \Sigma^*$ and u, v are palindromes.*

Proof. We first show the converse. Let $w = u\theta(x^R)x$, for a palindrome u such that $u, x \in \Sigma^*$. Then, $\theta(x)u\theta(x^R) \in C_\theta(w)$ is a palindrome. Similarly, for $w = yv\theta(y^R)$ where $v, y \in \Sigma^*$ and v is a palindrome, $y^R\theta(v)y \in C_\theta(w)$ is a palindrome. Therefore, when $w = u\theta(x^R)x$ or $w = yv\theta(y^R)$ for palindromes u and v, $C_\theta(w)$ contains at least one palindrome. Now, let there exist at least one palindrome in $C_\theta(w)$. Let $w = uv$ where $u, v \in \Sigma^*$ such that $\theta(v)u$ is a palindrome in $C_\theta(w)$. Then, we have the following cases:

1. Let $|u| < |v|$ and let $v = v_1 v_2$ such that $|v_2| = |u|$. Now, $\theta(v)u = \theta(v_2)\theta(v_1)u$. Since, $\theta(v)u$ is a palindrome and $|v_2| = |u|$, we get $\theta(v_2) = u^R$ and $\theta(v_1)$ is a palindrome. Then,

$$w = uv = uv_1 v_2 = uv_1\theta(u^R).$$

   Since $\theta(v_1)$ is a palindrome, v_1 is a palindrome.
2. If $|u| = |v|$ then, $\theta(v) = u^R$, i.e., $v = \theta(u^R)$, and hence, $w = uv = u\theta(u^R)$.
3. Let $|u| > |v|$ and let $u = u_1 u_2$ such that $|u_2| = |v|$. Since, $\theta(v)u = \theta(v)u_1 u_2 = u^R\theta(v^R)$ we obtain, $u_2 = \theta(v^R)$ and u_1 a palindrome. Then, $w = uv = u_1 u_2 v = u_1\theta(v^R)v$.

Hence, in all cases, either $w = u\theta(x^R)x$ or $w = yv\theta(y^R)$ where $u, v, x, y \in \Sigma^*$ and u, v are palindromes. $\qquad\qquad\qquad\qquad\qquad\qquad\qquad\qquad\qquad\qquad\square$

It is evident from the definition of θ-conjugacy of a word that, $C_\theta(w)$ contains both w and $\theta(w)$. Hence, if w is a palindrome, then $C_\theta(w)$ contains at least two palindromes w and $\theta(w)$. In the following, we show that for a palindrome w, w and $\theta(w)$ are the only palindromes in the set of all θ-conjugates of w.

Theorem 20. *For a palindrome w, the number of palindromes in $C_\theta(w)$ is atmost two and is exactly two if $w \neq \theta(w)$.*

Proof. Let w be a palindrome. Then $\theta(w)$ is also a palindrome. Suppose there exists a $w' = \theta(v)u \in C_\theta(w)$ where $w = uv$ such that w' is a palindrome, then $\theta(v)u = u^R\theta(v^R)$. We have the following cases.

Case I: If $|v| > |u|$, then there exists a $v' \in \Sigma^+$ such that $\theta(v')u = \theta(v^R)$. We then have, $\theta(u)v' = v^R$ i.e., $v = v'^R\theta(u^R)$. Now, $w = uv = uv'^R\theta(u^R)$. As w is a palindrome, $u^R = \theta(u^R)$, i.e., $u = \theta(u)$. Then, $w' = \theta(v)u = \theta(v)\theta(u) = \theta(uv) = \theta(w)$.

Case II: If $|v| = |u|$, then $\theta(v) = u^R$ and since w is a palindrome, we have, $v = u^R$ which implies $v = \theta(v)$ and $u = \theta(u)$. Thus, $w = uu^R$ and $w' = \theta(v)u = \theta(u^R)u\theta(u^R)\theta(u) = \theta(w)$.

Case III: If $|u| > |v|$, then v^R is a prefix of u and $\theta(v^R)$ is a suffix of u since both w and w' are palindromes. If $|u| \leq 2|v|$ and since v^R is a prefix of u and $\theta(v^R)$ is a suffix of u, then $u = v_2^R v_1^R\theta(v_2^R)$ with $v = v_1v_2$ such that $|v_1| = 2|v| - |u|$ and $v_1^R = \theta(v_1^R)$. Thus, $\theta(u) = u$, and hence, $\theta(w) = \theta(v)\theta(u) = w'$. If $|u| > 2|v|$, then $u = v^R\alpha\theta(v^R)$ for some $\alpha \in \Sigma^+$. Since $w = uv$, $w' = \theta(v)u$ and $\theta(w)$ are palindromes, we get

$$w = uv = v^R\alpha\theta(v^R)v = v^Ru^R = v^R\theta(v)\alpha^Rv; \qquad (2)$$

$$\theta(w) = \theta(v)\theta(u) = \theta(v)v^R\theta(\alpha)\theta(v^R) = \theta(u^R)\theta(v^R) = \theta(v)\theta(\alpha^R)v\theta(v^R). \quad (3)$$

Equations 2 and 3 gives, $\alpha\theta(v^R) = \theta(v)\alpha^R$ and $v^R\theta(\alpha) = \theta(\alpha^R)v$, respectively. Since w' is a palindrome, $v^R\alpha = \alpha^Rv$ and $\theta(w')$ is a palindrome. Now

$$\theta(w') = \theta(u)v = v^R\theta(\alpha)\theta(v^R)v = \theta(\alpha^R)v\theta(v^R)v = (\theta(w'))^R = v^R\theta(v)\theta(\alpha^R)v.$$

Then, we get,

$$\theta(\alpha^R)v\theta(v^R) = v^R\theta(v)\theta(\alpha^R).$$

Then by Lemma 3, $v^R\theta(v) = xy$, $\theta(\alpha^R) = (xy)^ix$ and $v\theta(v^R) = yx$ where $i \geq 0$, $y \in \Sigma^*$ and $x \in \Sigma^+$. Now $v^R\theta(v) = \theta(v\theta(v^R))$, i.e., $\theta(yx) = xy$. So x and y are θ palindromes and hence,

$$\theta(w') = v^R\theta(\alpha)\theta(v^R)v = \theta(\alpha^R)v\theta(v^R)v = \theta(\alpha^R)yxv = (xy)^ixyxv = x(yx)^{i+1}v.$$

Then using Eq. 2, we get,

$$w = uv = v^R\alpha\theta(v^R)v = v^R\theta(v)\alpha^Rv = xyx(yx)^iv = x(yx)^{i+1}v = \theta(w').$$

So, $\theta(w) = w'$.

Hence, in all the cases, we are done.   □

Consider the word $w = uu\theta(u)$ where u is a palindrome but not a θ-palindrome. Then, uuu, $u\theta(u)u \in C_\theta(w)$ are palindromes. Moreover the word $w = u^{2i}\theta(u)^i$, where u is a palindrome but not a θ-palindrome, has at least two palindromes. It is evident that there exists a non-palindrome w such that $C_\theta(w)$ contains more than one palindrome.

6   Theta Palindromes in the Theta-Conjugacy Set of a Word

In this section, for a given word w, we study the number of θ-palindromes in the set $C_\theta(w), w \in \Sigma^*$. We find the structure of words which have at least one θ-palindrome in the set of their θ-conjugates. We also show that if a word is a θ-palindrome, then there can be at most one θ-palindrome among its θ-conjugates.

We first give examples of words that have zero and one θ-palindrome in their $C_\theta(w)$.

Example 21. Let $\Sigma = \{a, b\}$, and consider θ such that $\theta(a) = b$ and $\theta(b) = a$. Then

1. $C_\theta(aaa) = \{aaa, baa, bba, bbb\}$. Thus, it has zero θ-palindromes.
2. $C_\theta(abab) = \{abab, aaba, abaa\}$. The word $abab$ has exactly one θ-palindrome $abab$.

We now find the structure of words with at least one palindrome among their θ conjugates.

Theorem 22. *Given $w \in \Sigma^*$, $C_\theta(w)$ contains at least one θ-palindrome iff $w = uxu$ or $w = xuu$ where $u, x, \in \Sigma^*$ and x is a θ-palindrome.*

Proof. Let there exist at least one θ-palindrome in $C_\theta(w)$ and let $w = uv$ where $u, v \in \Sigma^*$ such that $\theta(v)u$ is a θ-palindrome in $C_\theta(w)$. Then, we have the following cases:

1. Let $|u| < |v|$. Let $v = v_1v_2$ such that $|v_2| = |u|$. Now, $\theta(v)u = \theta(v_2)\theta(v_1)u$. Since $\theta(v)u$ is a θ-palindrome and $|v_2| = |u|$, we get $v_2 = u$ and v_1 is a θ-palindrome. Then, $w = uv = uv_1v_2 = uv_1u$ and v_1 is a θ-palindrome.
2. Let $|u| = |v|$. Since $\theta(v)u$ is a θ-palindrome and $|u| = |v|$, $v = u$. Then, $w = uv = uu$.
3. Let $|u| > |v|$. Let $u = u_1u_2$ such that $|u_2| = |v|$. Now, $\theta(v)u = \theta(v)u_1u_2$. Since $\theta(v)u$ is a θ-palindrome and $|u_2| = |v|$, $u_2 = v$ and u_1 is a θ-palindrome. Then, $w = uv = u_1u_2v = u_1vv$ where u_1 is a θ-palindrome.

Hence, in all the cases either $w = uxu$ or $w = xuu$ where $u, x, \in \Sigma^*$ and x is a θ-palindrome.

Conversely, let $x \in \Sigma^*$ be a θ-palindrome. If $w = uxu$ for some $u \in \Sigma^*$ then, $\theta(xu)u \in C_\theta(w)$ is a θ-palindrome. Similarly, for $w = xuu$ where $u \in \Sigma^*$, $\theta(u)xu \in C_\theta(w)$ is a θ-palindrome. Therefore, when $w = uxu$ or $w = xuu$ where $u, x \in \Sigma^*$ and x is θ-palindrome, $C_\theta(w)$ contains at least one θ-palindrome.   □

Consider $w = uv$ such that w is not a θ-palindrome, but $C_\theta(w)$ has a θ-palindrome say $\theta(v)u$. Since, the θ conjugacy relation is not an equivalence relation, we cannot predict the number of θ-palindromes in $C_\theta(uv)$ using the fact the $\theta(v)u$ is a θ-palindrome. But, for a θ-palindrome w, we find (Theorem 23) the exact number of θ-palindromes in the set $C_\theta(w)$.

Theorem 23. *The set $C_\theta(w)$ for a θ-palindrome w has exactly one θ-palindrome which is w itself.*

Proof. We prove the statement by induction on the length of w. For a word of length 1, the case is trivial. For a θ-palindrome of length 2, say a_1a_2, for $a_i \in \Sigma$, $C_\theta(a_1a_2)$ is $\{a_1a_2, \theta(a_2)a_1\}$. Assume that a_1a_2 and $\theta(a_2)a_1$ are distinct θ-palindromes, then $\theta(a_2)a_1 = \theta(a_1)a_2$ and $a_1a_2 = \theta(a_2)\theta(a_1)$. This implies $a_1 = \theta(a_2) = \theta(a_1) = a_2$ which is a contradiction. Hence, $a_1a_2 = \theta(a_2)a_1$ and there is only one θ-palindrome in $C_\theta(a_1a_2)$. We assume that for a word α of length less than $|w|$, if there is a θ-palindrome β in the $C_\theta(\alpha)$, then $\alpha = \beta$. Let w be a θ-palindrome. Suppose there exist a $w' = \theta(v)u \in C_\theta(w)$ where $w = uv$ such that w' is a θ-palindrome, then $\theta(v)u = \theta(u)v$. We have the following cases.

Case I: If $|u| < |v|$, then as $\theta(u)$ is a suffix of v and u is the suffix of v, this implies that u is a θ-palindrome. Thus, $w = uv = \theta(v)\theta(u) = \theta(v)u = w'$.

Case II: If $|u| = |v|$, then $u = \theta(v) = \theta(u) = v$, we have, $w = uv = \theta(v)u = w'$.

Case III: If $|u| > |v|$, then $\theta(v)$ is a prefix of u and v is a suffix of u since both are θ-palindromes. If $|u| \leq 2|v|$ and since $\theta(v)$ isa prefix of u and v is a suffix of u, then $u = \theta(v_2)v_1v_2$ with $v = v_1v_2$ such that $|v_1| = 2|v| - |u|$ and v_1 is a θ-palindrome. Then $\theta(u) = u$, and hence, $\theta(w) = \theta(v)u = w'$. If $|u| > 2|v|$, then $u = \theta(v)u_1v$ where $u_1 \in \Sigma^+$. As w is a θ-palindrome, $uv = \theta(v)\theta(u)$, this implies $\theta(v)u_1vv = \theta(v)\theta(v)\theta(u_1)v$. We have, $u_1v = \theta(v)\theta(u_1)$. Also, as w' is a θ-palindrome, $\theta(v)u = \theta(u)v$, this implies $\theta(v)\theta(v)u_1v = \theta(v)\theta(u_1)vv$. We have, $\theta(v)u_1 = \theta(u_1)v$. Now, $u_1v = \theta(v)\theta(u_1)$ and $\theta(v)u_1 = \theta(u_1)v$. Then, by induction hypothesis, as u_1v and $\theta(v)u_1$ are both θ-conjugates of u_1v and are both θ-palindromes, we have $u_1v = \theta(v)u_1$, thus,

$$w = uv = \theta(v)u_1vv = \theta(v)\theta(v)u_1v = \theta(v)u = w'.$$

In all the cases, we are done.   □

Consider the word $w = uxxuxx$ where x, u are distinct θ-palindromes. Then, $\theta(x)uxxux, \theta(uxx)uxx \in C_\theta(w)$. Moreover, the word $w' = (u^ix^{2i})^{2i}$ has at least two θ-palindromes in the set $C_\theta(w')$. It is evident that there exists words w such that $C_\theta(w)$ contains more than one θ palindrome.

7 Conclusions

We have studied the distribution of palindromes and θ-palindromes among the conjugates and θ-conjugates of a word. We have characterized the words which have the maximum number of θ-conjugates. We have found structures of words which have at least one palindrome and θ-palindrome in the set of their θ-conjugates. We have enumerated palindromes and θ-palindromes in the set $C_\theta(w)$ where w is a palindrome and a θ-palindrome, respectively. The maximum number of palindromes and θ-palindromes in the set of θ-conjugates of a word is still unknown in general. After checking several examples, we believe that the maximum number of palindromes and θ-palindromes in the set $C_\theta(w)$ for a word w is two. We have also given examples of the words that achieve the above bound. One of our immediate future work is to prove this bound.

References

1. Amir, A., Aumann, Y., Landau, G.M., Lewenstein, M., Lewenstein, N.: Pattern matching with swaps. J. Algorithms **37**(2), 247–266 (2000)
2. Blanchet-Sadri, F., Luhmann, D.: Conjugacy on partial words. Theoret. Comput. Sci. **289**(1), 297–312 (2002)
3. Czeizler, E., Kari, L., Seki, S.: On a special class of primitive words. Theoret. Comput. Sci. **411**(3), 617–630 (2010)
4. Daley, M., McQuillan, I.: On computational properties of template-guided DNA recombination. In: Carbone, A., Pierce, N.A. (eds.) DNA 2005. LNCS, vol. 3892, pp. 27–37. Springer, Heidelberg (2006). https://doi.org/10.1007/11753681_3
5. Domaratzki, M.: Hairpin structures defined by DNA trajectories. Theory Comput. Syst. **44**, 432–454 (2007)
6. Garzon, M.H., Phan, V., Roy, S., Neel, A.J.: In search of optimal codes for DNA computing. In: Mao, C., Yokomori, T. (eds.) DNA 2006. LNCS, vol. 4287, pp. 143–156. Springer, Heidelberg (2006). https://doi.org/10.1007/11925903_11
7. Guo, C., Shallit, J., Shur, A.M.: On the combinatorics of palindromes and antipalindromes. arXiv e-prints arXiv:1503.09112, March 2015
8. Hopcroft, J.E., Ullman, J.D.: Formal Languages and Their Relation to Automata. Addison-Wesley Longman Inc., Boston (1969)
9. Kari, L., Mahalingam, K.: Watson-Crick conjugate and commutative words. In: Garzon, M.H., Yan, H. (eds.) DNA 2007. LNCS, vol. 4848, pp. 273–283. Springer, Heidelberg (2008). https://doi.org/10.1007/978-3-540-77962-9_29
10. Kari, L., Mahalingam, K.: Watson-Crick palindromes in DNA computing. Nat. Comput. **9**(2), 297–316 (2010)
11. Lipsky, O., Porat, B., Porat, E., Shalom, B.R., Tzur, A.: Approximate string matching with swap and mismatch. In: Tokuyama, T. (ed.) ISAAC 2007. LNCS, vol. 4835, pp. 869–880. Springer, Heidelberg (2007). https://doi.org/10.1007/978-3-540-77120-3_75
12. Lipsky, O., Porat, B., Porat, E., Riva Shalom, B., Tzur, A.: String matching with up to k swaps and mismatches. Inf. Comput. **208**(9), 1020–1030 (2010)
13. Lothaire, M.: Combinatorics on Words. Cambridge University Press, Cambridge (1997)
14. de Luca, A., Luca, A.D.: Pseudopalindrome closure operators in free monoids. Theoret. Comput. Sci. **362**(1), 282–300 (2006)
15. Lyndon, R.C., Schützenberger, M.P.: The equation $a^M = b^N c^P$ in a free group. Michigan Math. J. **9**, 289–298 (1962)
16. Marathe, A., Condon, A., Corn, R.M.: On combinatorial DNA word design. In: DNA Based Computers (1999)
17. Shyr, H.: Free Monoids and Languages. Hon Min Book Company, Taichung (2001)

Line Reconfiguration by Programmable Particles Maintaining Connectivity

Nooshin Nokhanji$^{(\boxtimes)}$ and Nicola Santoro

School of Computer Science, Carleton University, Ottawa, Canada
nooshinnokhanji@cmail.carleton.ca, santoro@scs.carleton.ca

Abstract. In the geometric *Amoebot* model, programmable matter is viewed as a very large number of identical micro/nano-sized entities, called *particles*, operating on a hexagonal tessellation of the plane, with limited computational capabilities, interacting only with neighboring particles, and moving from a grid node to an empty neighboring node. An important requirement, common to most research in this model, is that the particles must be *connected* at all times.

Within this model, a central concern has been the formation of geometric shapes; in particular, the *line* is the elementary shape used as the basis to form more complex shapes, and as a step to solve complex tasks. If some of the particles on the line are faulty it might be necessary for the non-faulty particles to reconstruct a line that does not contain faulty particles. In this paper we study the `Connected Line Recovery` problem of reconstructing the line without violating the connectivity requirement. We provide a complete feasibility characterization of the problem, identifying the conditions necessary for its solvability, and constructively proving the sufficiency of those conditions. Our algorithm allows the non-faulty particles to solve the problem, regardless of the initial distribution of the faults and of their number.

Keywords: Swarm intelligence · Programmable matter · Shape reconstruction · Fault tolerance

1 Introduction

1.1 Framework

Lately, several unconventional types of parallel and distributed models have been proposed to formalize and investigate the computational universes within the interdisciplinary field of *Programmable Matter*. In this field, matter is envisioned as a very large number of identical micro- and nano-sized entities with limited computational, communication and movement capabilities, which are programmed to collectively perform a task without the need for external intervention. The proposed models range from DNA self-assembly systems (e.g., [14,15])

Supported in part by NSERC under the Discovery Grant program.

C. Martín-Vide et al. (Eds.): TPNC 2020, LNCS 12494, pp. 157–169, 2020.
https://doi.org/10.1007/978-3-030-63000-3_13

to metamorphic robots (e.g., [2, 16]), to nature-inspired synthetic insects and micro-organisms (e.g., [13]).

In this paper we consider the popular geometric *Amoebot* model, introduced in [9]. In this model, programmable matter is viewed as a swarm of decentralized autonomous self-organizing entities, operating on a hexagonal tessellation of the plane (i.e., an infinite triangular grid). These entities, called *particles*, are identical and anonymous (i.e., no IDs), and are constrained by having simple computational capabilities (they are finite-state machines), strictly local interaction and communication capabilities (only with particles located in neighboring nodes of the grid), and limited motorial capabilities (from a grid node to an empty neighboring node). They move by repeating an *expansion* operation, in which the particle expands to occupy two neighbouring nodes of the grid, and a *contraction* operation, in which an expanded particle contracts to a single node of the grid. Additionally, the particles are provided with an *handover* capability that allows each particle to coordinate its movement with one of its neighbours.

A particle (implicitly) labels the incident edges of a node in a cyclic (i.e., clockwise or counterclockwise) order with the integers from 0 to 5. The cyclic order of each particle is invariant; if all particles share the same order, they are said to have *chirality*. An important requirement, common to most research on programmable particles, is that the particles must be *connected* at all times e.g. to prevent them drifting apart in an uncontrolled manner like in fluids; that is, the graph formed by the grid locations occupied by the particles is connected at any time [3–6, 8].

Research using this model is being carried out within the parallel, distributed, and molecular computing fields (e.g., see [1, 3, 5–8, 10–12]; for a recent survey see [4]), With the goal of understanding of the nature and limits of this distributed computational universe, researchers have been examining a variety of problems, such as *Coating, Gathering, Election*. In particular the research focus has been on *Shape Formation* (e.g., [5, 6, 8, 11, 12]); this problem requires the entities to move so to form a predefined shape in a finite time and terminate, and it is a prototypical problem for systems of self-organizing entities.

Let us point out that the construction of some elementary shapes, in particular the *line*, is used as the basis for the formation of more complex shapes, or as a preliminary step for the resolution of complex tasks (e.g., [6, 11]).

A shared assumption of the existing studies is that the particles never fail. Clearly, the possibility that some particles might stop functioning, partially or completely, opens new research directions to be explored. The first step in this direction has been taken in [10] where they consider the Line Recovery problem: given a set of particles forming a line in the grid, where some of the particles are faulty, within finite time, the correct particles must rearrange themselves so to form a continuous segment without including any faulty particle, and terminate. They consider complete failures (i.e., a faulty particle is unable both to move and to communicate) but detectable, and propose a solution that works without chirality in a strong adversarial setting (i.e., semi-synchronous scheduler). However, this solution does not maintain connectivity.

In this paper, we consider the problem of re-configuring the line while maintaining connectivity; that is, in the graph formed by the grid locations occupied by all particles, the non-faulty particles are connected at all times.

1.2   Contributions

In this paper we investigate the feasibility of Connected Line Recovery and provide a complete characterization.

We first study under what conditions the problem is *not* feasible; i.e., non-faulty particles cannot form a continuous line segment without breaking connectivity. It is known that, without chirality, connectivity may be broken [10]. We prove that, while necessary, chirality is not sufficient: even with chirality, Connected Line Recovery is unsolvable if the failures affect not only the mobility but also the communication ability of the particles. In other words, to maintain connectivity, only mobility failures can possibly be tolerated.

The question then becomes under what conditions can the problem Connected Line Recovery be solved. We prove that, with chirality the problem is solvable tolerating any number of mobility failures. The proof is constructive. We provide a set of rules (the "algorithm") that allows the non-faulty particles to form a contiguous segment of a line within finite time without ever breaking connectivity, regardless of the initial distribution of the faults and of their number.

Moreover, the impossibility results hold even in the weakest adversarial setting (i.e., fully synchronous scheduler), while the algorithm works even in the stronger adversarial setting (i.e., semi-synchronous scheduler). Due to space constraints, the code of the algorithm and the proofs are omitted.

2   Model, Problem, and Impossibility

2.1   The Model

In the geometric *Amoebot* model, introduced in [9], the space is an infinite triangle grid $\mathcal{G}$ embedded in the Euclidean plane, where nodes are anonymous and edges are bidirectional; in this space operates a set $\mathcal{P}$ of mobile computational elements, called *particles*. A particle may occupy either one node of $\mathcal{G}$ or two adjacent nodes: in the first case, the particle is said to be *contracted*; otherwise, it is *expanded*; When it is expanded, one of the nodes it occupies is called its *head*, and the other node is its *tail*.

A particle may move through G by repeatedly expanding toward an empty adjacent node, which becomes the particle's head, and then contracting there. Two particles are said to be *neighbours* if they occupy adjacent nodes. Neighbouring particles are able to coordinate their movement by a special operation called *handover*, which can happen in two ways. An expanded particle q can perform a *pull* handover with a contracted neighbour p by contracting and causing p to expand into the node it is leaving; conversely, a contracted particle p can perform a *push* handover with an expanded neighbour q by forcing the contraction of q and expanding to the node previously occupied by q. For each node v, a particle p implicitly labels the six incident edges in a cyclic (i.e., clockwise or counterclockwise) order with the integers from 0 to 5, called *port numbers*. The cyclic order of each particle is invariant; however the cyclic order of different particles might be different; if all particles share the same order, they are said to have *chirality*. Even in presence of chirality, different particles may have different port labels for the same incident link of a node v, depending on what edge is assigned the label 0.

Neighbouring particles form a *bond*, enabling them to communicate. Each particle has a shared, constant size memory associated with each of its local ports; this memory can be read and written to by the corresponding neighboring particle. Moreover, each particle has a constant size memory used to store its state, readable from all neighbouring particles. In particular, a particle q can determine whether a neighbor p is contracted or expanded, and it knows if it is bonded with the tail or the head of p.

For ease of description, in the following (as in [10]) we will use a *message passing* terminology to describe the communication between neighbours: we say that a particle p sends a message Msg to a neighbor q, to describe the action of p writing Msg in the shared memory of the corresponding port of q; likewise, we say that q receives Msg, to mean that q reads Msg in the port's memory.

The system works in rounds; in each round, a particle is either active or inactive. When active, a particle executes the following three operations:

- *Look*: It reads the shared memories of its local ports (i.e., the last received message from its neighbours), and determines the state of its neighbours (if any) and their status (i.e., whether contracted or expanded).
- *Compute*: Using the information from the previous operation and its local state as input, it executes its program. As part of this execution, it updates its internal memory, possibly writes to the shared memories of (i.e., sends messages to) its neighbours and decides the movement it wants to perform: none (i.e., stay still); expand to a specific unoccupied adjacent node; contract to its head or to its tail.
- *Move*: It performs the movement action decided in previous operation.
  The activation of the particles is determine by an *adversarial scheduler*. The weakest adversary is the *fully synchronous* one ($\mathcal{FSYNC}$), which activates all the particles in all rounds; a frequently assumed adversary is the *sequential* one ($\mathcal{SEQNL}$), which activates each particle infinitely often but only one per round; a stronger adversary (which includes the other two as limited special cases) is the *semi-synchronous* one ($\mathcal{SSYNC}$) which activates an arbitrary subset of the particles in each round, but every particle is activated infinitely often.

2.2   The Problem

A set of particles $\mathcal{P}$ *forms a line* if the sub-graph induced by their positions is a continuous line segment. A subset $\mathcal{Q} \subseteq \mathcal{P}$ of the particles is said to be *connected* at round r if they are connected in the graph of the positions of all particles at round r. Initially, at round $r = 0$, all the particles are contracted and form a continuous line segment located on line L_0.

Some of the particles may be *faulty*. We distinguish between *communication failure*, in which the particle is no longer able to communicate with its neighbours (i.e., send and receive messages), and *movement failure*, in which the particle is no longer able to move (i.e., to expand). A particle experiencing both communication and a movement failure is said to have a *complete* failure.

The task to be performed, called CONNECTED LINE RECOVERY, is for the non-faulty particles to form within fine time a continuous segment on line L_0 not including and not surrounded by faulty particles, without ever breaking their connectivity, and terminate.

2.3   Impossibilities and Basic Limitations

First observe that, to solve the CONNECTED LINE RECOVERY problem, the particles need *chirality*; that is, they need to agree on the same circular orientation of the space. This is due to the following property established in [10]:

Theorem 1 [10]. *If the particles have no chirality, then an adversary can prevent the non-faulty particles from forming a single connected line, even in $\mathcal{FSYNC}$ and with communication capability of the particles not disabled by the faults.*

In other words, chirality is necessary even if faulty particles continue to be able to communicate with other particles. However, the presence of chirality is not sufficient for the problem to be solvable, as shown by the following.

Theorem 2. *If failures disable also the communication capability of the particles, the* CONNECTED LINE RECOVERY *problem is unsolvable even in $\mathcal{FSYNC}$, with reliable fault-detection and chirality.*

Proof (Sketch). Let faults disable also the communication capability of the affected particles. By contradiction, let $\mathcal{A}$ be a protocol that allows the particles to solve the CONNECTED LINE RECOVERY problem regardless of the number and location of the faults. Consider the following two scenarios. In the first scenario, all non-faulty particles form a continuous segment S, surrounded by faulty particles. In the second scenario, there are two continuous segments, S' and S'' of non-faulty particles, each of size $|S|$, surrounded by faulty particles. The choice of the scenario is made by an adversary. Since the faulty particles are assumed to be unable to communicate, a non-faulty particle p, even-though capable to communicate with its non-faulty neighbours and to detect whether a neighbouring particle is faulty, is unable to distinguish between the two scenarios. In the first scenario, within finite time, the entire segment has to move so to reach a placement away from (before or after) all the faulty particles. On the other hand, as soon as any subset of the particles (possibly all) of a segments decide to move in a given direction, the adversary will choose the second scenario, as well as the placement of S' and S'' in the line (and which segment to activate), so that the empty locations left by the moving particles disconnects the two sets, contradicting the claimed correctness of the protocol.   □

As a consequence of Theorems 1 and 2, both chirality and functioning of the communication capabilities of faulty particles are necessary conditions for the solvability of the CONNECTED LINE RECOVERY problem. Thus, in the following we will assume both conditions.

Since all particles are on the same line L_0, the presence of chirality provides the particles a common left-right direction. In the following, when no ambiguity arises, "first" and "last" are used to mean "rightmost" and "leftmost" respectively. Without loss of generality, we can assume that the rightmost and leftmost particles in the line segment (i.e. with only one neighbour) are initially in the special state *Leader* and *Marker*, respectively; furthermore, every particle knows its *parent* (i.e., the right neighbour, if any) and its *child* (i.e., the left neighbour, if any). Moreover, they agree on the ordering of the lines parallel to L_0; i.e., on which neighbouring line is L_1 and which is L_{-1}. Notice that, since all particles including the faulty ones are able to communicate, should this information be initially not available, it can be determined with a simple pre-processing step.

3   Line-Recovery Algorithm

The proposed algorithm, called LINE-RECOVERY, is composed of the INITIALIZATION, FAULT RECOVERY, and LINE FORMATION phases detailed below.

The algorithm uses the following set of particle states $S = \{idle,\ faulty,\ correct,\ Single,\ segLead,\ segMark,\ segMark\&Lead,\ Lead\&segMark,\ Mark\&segLead,\ Delimiter\}$. Initially, all particles are *idle*, except for the first and the last in the line which are in state *Leader* and *Marker*, respectively. There is no restriction on the number f of faulty particles, except $f < n$ (i.e., there is at least one non-faulty particle), nor on their location.

3.1   Initialization

3.1.1   Basic Set-Up Rules

The INITIALIZATION phase is started by the particles that have suffered a failure. Any such a particle, regardless of its initial state, sends a *WakeUp* message to its neighbours to alert them that it is faulty. Upon receiving such a message, any non-faulty particle becomes aware that the recovery process is starting; it forwards the message to its other neighbour, if one exists, notifying that, while itself is not-faulty, the process should start. Thus, within finite time all particles are activated, and know which of their neighbours are faulty (if any). As part of this wakeup process, with the exception of the *Leader* and the *Marker*, each particle p determines its new state as follows:

- (i) if it is faulty, it changes its state to *faulty*;
- (ii) if non-faulty and both neighbours are not-faulty, it becomes *correct*;

- (iii) if it is non-faulty and both its neighbours are faulty, it changes its state to *segMark&Lead* and sets its *child* and *parent* to *nil*;
- (iv) if non-faulty and only its child is faulty, it changes its state to *segMark* sets its *child* to *nil*;
- (v) if non-faulty and only its parent is faulty, it changes its state to *segLead* and sets its *parent* to *nil*.

An example is shown in Fig. 1 where squares denote faulty particles. Initially (Fig. 1(a)) all particles are in state *idle* (green) except for the *Marker* (red) and the *Leader* (yellow). After the basic set-up, (Fig. 1(b)) some particles have changed their state to *faulty* (black), *segMark* (gray), *segLead* (turquoise), *segMark&Lead* (purple), or *correct* (brown).

(a) Initially all particles are *idle* except the *Leader* and the *Marker*

(b) Particles determine their new states

Fig. 1. States of the particles (a) before and (b) after the execution of basic set-up (Color figure online)

3.1.2   Rules for Faulty Leader and Marker
Since there is are no restriction on which particles can become faulty nor on their number, it is possible that the *Leader* and/or the *Marker* could be faulty. To address these cases, they follow the rules described below:

- (i) If the *Marker* is faulty, it passes its role to the closest non-faulty particle: it becomes *faulty* and sends a *MarkerIsRequired* message to its parent; this message is forwarded until its arrives to the first non-faulty particle; this particle (which by necessity is either *segMark*, or *segMark&Lead*), changes its state to *Marker*.
- (ii) If the *Leader* is faulty, it passes its role to the closest non-faulty particle: it becomes *Delimiter* and it sends a *LeaderIsRequired* message to its child; this message is forwarded until its arrives to the first non-faulty particle; this particle changes its state to *Leader*.

3.1.3   Rules for Single Particle, Single Leader, Single Marker
If there is only one non-faulty particle, say p, that particle will detect it as it will be (requested to be) both the *Leader* and the *Marker*. In this case, p becomes *Single*, and starts directly the LINE FORMATION phase.

On the other hand, if $f < n - 1$, within finite time there are two non-faulty particles in state *Leader* and *Marker* respectively. In this case, one more test and possible state change is performed by those two particles:

- (i) if the child of the *Leader* is faulty, then the *Leader* becomes *Lead&segMark* sets its *child* to *nil*;
- (ii) if the parent of the *Marker* is faulty, then the *Marker* becomes *Mark&segLead* and sets its *parent* to *nil*.

Figure 2 shows an example where the *Leader* and the *Marker* become *Lead&segMark* (orange) and *Mark&segLead* (pink), respectively.

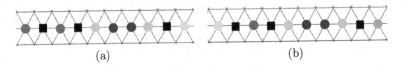

(a)   (b)

Fig. 2. (a) *Leader* and *Marker* perform the "single" test and (b) change their state (Color figure online)

3.1.4   Delimiter Determination

Part of the INITIALIZATION phase is to create a landmark, to be used in the LINE FORMATION phase of the algorithm, by having the first faulty particle in the line entering state *Delimiter*. This is done as follows.

- (i) If the original *Leader* is non-faulty, then upon receiving a *Wakeup* message it sends a *DelimiterIsRequired* message to its child; this message is forwarded until it reaches the first *faulty* particle, which then changes its state to *Delimiter*.
- (ii) If instead the original *Leader* is faulty, then, as already described, this particle becomes the *Delimiter*.

3.1.5   Properties of Initialization

Lemma 3. *Let the faults divide the non-faulty particles into $k \geq 1$ connected segments of the line, separated by faulty particles. Then, within finite time after* INITIALIZATION *starts, under the* SSYNC *adversarial scheduler, the following properties hold.*

- (1) *Let $k = 1$. If the segment is composed of more than one particle, the first is in state* Leader *and the last is in state* Marker; *otherwise, the sole particle is in state* Single.
- (2) *Let $k > 1$. In the first segment, if it contains more than one particle, the first one is in state* Leader *and the last is in state* segMark; *else, the sole particle is in state* Lead&segMark.
- (3) *Let $k > 1$. In the last segment, if composed by more than one particle, the last one is in state* Marker *and the first is in state* segLead; *else, the sole particle is in state* Mark&segLead

- (4) *Let* $k > 2$. *Every segment other than the first and the last, if composed of more than one particle starts with a* segLead *and ends with a* segMark; *else, the sole particle is in state* segMark&Lead.
- (5) *The first* faulty *particle is in state* Delimiter. *Furthermore, during the execution, the non-faulty particles remain connected.*

3.1.6   Subsequent Action

If $k > 1$, then the particles start the FAULT RECOVERY phase; if $k = 1$ they execute directly the LINE FORMATION phase. Both the FAULT RECOVERY phase and the LINEFORMATION phase, require a segment of non-faulty particles to move. Their movement is through expansion, contraction, and handover. To bypass faulty particles, the movement is carried out using line L_1 and returning to line L_0 whenever possible.

3.2   Fault Recovery

The FAULT RECOVERY phase proceeds through a sequence of identical actions, each composed of three operations: Notification, Advance and Merge. As a result of each action, the last two segments become physically connected ("are merged") reducing by one the number of segments. This process is repeated until there is only one segment. A special Preliminary Action is taken initally only in the particular case when the last segment is composed of a single particle.

3.2.1   Preliminary Action

Let the last segment be composed of a single particle, say M; by Lemma 3, M is in state *Mark&segLead*. Then particle M acts as follows:

- (i) It chooses L_1 (the adjacent horizontal line above L_0) as the movement line and expands to it in the right direction.
- (ii) It goes over the faulty particle(s) (given that the it does not have any child, it is able to expand and contract without any limitation) until it finds a non-faulty particle p on L_0; by necessity, p's state is either *segMark*, *segMark&Lead*, or *Lead&segMark*.
- (iii) When this occurs, M sets p to be its parent and changes its state to *Marker*.
- (iv) It sends *StartRecovery* message to p.

Once p receives the *StartRecovery* message, it sets M to be its child; it then changes state to *correct* if it was *segMark*, to *segLead* if it was *segMark&Lead*, and to *Leader* if instead it was *Lead&segMark*.

Hence, within finite time, M has joined the previous segment. From this moment on, it will no longer change its state from *Marker*, and the algorithm proceeds with the regular sequence of actions, each composed of three operations (notification, advance and merge) described in the following.

3.2.2 Notification

In each action, the Notification is started by a different non-faulty particle N; initially, it is started by the *Marker*.

The Notification operation is as follows: if N is in the state *Marker*, it sends a *MarkerIsHere* message to its parent; otherwise, N sends a *StartRecovery* message to its parent. In either case, the message is forwarded until it reaches the furthermost non-faulty particle, say S, in its segment. Particle S is by necessity either in state *segLead* or *Leader*.

If S is the *Leader*, all the correct particles are in this segment. In this case, the FAULT RECOVERY phase terminates, and the LINEFORMATION phase starts.

If instead S is in state *segLead*, upon rreceiving *MarkerIsHere* or *StartRecovery*, S starts the Advance operation of the FAULT RECOVERY phase.

3.2.3 Advance

The *segLead* S chooses L_1 (the adjacent horizontal line above L_0) and expands to it in the right direction. It then goes over the fault(s) pulling all the particles in its segment. It continues to move on L_1, followed by all other particles in the segment, until it encounters a non-faulty particle on L_0. By Lemma 3, this particle, say Q is either in the *segMark*, *segMark&Lead*, or *Lead&segMark* states. When this happens, the two segments merge. An example of this condition is shown in Fig. 3, where the black triangle is the *Delimiter*.

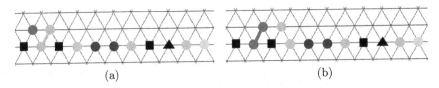

(a)   (b)

Fig. 3. The *segmentLeader* (a) expands to L_1; (b) it finds a non-faulty particle on L_0

3.2.4 Merge

The Merging operation is done as following: S sets Q as its parent, changes its state to *correct*, and notifies Q (i.e. it sends *StartRecovery* message) which then sets S as its child. What is done next depends on the current state of Q:

- (i) If Q is in state *segMark*, it becomes *correct* and executes the Notification operation of the next step (i.e., $N = Q$);
- (ii) if Q is in state *segMark&Lead*, it becomes *segLead* and starts the Advance operation of the next step;
- (iii) if Q is in state *Lead&segMark* then it becomes *Leader* and starts the LINE FORMATION phase.

An example of Merge operation, is shown in Fig. 4.

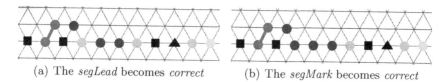

| (a) The *segLead* becomes *correct* | (b) The *segMark* becomes *correct* |

Fig. 4. An example of Merge operation, continuing the example of Fig. 3(b)

3.2.5   Properties of Fault Recovery

Lemma 4. *Within finite time after* FAULT RECOVERY *starts under the* $\mathcal{SSYNC}$ *adversarial scheduler:*

- *(1) The non-faulty particles form a single connected segment;*
- *(2) the first is in state* Leader *and the last is in state* Marker.
- *(3) The first* faulty *particle is in state* Delimiter.

Furthermore, during the execution, the non-faulty particles remain connected.

The FAULT RECOVERY phase is executed only if $f < n - 1$. The end of the phase is determined by the *Leader*, which then starts LINE FORMATION phase.

3.3   Line Formation

By Lemma 4, within finite time, the non-faulty particles will form a single connected segment. When this occurs, it is possible that some particles are on line L_0 while others are on L_1. Also, unless the original *Leader* was not-faulty, there might be *faulty* particles in front of the non-faulty particle in state *Leader* or *Single*. The purpose of the LINE FORMATION phase is to ensure that all non-faulty particles re-form a connected contracted line on L_0 with no faulty particles in front. To reach this goal, all the non-faulty particles must pass the faulty particle in state *Delimiter* determined in the INITIALIZATION phase.

3.3.1   Segment with One Particle
Consider first the case $f = n - 1$; that is, the segment is composed of a just one particle X in state *Single*. In this case, x does as follows:

- (i) If the position (on L_0) in front of X is occupied (necessarily by a *faulty* particle), X moves forward (expanding to line L_1) until it passes the *Delimiter*; it then goes back to L_0, contracts, and terminates.
- (ii) If instead the position in front of X is not occupied, then X terminates.

3.3.2   Segment with More Than One Particle
Consider next the case $f < n - 1$; i.e., there are two or more particles in the segment. In this case the *Leader* moves forward (expanding to line L_1 if the position on L_0 is occupied by a *faulty* particle, and returning to L_0 as soon as

possible), pulling all the particles in the segment. This process continues until the *Marker* passes the *Delimiter* and moves back on L_0. When this happens, the *Marker* sends the *Termination* message to its parent. This message is forwarded until it is received by the *Leader*,

The *Leader* then completes the move it is currently performing (if any), sends a *Contract* message to its child and terminates. Upon receiving the *Contract* message, a non-faulty particle completes the move it is currently performing (if any); if in state *correct* it becomes *idle* and sends the *Contract* message to its child; and terminates. Within finite time, the entire segment will form a contracted line.

3.3.3 Segment in Final Shape

Consider finally the special case when $f < n - 1$, the non-faulty particles are in the final shape from the beginning, and there is no fault in front of the initial *Leader*. This case is detected by the *Leader* when it receives the *MarkerIsHere* message. It then sends a *Stop* message to its child and terminates. The message is forwarded down the segment and all particles become *idle* and terminates, except the *Marker* that just terminates.

3.3.4 Properties of Line Formation

Lemma 5. *The execution of* LINE FORMATION *under the* $SS\mathcal{YNC}$ *adversarial scheduler, leads the non-faulty particles to form a contracted connected line with no faulty particles ahead.*

Furthermore, during the execution, the non-faulty particles remain connected.

3.4 Conclusion

Theorem 6. *Given a continuous segment on line* L_0 *of n particles with chirality of which* $f < n$ *have mobility failure, the execution of algorithm* LINE-RECOVERY *under the* $SS\mathcal{YNC}$ *adversarial scheduler allows the non-faulty particles to form a continuous segment on line* L_0 *within fine time, without ever breaking their connectivity, and terminate.*

That is, algorithm LINE-RECOVERY solves the CONNECTED LINE RECOVERY problem under the minimal necessary conditions and a strong adversary.

References

1. Cannon, S., Daymude, J., Randall, D., Richa, A.: A Markov chain algorithm for compression in self-organizing particle systems. In: Proceedings of 35th Symposium on Principles of Distributed Computing (PODC), pp. 279–288 (2016)
2. Chirikjian, G.: Kinematics of a metamorphic robotic system. In: Proceedings of the International Conference on Robotics and Automation, pp. 1:449–1:455 (1994)

3. Daymude, J.J., Gmyr, R., Richa, A.W., Scheideler, C., Strothmann, T.: Improved leader election for self-organizing programmable matter. In: Fernández Anta, A., Jurdzinski, T., Mosteiro, M.A., Zhang, Y. (eds.) ALGOSENSORS 2017. LNCS, vol. 10718, pp. 127–140. Springer, Cham (2017). https://doi.org/10.1007/978-3-319-72751-6_10

4. Daymude, J., Hinnenthal, K., Richa, A., Scheideler, C.: Computing by programmable particles. In: Flocchini, P., Prencipe, G., Santoro, N. (eds.) Distributed Computing by Mobile Entities, pp. 615–681. Springer, Cham (2019). https://doi.org/10.1007/978-3-030-11072-7_22

5. Derakhshandeh, Z., Gmyr, R., Richa, A., Scheideler, C., Strothmann, T.: An algorithmic framework for shape formation problems in self-organizing particle systems. In: Proceedings of NanoCom, pp. 21:1–21:2 (2015)

6. Derakhshandeh, Z., Gmyr, R., Richa, A., Scheideler, C., Strothmann, T.: Universal shape formation for programmable matter. In: Proceedings of the 28th ACM Symposium on Parallelism in Algorithms and Architectures (SPAA), pp. 289–299 (2016)

7. Derakhshandeh, Z., Gmyr, R., Richa, A., Scheideler, C., Strothmann, T.: Universal coating for programmable matter. Theoret. Comput. Sci. **671**, 56–68 (2017)

8. Derakhshandeh, Z., Gmyr, R., Strothmann, T., Bazzi, R., Richa, A.W., Scheideler, C.: Leader election and shape formation with self-organizing programmable matter. In: Phillips, A., Yin, P. (eds.) DNA 2015. LNCS, vol. 9211, pp. 117–132. Springer, Cham (2015). https://doi.org/10.1007/978-3-319-21999-8_8

9. Derakhshandeh, Z., Dolev, S., Gmyr, R., Richa, A.W., Scheideler, C., Strothmann, T.: Brief announcement: Amoebot - a new model for programmable matter. In: Proceedings of 26th ACM Symposium on Parallelism in Algorithms and Architectures, pp. 220-222 (2014)

10. Di Luna, G., Flocchini, P., Prencipe, G., Santoro, N., Viglietta, G.: Line recovery by programmable particles. In: Proceedings of the International Conference on Distributed Computing and Networking (ICDCN), pp. 4.1–4.10 (2018)

11. Di Luna, G.A., Flocchini, P., Santoro, N., Viglietta, G., Yamauchi, Y.: Shape formation by programmable particles. Distrib. Comput. **33**(1), 69–101 (2019). https://doi.org/10.1007/s00446-019-00350-6

12. Di Luna, G.A., Flocchini, P., Santoro, N., Viglietta, G., Yamauchi, Y.: Mobile RAM and shape formation by programmable particles. In: Malawski, M., Rzadca, K. (eds.) Euro-Par 2020. LNCS, vol. 12247, pp. 343–358. Springer, Cham (2020). https://doi.org/10.1007/978-3-030-57675-2_22

13. Dolev, S., Frenkel, S., Rosenbli, M., Narayanan, P., Venkateswarlu, K.: In-vivo energy harvesting nano robots. In: Proceedings of ICSEE, pp. 1–5 (2016)

14. Patitz, M.J.: An introduction to tile-based self-assembly and a survey of recent results. Natural Comput. **13**(2), 195–224 (2013). https://doi.org/10.1007/s11047-013-9379-4

15. Rothemund, P.: Folding DNA to create nanoscale shapes and patterns. Nature **440**(7082), 297–302 (2006)

16. Walter, J., Welch, J., Amato, N.: Distributed reconfiguration of metamorphic robot chains. Distrib. Comput. **17**(2), 171–189 (2004)

Author Index